AF624349

HUMAN RIGHTS AND SOCIAL JUSTICE

R.K. Narasimham

Commonwealth

Human Rights and Social Justice

© Reserved

ISBN : 81-7169-570-1

Edition : 2027

Published by :
COMMONWEALTH PUBLISHERS (P) LTD.
4831/24, Govind Lane,
Ansari Road, Darya Ganj,
New Delhi - 110002
Ph. : 23272541, 23242541
e-mail : commonwealthpublishers2016@gmail.com

Distributed by :
ARJUN PUBLISHING HOUSE
4831/24, Govind Lane,
Ansari Road, Darya Ganj,
New Delhi - 110002
Ph. : 23272541, 23242541
e-mail : arjunbooks2001@gmail.com

Laser Typesetting by :
Dimple Computers
Delhi

Printed at :
Balaji Digital
Delhi

Preface

The experiences of the Second World War disclosed many gaps in the protection of the victims of war. Although considerable protection was afforded to prisoners of war by the 1929 Convention when both belligerents were parties to it, the appalling experiences of Russian prisoners of war in German hands, and of all prisoners of war in Japanese hands illustrated what could happen in situation to which the 1929 Convention was not considered to apply. Furthermore, the occupation of a number of countries in Europe and in Asia disclosed how inadequate was the protection afforded by existing rules of international law to civilians in the hands of an occupying power. Four new Conventions were drawn up in Geneva in 1949 at a diplomatic conference on the basis of texts already prepared under the aegis of the International Red Cross. Three of the 1949 Geneva Conventions; were revisions of existing Conventions: the fourth was an entirely new Convention relative to the Protection of Civilian Persons in Time of War. These four instruments although each of them can be accepted conventions on the Protection of the Victims of War. This essential unity is emphasised by the fact that there are at the beginning of each Convention a group of articles common to all four Conventions.

The territories of the parties to the conflict and to occupied territories, the Civilian Convention contains, provisions about the status and treatment of protected persons, which are common to both. Such person are "entitled in all circumstances to respect for their persons, their honour, their family rights, their religious convictions and practices and their manners and customs." They are at all times to be humanely treated, and women are to be especially protected against any attack on their honour, in particular against rape, enforced prostitution, or any form of indecent assault.

Clearly human rights is closely linked and represent some of the most important issues before the global community today. The human rights violation at all levels is a heinous crime against the society.

Publisher

Contents

1 Universal Declaration of Human Rights

Whereas recognition of the inherent dignity and of the equal and inalienable rights of all members of the human family is the foundation of freedom, justice and peace in the world,

Whereas disregard and contempt for human rights have resulted in barbarous acts which have outraged the conscience of mankind, and the advent of a world in which human beings shall enjoy freedom of speech and belief and freedom from fear and want has been proclaimed as the highest aspiration of the common people,

Whereas it is essential, if man is not to be com-pelled to have recourse, as a last resort, to rebellion, against tyranny and oppression, that human rights should be protected by the rule of law,

Whereas it is essential to promote the develop-ment of friendly relations between nations,

Whereas the peoples of the United Nations have in the Charter reaffirmed their faith in fundamental human rights, in the dignity and worth of the human person and in the equal rights of men and women and have determined to promote social progress and better standards of life in larger freedom,

Whereas Member States have pledged themselves to achieve, in co-operation with the United Nations, the promotion of universal respect for the observance of human rights and fundamental freedoms,

Whereas a common understanding of these rights and freedoms is of the greatest importance for the full realization of this pledge,

Now, therefore, the General Assembly Proclaims

This Universal Declaration of Human Rights as a common standard of achievement for all peoples and all nations, to the end that every individual and every organ of society, keeping this Declaration constantly in mind, shall strive by teaching and education to promote respect for these rights and freedoms and by progressive measures, national and international, to secure their universal and effective recognition and observance, both among the peoples of Member States themselves and among the peoples of territories under their jurisdiction.

Article 1

All human beings are born free and equal in dignity and rights. They are endowed with reason and conscience and should act towards one another in a spirit or brotherhood.

Article 2

Everyone is entitled to all the rights and freedoms set forth in this Declaration, without distinction of any kind, such as race, colour, sex, language, religion, political or other opinion, national or social origin, property, birth or other status.

Furthermore, no distinction shall be made on the basis of the political, jurisdictional or international status of the country or territory to which a person belongs, whether it be independent, trust, non-self-governing or under any other limitation of sovereignty.

Article 3

Everyone has the right to life, liberty and security of person.

Article 4

No one shall be held in slavery or servitude; slavery and the slave trade shall be prohibited in all their forms.

Article 5

No one shall be subjected to torture or to cruel, inhuman or degrading treatment or punishment.

Article 6

Everyone has the right to recognition everywhere as a person before the law.

Article 7

All are equal before the law and are entitled without any discrimination to equal protection of the laws. All are entitled to equal protection against any discrimination in violation of this Declaration and against any incitement to such discrimination.

Article 8

Everyone has the right to an effective remedy by the competent national tribunals for acts violating the fundamental rights granted him by the constitution or by law.

Article 9

No one shall be subjected to arbitrary arrest, detention or exile.

Article 10

Everyone is entitled in full equality to a fair and public hearing by an independent and impartial tribunal, in the determination of his rights and obligations and of any criminal charge against him.

Article 11

1. Everyone charged with a penal offence has the right to be presumed innocent until proved guilty according to law in a public trial at which has all the guarantees necessary for his defence.
2. No one shall be held guilty of any penal offence on account of any act or omission which did not constitute a penal offence, under national or international law, at the time when it was committed. Nor shall a heavier penalty be imposed than the one

that was applicable at the time the penal offence was committed.

Article 12

No one shall be subjected to arbitrary interference with his privacy, family, home or correspondence, nor to attacks upon his honour and reputation. Everyone has the right to the protection of the law against such interference or attacks.

Article 13

1. Everyone has the right to freedom of movement and residence within the borders of each state.
2. Everyone has the right to leave any country, including his own, and to return to his country.

Article 14

1. Everyone has the right to seek and to enjoy in other countries asylum from prosecution.
2. This right may not be invoked in the case of prosecutions genuinely arising from non-political crimes or from acts contrary to the purposes and principles of the United Nations.

Article 15

1. Everyone has the right to a nationality.
2. No one shall be arbitrarily deprived of his nationality nor denied the right to change his nationality.

Article 16

1. Men and women of full age, without any limitation due to race, nationality or religion, have the right to marry and to found a family. They are entitled to equal rights as to marriage, during marriage and at its dissolution.
2. Marriage shall be entered into only with the free and full consent of the intending spouses.
3. The family is the natural and fundamental group unit of society and is entitled to protection by society and the State.

Article 17

1. Everyone has the right to own property alone as well as in association with others.
2. No one shall be arbitrarily deprived of his property.

Article 18

Everyone has the right to freedom of thought, conscience and religion; this right includes freedom to change his religion or belief, and freedom, either alone or in community with others and in public or private, to manifest his religion or belief in teaching, practice, worship and observance.

Article 19

Everyone has the right to freedom of opinion and expression; this right includes freedom to hold opinions without interference and to seek, receive and impart information and ideas through any media and regardless of frontiers.

Article 20

1. Everyone has the right to freedom of peaceful assembly and association.
2. No one may be compelled to belong to an association.

Article 21

1. Everyone has the right to take part in the government of his country, directly or through freely chosen representatives.
2. Everyone has the right of equal access to public service in his country.
3. The will of the people shall be the basis of the authority of government; this will shall be expressed in periodic and genuine elections which shall be universal and equal suffrage and shall be held by secret vote or by equivalent free voting procedures.

Article 22

Everyone, as a member of society, has the right to social

security and is entitled to realization, through national effort and international cooperation and in accordance with the organization resources of each State, of the economic, social and cultural rights indispensable for his dignity and the free development of his personality.

Article 23

1. Everyone has the right to work, to free choice of employment, to just and favourable conditions of work and to protection against unemployment.
2. Everyone, without any discrimination, has the right to equal pay for equal work.
3. Everyone who works has the right to just and favourable remuneration ensuring for himself and his family an existence worthy of human dignity, and supplemented, if necessary, by other means of social protection.
4. Everyone has the right to form and to join trade unions for the protection of his interests.

Article 24

Everyone has the right to rest and leisure, including reasonable limitation of working hours and periodic holidays with pay.

Article 25

1. Everyone has the right to a standard of living adequate for the health and well-being of himself and of his family, including food, clothing housing and medical care and necessary social services, and the right to security in the event of unemployment, sickness, disability, widowhood, old age or other lack of livelihood in circumstances beyond his control.
2. Motherhood and childhood are entitled to special care and assistance. All children, whether born in or out of wedlock, shall enjoy the same social protection.

Article 26

1. Everyone has the right to education. Education shall

be free, at least in the elementary and fundamental stages. Elementary education shall be compulsory. Technical and professional education shall be made generally available and higher education shall be equally accessible to all on the basis of merit.

2. Education shall be directed to the full development of the human personality and to the strengthening of respect for human rights and fundamental freedoms. It shall promote understanding, tolerance and friendship among all nations, racial or religious groups, and shall further the activities of the United Nations for the maintenance of peace.
3. Parents have a prior right to choose the kind of education that shall be given to their children.

Article 27

1. Everyone has the right freely to participate in the cultural life of the community, to enjoy the art and to share in scientific advancement and its benefits.
2. Everyone has the right to the protection of the moral and material interests resulting from any scientific, literary to artistic production of which he is the author.

Article 28

Everyone is entitled to a social and international order in which the rights and freedoms set forth in this Declaration can be fully realized.

Article 29

1. Everyone has duties to the community in which alone the free and full development of his personality is possible.
2. In the exercise of his rights and freedoms, everyone shall be subject only to such limitations as are determined by law solely for the purpose of securing due recognition and respect for the rights and freedoms of others and of meeting the just

requirements of morality, public order and the general welfare in a democratic society.

3. These rights and freedoms may in no case be exercised contrary to the purposes and principles of the United Nations.

Article 30

Nothing in this Declaration may be interpreted as implying for any State, group or person any right to engage in any activity or to perform any act aimed at the destruction of any of the rights and freedoms set forth herein.

2 Protection and Welfare of Children

The General Assembly,

Recalling its resolutions 36/167 of 16 December 1981, 37/115 of 16 December 1982, 38/142 of 19 December 1983 and 39/89 of 13 December 1984, and its decision 40/422 of 11 December 1985,

Taking Note of the draft Declaration on Social and Legal Principles relating to the Protection and Welfare of Children, with Special Reference to Foster Placement and Adoption Nationally and Internationally, as submitted by the Economic and Social Council by its resolution 1979/28 of 9 May 1979,

Taking Note with appreciation of the work done on this question in the Third and Sixth Committees, as well as the efforts made by Member States representing different legal systems, during the consultations held at Headquarters from 16 to 27 September 1985 and early in the forty-first session, to join in the common endeavour of completing the work on the draft Declaration,

Adopts the Declaration on Social and Legal Principles relating to the Protection and Welfare of Children, with Special Reference to Foster Placement and Adoption Nationally and Internationally, the text of which is annexed to the present resolution.

Annex

Declaration on social and Legal Principles relating to the Protection and Welfare of Children, with special

Reference to Foster Placement and Adoption Nationally and Internationally

The General Assembly,
Recalling the Universal declaration of Human Rights, the International Covenant on Economic, Social and Cultural Rights, the International Covenant on Civil and Political Rights, the International Convention on the Elimination of All Forms of Racial Discrimination and the Convention on the Elimination of All Forms of Discrimination against Women;

Recalling also the Declaration of the Rights of the Child, which it proclaimed by its resolution 1386(XIV) of 20 November 1959.

Reaffirming principle 6 of that Declaration, which states that the child shall, wherever possible, grow up in the care and under the responsibility of his parents and, in any case, in an atmosphere of affection and of moral and material security.

Concerned at the large number of children who are abandoned or become orphans owing to violence, internal disturbance, armed conflicts, natural disasters, economic crises or social problems.

Bearing in mind that in all foster placement and adoption procedures the best interests of the child should be the paramount consideration.

Recognizing that under the principal legal systems of the world, various valuable alternative institutions exist, such as the Kafala of Islamic Law, which provide substitute care to children who cannot be cared for by their own parents;

Recognizing further that only where a particular institution is recognized and regulated by the domestic law of a State would the provisions of this Declaration relating to that institution be relevant and that such provisions would in no way affect the existing alternative institutions in other legal systems,

Conscious of the need to proclaim universal principles to be taken into account in in cases where procedures are instituted relating to foster placement or adoption of a child, either nationally or internationally,

Bearing in mind, however, that the principles set forth hereunder do not impose on States such legal institutions as foster placement or adoption.

Proclaims the following principles:

A. General Family and Child Welfare

Article 1

Every State should give a high priority to family and child welfare.

Article 2

Child welfare depends upon good family welfare.

Article 3

The first priority for a child is to be cared for by his or her own parents.

Article 4

When care by the child's own parents is unavailable or inappropriate, care by relatives of the child's parents by another substitute-foster or adoptive-family or, if necessary, by an appropriate institution should be considered.

Article 5

In all matters relating to the placement of a child outside the care of the child's own parents, the best interests of the child, particularly his or her need for affection and right to security land continuing care should be the paramount consideration.

Article 6

Persons responsible for foster placement or adoption procedures should have professional or other appropriate training.

Article 7

Government should determine the adequacy of their national child welfare services and consider appropriate actions.

Article 8

The child should at all times have a name, a nationality and a legal representative. The child should not, as a result of foster placement, adoption or any alternative regime, be deprived or his or her name, nationality or legal representative unless the child thereby acquires a new name, nationality or legal representative.

Article 9

The need of a foster or an adopted child to know about his or her background should be recognized by persons responsible for the child's care unless this is contrary to the child's best interests.

B. Foster Placement

Article 10

Foster placement of children should be regulated by law.

Article 11

Foster family care, though temporary in nature, may continue, if necessary, until adulthood but should not preclude either prior return to the child's own parents or adoption.

Article 12

In all matters of foster family care, the prospective foster parents and, as appropriate, the child and his or her own parents should be properly involved. A competent authority or agency should be responsible for supervision to ensure the welfare of the child.

C. Adoption

Article 13

The primary aim of adoption is to provide the child

who cannot be cared for by his or her own parents with a permanent family.

Article 14

In considering possible adoption placements persons responsible for them should select the most appropriate environment for the child

Article 15

Sufficient time and adequate counselling should be given to the child's own parents, the prospective adoptive parents and, as appropriate, the child in order to reach a decision on the child's future as early as possible.

Article 16

The relationship between the child to be adopted and the prospective adoptive parents should be observed by child welfare agencies or services prior to the adoption. Legislation should ensure that the child is recognized in law as a member of the adoptive family and enjoys all the rights pertinent thereto.

Article 17

If a child cannot be placed in a foster or an adoptive family or cannot in any suitable manner be cared for in the country of origin, intercountry adoption may be considered as an alternative means of providing the child with a family.

Article 18

Governments should establish policy, legislation and effective supervision for the protection of children involved in intercountry adoption. Intercountry adoption should wherever possible, only be undertaken when such measures have been established in the States concerned.

Article 19

Policies should be established and laws enacted, where necessary, for the prohibition of abduction and of any other act for illicit placement of children.

Article 20

In intercountry adoption, placements should as a rule, be made through competent authorities or agencies with application of safeguards and standards equivalent to those existing in respect of national adoption. In no case should the placement result in improper financial gain for those involved in it.

Article 21

In intercountry adoption through persons acting as agents for prospective adoptive parents, special precautions should be taken in order to protect the child's legal and social interests.

Article 22

No intercountry adoption should be considered before it has been established that the child is legally free for adoption and that any pertinent documents necessary to complete the adoption, such as the consent of competent authorities, will become available. It must also be established that the child will be able to migrate and to join the prospective adoptive parents and may obtain their nationality.

Article 23

In intercountry adoption, as a rule, the legal validity of the adoption should be assured in each of the countries involved.

Article 24

Where the nationality of the child differs from that of the prospective adoptive parents, all due weight shall be given to both the law of the State of which the child is a national and the law of the State of which the prospective adoptive parents are nationals. In this connection due regard shall be given to the child's cultural and religious background and interests.

3 Convention on the Nationality of Married Women

The Contracting States,

Recognizating that, conflicts law in practice with reference to nationality arise as a result of provisions concerning the loss or acquisition of nationality by women as a result of marriage.

Recognizing that, in article 15 of the Universal Declaration of Human Rights, the General Assembly of the United Nations has proclaimed that "everyone has the right to a nationality" and that "no one shall be arbitrarily deprived of hi snationality nor denied the right to change his nationality",

Desiring to co-operate with the United Nations in promoting universal respect for, and observance of human rights and fundamental freedoms for all without distinction as to sex,

Hereby agree as hereinafter provided:

Article 1

Each Contracting State agrees that neither the celebration nor the dissolution of a marriage between one of its nationals and an alien, nor the change of nationality by the husband during marriage, shall automatically affect the nationality of the wife.

Article 2

Each Contracting State agrees that neither the voluntary acquisition of the nationality of another State nor the renunciation of its nationality by one of its nationals shall prevent the retention of its nationality by the wife of such national.

Article 3

1. Each Contracting State agrees that the alien wife of one of its nationals may, at her request, acquire the nationality of her husband through specially privileged naturalization procedures; the grant of such nationality may be subject to such limitations as may be imposed in the interests of national security or public policy.
2. Each Contracting State agrees that the present Convention shall not be construed as affecting any legislation or judicial practice by which the alien wife of one of its nationals may, at her request, acquire her husband's nationality as a matter of right.

Article 4

1. The present Convention shall be open for signature and ratification on behalf of any State Member of the United Nations and also on behalf of any other State which is or hereafter becomes a member of any specialized agency of the United Nations, or which is or hereafter becomes a Party to the Statute of the International Court of Justice, or any other State to which an invitation has been addressed by the General Assembly of the United Nations.
2. The present Convention shall be ratified and the instruments of ratification shall be deposited with the Secretary-General of the United Nations.

Article 5

1. The present Convention shall be open for accession to all States referred to paragraph 1 of article 4.
2. Accession shall be effected by the deposit of an instrument of accession with the Secretary-General of the United Nations.

Article 6

1. The present Convention shall come into force on the ninetieth day following the date of deposit of the sixth instrument of ratification or accession.
2. For each State ratifying or acceding to the Convention after the deposit of the sixth instrument of ratification or accession, the Convention shall enter into force on the ninetieth day after deposit by such State of its instrument of ratification or accession.

Article 7

1. The present Convention shall apply to all non-self-governing, trust, colonial and other non-metropolitan territories for the international relations of which any Contracting State is responsible; the Contracting State concerned shall, subject to the provisions of paragraph 2 of the present article, at the time of signature, ratification or accession declare the non-metropolitan territory or territories to which the Convention shall apply *ipso facto* as a result of such signature, ratification of accession.
2. In any case in which, for the purpose of nationality, a non-metropolitan territory is not treated as one with the metropolitan territory, or in any case in which the previous consent of a non-metropolitan territory is required by the constitutional laws or practices of the Contracting State or of the non-metropolitan territory for the application of the Convention to that territory, that Contracting State shall endeavour to secure the needed consent of the non-metropolitan territory within the period of twelve months from the date of signature of the Convention by that Contracting State, and when such consent has been obtained the Contracting State shall notify the Secretary-General of the United Nations. The present Convention shall apply to the territory or territories named in such notification from the date of its receipt by the Secretary-General.

3. After the expiry of the twelve-month period mentioned in paragraph 2 of the present article, the Contracting States concerned shall inform the Secretary-General of the results of the consultations with those non-metropolitan territories for whose international relations they are responsible and whose consent to the application of the present Convention may have been withheld.

Article 8

1. At the time of signature, ratification or accession, any State may make reservations to any article of the present Convention other than articles 1 and 2.
2. If any State makes a reservation in accordance with paragraph 1 of the present article, the Convention, with the exception of those provisions to which the reservation relates, shall have effect as between the reserving State and the other Parties. The Secretary-General of the United Nations shall communicate the text of the reservation to all State which are or may become Parties to the Convention. Any State Party to the Convention or which thereafter becomes a Party may notify the Secretary-General that it does not agree to consider itself bound by the Convention with respect to the State making the reservation. This notification must be made, in the case of a State already a Party, within ninety days from the date of the communication by the Secretary-General; and, in the case of a State subsequently becoming a Party, within ninety days from the date when the instrument of ratification or accession is deposited. In the event that such a notification is made, the Convention shall not be deemed to be in effect as between the State making the notification and the State making the reservation.
3. Any State making a reservation in accordance with paragraph 1 of the present article may at any time

withdraw the reservation, in whole or in part, after it has been accepted, by a notification to this effects addressed to the Secretary- General of the United Nations. Such notification shall take effects on the date on which it is received.

Article 9

1. Any Contracting State may denounce the present Convention by written notification to the Secretary-General of the United Nations. Denunciation shall take effect one year after the date of receipt of the notification by the Secretary-General.
2. The present Convention shall cease to be in force as from the date when the denunciation which reduces the number of Parties to less than six becomes effective.

Article 10

Any dispute which may arise between any two or more Contracting States concerning the interpretation or application of the present Convention which is not settled by negotiation, shall, at the request of any one of the parties to the dispute, be referred to the International Court of Justice for decision, unless the parties agree to another mode of settlement.

Article 11

The Secretary-General of the United Nations shall notify all States Members of the United Nations and the non-member States contemplated in paragraph 1 of article 4 of the present Convention of the following:

(a) Signatures and instruments of ratification received in accordance with article 4;

(b) Instruments of accession received in accordance with article 5;

(c) The date upon which the present Convention enters into force in accordance with article 6;

(d) Communications and notifications received in accordance with article 8;

(e) Notifications of denunciation received in accordance with paragraph 1 of article 9;

(f) Abrogation in accordance with paragraph 2 of article 9.

Article 12

1. The present Convention, of which the Chinese, English, French, Russian and Spanish texts shall be equally authentic, shall be deposited in the archives of the United Nations.
2. The Secretary-General of the United Nations shall transmit a certified copy of the Convention to all States Members of the United Nations and to the non-member States contemplated in paragraph 1 of article 4.

4 Slavery Convention

Entry into Force: 9 March 1927, in accordance with article 12. The Convention was amended by the Protocol done at the Headquarters of the United Nations, New York, on 7 December 1953; the amended Convention entered into force on 7 July 1955, the date on which the amendments, set forth in the annex to the Protocol of 7 December 1953, entered into force in accordance with article III of the Protocol.

Whereas the signatories of the General Act of the Brussels Conference of 1889-90 declared that they were equally animated by the firm intention of putting an end to the traffic in African slaves,

Whereas the signatories of the Convention of Saint-German-en-Laye of 1919, to revise the General Act of Berlin of 1885 and the General Act and Declaration of Brussels of 1890, affirmed their intention of securing the complete suppression of slavery in all its forms and of the slave trade by land and sea,

Taking into consideration the report of the Temporary Slavery Commission appointed by the Council of the League of Nations on June 12th, 1924,

Desiring to complete and extend the work accomplished under the Brussels Act and to find a means of giving practical effect throughout the world to such intentions as were expressed in regard to slave trade and slavery by the signatories of the Convention of Saint-

German-en-Laye, and recognising that it is necessary to conclude to that end more detailed arrangements than are contained in that Convention,

Considering moreover, that it is necessary to prevent forced labour from developing into conditions ????

Convention and have accordingly appointed as their Plenipotentiaries [names omitted]

...have agreed as follows:

Article 1

For the purpose of the present Convention, the following definitions are agreed upon:

(1) Slavery is the status or condition of a person over whom any or all of the Powers attaching to the right of ownership are exercised.

(2) The slave trade includes all acts involved in the capture, acquisition or disposal of a person with intent to reduce him to slavery; all acts involved in the acquisition of a slave with a view to selling or exchanging him; all acts of disposal by sale or exchange of a slave acquired with a view to being sold or exchanged, and, in general, every act of trade or transport in slaves.

Article 2

The High Contracting Parties undertake, each in respect of the territories placed under its sovereignty, jurisdiction, protection, suzerainty or tutelage, so far as they have not already taken the necessary steps:

(a) To prevent and suppress the slave trade;

(b) To bring about, progressively and as soon as possible, the complete abolition of slavery in all its forms.

Article 3

The High Contracting Parties undertake to adopt all appropriate measures with a view to preventing and suppressing the embarkation, disembarkation and transport of slaves in their territorial waters and upon all vessels flying their respective flags.

The High Contracting Parties undertake to negotiate as soon as possible a general Convention with regard to the slave trade which will give them rights and impose upon them duties of the same nature as those provided for in the Convention of June 17th, 1925, relative to the International Trade in Arms (Articles 12, 20, 21, 22, 23, 24 and paragraphs 3, 4 and 5 of Section II of annex II), with the necessary adaptations, it being understood that this general Convention will not place the ships (even of small tonnage) of any High Contracting Parties in a position different from that of the other High Contracting Parties.

It is also understood that, before or after the coming into force of this general Convention, the High Contracting Parties are entirely free to conclude between themselves, without, however, derogating from the principles laid down in the preceding paragraph, such special agreements as, by reason of their peculiar situation, might appear to be suitable in order to bring about as soon as possible the complete disappearance of the slave trade.

Article 4

The High Contracting Parties shall give to one another assistance with the object of securing the abolition of slavery and the slave trade.

Article 5

The High Contracting Parties recognise that resource to compulsory or forced labour may have grave consequences and undertake, each in respect of the territories placed under its sovereignty, jurisdiction, protection, suzerainty or tutelage, to take all necessary measures to prevent compulsory or forced labour from developing into conditions analogous to slavery.

It is agreed that:

(1) Subject to the transitional provisions laid down in paragraph (2) below, compulsory or forced labour may only be exacted for public purpoes.

(2) In territories in which compulsory or forced labour for other than public purposes still survives, the High Contracting Parties shall endeavour progressively and as soon as possible to put an end to the practice. So long as such forced or compulsory labour exists, this labour shall invariably be of an exceptional character, shall always receive adequate remuneration, and shall not involve the removal of the labourers from their usual place of residence.

(3) In all cases, the responsibility for any recourse to compulsory or forced labour shall rest with the competent central authorities of the territory concerned.

Article 6

Those of the High Contracting Parties whose laws do not at present make adequate provision for the punishment of infractions of laws and regulations enacted with a view to giving effect to the purposes of the present Convention undertake to adopt the necessary measures in order that severe penalties may be imposed in respect of such

Article 7

The High Contracting Parties undertake to communicate to each other and to the Secretary-General of the League of Nations any laws and regulations which they may enact with a view to the application of the provisions of the present Convention.

Article 8

The High Contracting Parties agree that disputes arising between them relating to the interpretation or application of this Convention shall, if they cannot be settled by direct negotiation, be referred for decision to the Permanent Court of International Justice. In case either or both of the States Parties to such a dispute should not be Parties to the Protocol of December 16th, 1920, relating to the Permanent Court of International Justice, the dispute shall be referred, at the choice of the Parties and in accordance with the constitutional procedure of each State, either to the Permanent Court of International Justice or to a court of arbitration constituted in accordance with the Convention of October 18th, 1907, for the Pacific Settlement of International disputes, or to some other court of arbitration.

Article 9

At the time of signature or of ratification or of accession, any High Contracting Party may declare that its acceptance of the present Convention does not bind some or all of the territories placed under its sovereignty, jurisdiction, protection, suzerainty or tutelage in respect of all or any provisions of the Convention; it may subsequently accede separately on behalf of any one of them or in respect of any provision to which any one of them is not a Party.

Article 10

In the event of High Contracting Party wishing to denounce the present Convention, the denunciation shall be notified in writing to the Secretary-General of the League of Nations, who will at once communicate a certified true copy of the notification to all the other High Contracting Parties, informing them of the date on which it was received.

The denunciation shall only have effect in regard to the notifying State, and one year after the notification has reached the Secretary-General of the League of Nations.

Denunciation may also be made separately in respect of any territory placed under its sovereignty, jurisdiction, protection, suzerainty or tutelage.

Article 11

The present Convention, which will bear this day's date and of which the French and English texts are both authentic, will remain open for signature by the States Members of the League of Nations until April 1st, 1927.

The Secretary-General of the League of Nations will subsequently bring the present Convention to the notice of States which have not signed it, including states which are not Members of the League of Nations, and invite them to accede thereto.

A State desiring to accede to the Convention shall notify its intention in writing to the Secretary-General of the League of Nations and transmit to him the instrument of accession, which shall be deposited in the archives of the League.

The Secretary-General shall immediately transmit to all other High Contracting Parties a certified true copy of the notification and of the instrument of accession, informing them of the date on which he received them.

Article 12

The present Convention will be ratified and the instruments of ratification shall be deposited in the office of the Secretary-General of the League of Nations. The Secretary-General will inform all the High Contracting Parties of such deposit.

The Convention will come into operation for each State cn the date of the deposit of its ratification or of its accession.

In Faith Whereof the Plenipotentiaries signed the present Convention.

Done at Geneva the twenty-fifth day of September, one thousand nine hundred and twenty-six, in one copy, which will be deposited in the archives of the League of Nations. A certified copy shall be forwarded to each signatory State.

5 Convention Relating to the Status of Refugees

Preamble

The High Contracting Parties,

Considering that the Charter of the United Nations and the Universal Declaration of Human Rights approved on 10 December 1948 by the General

Assembly have affirmed the principle that human shall enjoy fundamental rights and freedoms without discrimination,

Considering that the United Nations has, on various occasions, manifested its profound concern for refugees and endeavoured to assure refugees the widest possible exercise of these fundamental rights and freedoms,

Considering that it is desirable to revise and consolidate previous international agreements relating to the status of refugees and to extend the scope of and the protection accorded by such instruments by means of a new agreement,

Considering that the grant of asylum may place unduly heavy burdens on certain countries, and that a satisfactory solution of a problem of which the United Nations has recognized the international scope and nature cannot therefore be achieved without international co-operation,

Expressing the wish that all States, recognizing the social and humanitarian nature of the problem of refugees, will do everything within their power to prevent this problem from becoming a cause of tension between States,

Noting that the United Nations High Commissioner for Refugees is charged with the task of supervising international conventions providing for the protection of refugees, and recognizing that the effective co-ordination of measures taken to deal with this problem will depend upon the co-operation of States with the High Commissioner,

Have Agreed as follows:

Chapter I: General Provisions

Article 1. -Definition of the term "refugee"

A. For the purposes of the present Convention, the term "refugee" shall apply to any person who:

(1) Has been considered a refugee under the Arrangements of 12 May 1926 and 30 June 1928 or under the Conventions of 28 October 1933 and 10 February 1938, the Protocol of 14 September 1939 or the Constitution of the International Refugee Organization;

Decisions of non-eligibility taken by the International Refugee Organization during the period of its activities shall not prevent the status of refugee being accorded to persons who fulfil the conditions of paragraph 2 of this section;

(2) As a result of events occurring before 1 January 1951 and owing to well-founded fear of being persecuted for reasons of race, religion, nationality membership of a particular social group or political opinion, is outside the country of his nationality and is unable, or owing to such fear, is unwilling to avail himself of the protection of that country; or who, not having a nationality and being outside the country of his former habitual residence as a result of such events, is unable or owing to such fear, is unwilling to return to it.

In the case of a person who has more than one nationality, the term "the country of his nationality" shall mean each of the countries of which he is a national, and a person shall not be deemed to be lacking the protection of the country of his nationality if, without any valid reason based on well-founded fear, he has not availed himself of the protection of one of the countries of which he is a national.

B. (1) For the purposes of this Convention, the words "events occurring before 1 January 1951" in article 1, section A, shall be understood to mean either (a) "events occurring in Europe before 1 January 1951"; or (b) "events occurring in Europe or elsewhere before 1 January 1951"; and each Contracting State shall make a declaration at the time of signature, ratification or accession, specifying which of these meanings it applies for the purpose of its obligations under this Convention.

(2) Any Contracting State which has adopted alternative (a) may at any time extend its obligations by adopting alternative (b) by means of a notification addressed to the Secretary-General of the United Nations.

C. This Convention shall cease to apply to any person falling under the terms of section A if:

(1) He has voluntarily re-availed himself of the protection of the country of his nationality; or

(2) Having lost his nationality, he has voluntarily reacquired it; or

(3) He has acquired a new nationality, and enjoys the protection of the country of his new nationality; or

(4) He has voluntarily re-established himself in the country which he left or outside which he remained owing to fear of persecution; or

(5) He can no longer, because the circumstances in connection with which he has been recognized as a

refugee have ceased to exist, continue to refuse to avail himself of the protection of the country of his nationality;

Provided that this paragraph shall not apply to a refugee falling under section A (1) of this article who is able to invoke compelling reasons arising out of previous persecution for refusing to avail himself of the protection of the country of nationality;

(6) Being a person who has no nationality he is, because the circumstances in connection with which he has been recognized as a refugee have ceased to exist, able to return to the country of his former habitual residence;

Provided that this paragraph shall not apply to a refugee falling under section A (1) of this article who is able to invoke compelling reasons arising out of previous persecution for refusing to return to the country of his former habitual residence.

D. This Convention shall not apply to persons who are at present receiving from organs or agencies of the United Nations other than the United Nations High Commissioner for Refugees protection or assistance.

When such protection or assistance has ceased for any reason, without the position of such persons being definitively settled in accordance with the relevant resolutions adpoted by the General Assembly of the United nations, these persons shall ipso facto be entitled to the benefits of this Convention.

E. This Convention shall not apply to a person who is recognized by the competent authorities of the country in which he has taken residence as having the rights and obligations which are attached to the possession of the nationality of that country.

F. The provisions of this Convention shall not apply to any person with respect to whom there are serious reasons for considering that:

(a) He has committed a crime against peace, a war crime, or a crime against humanity, as defined in the international instruments drawn up to make provision in respect of such crimes;

(b) He has committed a serious non-political crime outside the country of refuge prior to his admission to that country as a refugee;

(c) He has been guilty of acts contrary to the purposes and principles of the United Nations.

Article 2. - General obligations

Every refugee has duties to the country in which he finds himself, which require in particular that he conform to its laws and regulations as well as to measures taken for the maintenance of public order.

Article 3. - Non-discrimination

The Contracting States shall apply the provisions of this Convention to refugees without discrimination as to race, religion or country of origin.

Article 4. -Religion

The Contracting States shall accord to refugees within their territories treatment at least as favourable as that accorded to their nationals with respect to freedom to practise their religion and freedom as regards the religious education of their children.

Article 5. - Rights granted apart from this Convention

Nothing in this Convention shall be deemed to impair any rights and benefits granted by a Contracting State to refugees apart form this Convention.

Article 6 - The term "in the same circumstances"

For the purposes of this Convention, the term "in the same circumstances" implies that any requirements (including requirements as to length and conditions of sojourn or residence) which the particular individual would have to fulfil for the enjoyment of the right in question, if he were not a refugee, must be fulfilled by him, with the exception of requirements which by their nature a refugee is incapable of fulfilling.

Article 7. - Exemption from reciprocity

1. Except where this Convention contains more favourable provisions, a Contracting State shall accord to refugees the same treatment as is accorded to aliens generally.

2. After a period of three years' residence, all refugees shall enjoy exemption from legislative reciprocity in the territory of the Contracting States.

3. Each Contracting State shall continue to accord to refugees the rights and benefits to which they were already entitled, in the absence of reciprocity, at the date of entry into force of this Convention for that State.

4. The Contracting States shall consider favourably the possibility of according to refugees, in the absence of reciprocity, rights and benefits beyond those to which they are entitled according to paragraphs 2 and 3, and to extending exemption from reciprocity to refugees who do not fulfil the conditions provided for in paragraphs 2 and 3.

5. The provisions of paragraphs 2 and 3 apply both to the rights and benefits referred to articles 13, 18, 19, 21 and 22 of this Convention and to rights and benefits for which this Convention does not provide.

Article 8. -Exemption from exceptional measures

With regard to exceptional measures which may be taken against the person, property or interests of nationals of a foreign State, the Contracting States shall not apply such measures to a refugee who is formally a national of the said State solely on account of such nationality. Contracting States which, under their legislation, are prevented from applying the general principle expressed in this article, shall, in appropriate cases, grant exemptions in favour of such refugees.

Article 9. -Provisional measures

Nothing in this Convention shall prevent a Contracting State, in time of war or other grave and exceptional circumstances, from taking provisionally measures which it considers to be essential to the national security in the case of a particular person, pending a determination by the Contracting State that that person is in fact a refugee and that the continuance of such measures in necessary in his case in the intersts of national security.

Article 10. - Continuity of residence

1. Where a refugee has been forcibly displaced during the Second World War and removed to the territory of a Contracting State, and is resident there, the period of such enforced sojourn shall be considered to have been lawful residence within that territory.

2. Where a refugee has been forcibly displaced during the Second World War from the territory of a Contracting State and has, prior to the date of entry into force of this Convention, returned there for the purpose of taking up residence, the period of residence before and after such enforced displacement shall be regarded as one uninterrupted period for any purposes for which uninterrupted residence is required.

Article 11. -Refugee seamen

In the case of refugees regularly serving as crew members on board a ship flying the flag of a Contracting State, that State shall give sympathetic consideration to their establishment on its territory and the issue of travel documents to them or their temporary admission to its territory particularly with a view to facilitating their establishment in another country.

Chapter II: Juridical Status

Article 12. - Personal status

1. The personal status of a refugee shall be governed

by the law of the country of his domicile or, if he has no domicile, by the law of the country of his residence.

2. Rights previously acquired by a refugee and dependent on personal status, more particularly rights attaching to marriage, shall be respected by a Contracting State, subject to compliance, if this be necessary, with the formalities required by the law of that State, provided that the right in question is one which would have been recognized by the law of that State had he not become a refugee.

Article 13. - Movable and immovable property

The Contracting States shall accord to a refugee treatment as favorable as possible and, in any event, not less favorable than that accorded to aliens generally in the same circumstances, as regards the acquisition of movable and immovable property and other rights pertaining thereto, and to leases and other contracts relating to movable and immovable property.

Article 14. - Artistic rights and industrial property

In respect of the protection of industrial property, such as inventions, designs or models, trade marks, trade names, and of rights in literary, artistic and scientific works, a refugee shall be accorded in the country in which he has his habitual residence the same protection as is accorded to nationals of that country. In the territory of any other Contracting States, he shall be accorded the same protection as is accorded in that territory to nationals of the country in which he has his habitual residence.

Article 15. -Right of association

As regards non-political and non-profit-making associations and trade unions the Contracting States shall accord to refugees lawfully staying in their territory the most favorable treatment accorded to national of a foreign country, in the same circumstances.

Article 16. - Access to courts

1. A refugee shall have free access to the courts of law on the territory of all Contracting States.

2. A refugee shall enjoy in the Contracting State in which he has his habitual residence the same treatment as a national in matters pertaining to access to the courts, including legal assistance and exemption from cautio judicatum solvi.

3. A refugee shall be accorded in the matters referred to in paragraph 2 in countries other than that in which he has his habitual residence the treatment granted to a national of the country of his habitual residence.

Chapter III: Gainful Employment

Article 17. -Wage-earning employment

1. The Contracting States shall accord to refugees lawfully stating in their territory the most favorable treatment accorded to nationals of a foreign country in the same circumstances, as regards the right to engage in wage-earning employment.

2. In any case, restrictive measures imposed on aliens or the employment of aliens for the protection of the national labour market shall not be applied to a refugee who was already exempt from them at the date of entry into force of this Convention for the Contracting State concerned, or who fulfils one of the following conditions:

(a) He has completed three years' residence in the country;

(b) He has a spouse possessing the nationality of the country of residence. A refugee may not invoke the benefit of this provision if he has abandoned his spouse;

(c) He has one or more children possessing the nationality of the country of residence.

3. The Contracting States shall give sympathetic consideration to assimilating the rights of all refugees

with regard to wage-earning employment to those of nationals, and in particular of those refugees who have entered their territory pursuant to programmes of labour recruitment or under immigration schemes.

Article 18. -Self-employment

The Contracting States shall accord to a refugee lawfully in their territory treatment as favorable as possible and, in any event, not less favorable than that accorded to aliens generally in the same circumstances, as regards the right to engage on his own account in agriculture, industry, handicrafts and commerce and to establish commercial and industrial companies.

Article 19. -Liberal professions

1. Each Contracting State shall accord to refugees lawfully staying in their territory who hold diplomas recognized by the competent authorities of that State, and who are desirous of practising a liberal profession, treatment as favorable as possible and, in any event, not less favorable than that accorded to aliens generally in the same circumstances.

2. The Contracting States shall use their best endeavours consistently with their laws and constitutions to secure the settlement of such refugees in the territories, other than the metropolitan territory, for whose international relations they are responsible.

Chapter V: Warfare

Article 20. -Rationing

Where a rationing system exists, which applies to the population at large and regulates the general distribution of products in short supply, refugees shall be accorded the same treatment as nationals.

Article 21. - Housing

As regards housing, the Contracting States, in so far as the matter is regulated by laws or regulations or is subject to the control of public authorities, shall accord to refugees lawfully staying in their territory treatment as favourable as possible and, in any event, not less favourable than that accorded to aliens generally in the same circumstances.

Article 22. - Public education

1. The Contracting States shall accord to refugees the same treatment as is accorded to nationals with respect to elementary education.

2. The Contracting States shall accord to refugees treatment as favourable as possible, and, in any event, not less favourable than that accorded to aliens generally in the same circumstances, with respect to education other than elementary education and, in particular, as regards access to studies, the recognition of foreign school certificates, diplomas and degrees, the remission of fees and charges and the award of scholarships.

Article 23. - Public relief

The Contracting States shall accord to refugees lawfully staying in their territory the same treatment with respect to public relief and assistance as is accordance to their nationals.

Article 24. - Labour legislation and social security

1. The Contracting States shall accord to refugees lawfully staying in their territory the same treatment as is accorded to nationals in respect of the following matters;

(a) In so far as such matters are governed by laws or regulations or are subject to the control of administrative authorities: remuneration, including family allowances where these form part of remuneration, hours of work, overtime arrangements, holidays with pay, restrictions on home work, minimum age of employment, apprenticeship and training, women's work and the work of young persons, and the enjoyment of the benefits of collective bargaining;

(b) Social security (legal provisions in respect of employment injury, occupational diseases, maternity, sickness, disability, old age, death, unemployment, family responsibilities and any other contingency which, according to national laws or regulations, is covered by a social security scheme), subject to the following limitation:

(i) There may be appropriate arrangements for the maintenance of acquired rights and rights in course of acquisition;

(ii) National laws or regulations of the country of residence may prescribe special arrangements concerning benefits or portions of benefits which are payable wholly out of public funds, and concerning allowances paid to persons who do not fulfil the contribution conditions prescribed for the award of a normal pension.

2. The right to compensation for the death of a refugee resulting from employment injury or from occupational disease shall not be affected by the fact that the residence of the beneficiary is outside the territory of the Contracting State.

3. The Contracting States shall extend to refugees the benefits of agreements concluded between them, or which may be concluded between them in the future, concerning the maintenance of acquired rights and rights in the process of acquisition in regard to social security, subject only to the conditions which apply to nationals of the States signatory to the agreements in question.

4. The Contracting States will give sympathetic consideration to extending to refugees so far as possible the benefits of similar agreements which may at any time be in force between such Contracting States and non-contracting States.

Chapter V: Administrative Measures

Article 25. - Administrative assistance

1. When the exercise of a right by a refugee would normally require the assistance of authorities of a foreign country to whom he cannot have recourse, the Contracting States in whose territory he is residing shall arrange that such assistance be afforded to him by their own authorities or by an international authority.

2. The authority or authorities mentioned in paragraph 1 shall deliver or cause to be delivered under their supervision to refugees such documents or certifications as would normally be delivered to aliens by or through their national authorities.

3. Documents or certifications so delivered shall stand in the stead of the official instruments delivered to aliens by or through their national authorities, and shall be given credence in the absence of proof to the contrary.

4. Subject to such exceptional treatment as may be granted to indigent persons, fees may be charged for the services mentioned herein, but such fees shall be moderate and commensurate with those charged to nationals for similar services.]

5. The provisions of this article shall be without prejudice to article 27 and 28.

Article 26. - Freedom of movement

Each Contracting State shall accord to refugees lawfully in its territory the right to choose their place of residence and to move freely within its territory subject to any regulations applicable to aliens generally in the same circumstances.

Article 27. - Identity papers

The Contracting States shall issue identity papers to any refugee in their territory who does not possess a valid travel document.

Article 28. - Travel documents

1. The Contracting States shall issue to refugees lawfully staying in their territory, unless compelling reasons of national security or public order otherwise require, and the provisions of the Schedule to this Convention shall apply with respect to such documents. The Contracting States may issue such a travel document to any other refugee in their territory; they shall in particular give sympathetic consideration to the issue of such a travel document to refugees in their territory who are unable to obtain a travel document from the country of their lawful residence.

2. Travel documents issued to refugees under previous international agreements by Parties thereto shall be recognized and treated by the Contracting States in the same way as if they had been issued pursuant to this article.

Article 29. - Fiscal charges

1. The Contracting States shall not impose upon refugees duties, charges or taxes, of any description whatsoever, other or higher than those which are or may be levied on their nationals in similar situations.

2. Nothing in the above paragraph shall prevent the application to refugees of the laws and regulations concerning charges in respect of the issue to aliens of administrative documents including identity papers.

Article 30. - Transfer of assets

1. A Contracting State shall, in conformity with its laws and regulations, permit refugees to transfer assets which they have brought into its territory, to another country where they have been admitted for the purposes of resettlement.

2. A contracting State shall give sympathetic consideration to the application or refugees for permission to transfer assets wherever they may be and

which are necessary for their resettlement in another country to which they have been admitted.

Article 31. -Refugees unlawfully in the country of refuge

1. The Contracting States shall not impose penalties, on account of their illegal entry or presence, on refugees who, coming directly from a territory where their life or freedom was threatened in the sense of article 1, enter or are present in their territory without authorization, provided they present themselves without delay to the authorities and show good cause for their illegal entry or presence.

2. The Contracting States shall not apply to the movements of such refugees restrictions other than those which are necessary and such restrictions shall only be applied until their status in the country is regularized or they obtain admission into another country. The Contracting States shall allow such refugees a reasonable period and all the necessary facilities to obtain admission into another country.

Article 32. -Expulsion

1. The Contracting States shall not expel a refugee lawfully in their territory save on grounds of national security or public order.

2. The expulsion of such a refugee shall be only in pursuance of a decision reached in accordance with due process of law. Except where compelling reasons of national security otherwise require, the refugee shall be allowed to submit evidence to clear himself, and to appeal to and be represented for the purpose before competent authority or a person or persons specially designated by the competent authority.

3. The Contracting States shall allow such a refugee a reasonable period within which to seek legal admission into another country. The Contracting States reserve the right to apply during that period such internal measures as they may deem necessary.

Article 33. -Prohibition of expulsion or return ("refoulement")

1. No Contracting State shall expel or return ("refouler") a refugee in any manner whatsoever to the frontiers of territories where his life or freedom would be threatened on account of his race, religion, nationality, membership of a particular social group or political opinion.

2. The benefit of the present provision may not, however, be claimed by a refugee whom there are reasonable grounds for regarding as a danger to the security of the country in which he is, or who, having been convicted by a final judgement of a particularly serious crime, constitutes a danger to the community of that country.

Article 34. -Naturalization

The Contracting States shall as far as possible facilitate the assimilation and naturalization of refugees. They shall in particular make every effort to expedite naturalization preceedings and to reduce as far as possible the charges and costs of such proceedings.

Chapter VI: Executory and Transitory Provisions

Article 35. - Co-operation of the national authorities with the United Nations

1. The Contracting States undertake to co-operate with the Office of the United Nations High Commissioner for Refugees, or any other agency of the United Nations which may succeed it, in the exercise of its functions, and shall in particular facilitate its duty of supervising the application of the provisions of this Convention.

2. In order to enable the Office of the High Commissioner or any other agency of the United Nations which may succeed it, to make reports to the competent organs of the United Nations, the Contracting States undertake to provide them in the appropriate form with information and statistical data requested concerning:

(a) The condition of refugees,

(b) The implementation of this Convention, and

(c) Laws, regulations and decrees which are, or may hereafter be, in force relating to refugees.

Article 36. - Information on national legislation

The Contracting States shall communicate to the Secretary-General of the United Nations the laws and regulations which they may adopt to ensure the application of this Convention.

Article 37. - Relation to previous conventions

Without prejudice to article 28, paragraph 2, of this Convention, this Convention replaces, as between Parties to it, the Arrangements of 5 July 1922, 31 May 1924, 12 may 1926, 30 June 1928 and 30 July 1935, the Conventions of 28 October 1933 and 10 February 1938, the Protocol of 14 September 1939 and the Agreement of 15 October 1946.

Chapter VII: Final Clauses

Article 38. - Settlement of disputes

Any dispute between Parties to this Convention relating to its interpretation or applications, which cannot be settled by other means, shall be referred to the International Court of Justice at the request of any one of the parties to the dispute.

Article 39. - Signature, ratification and accession

1. This Convention shall be opened for signature at Geneva on 28 July 1951 and shall thereafter be deposited with the Secretary-General of the United Nations. It shall be open for signature at the European Office of the United Nations from 28 July to 31 August 1951 and shall be re-opened for signature at the Headquarters of the United Nations from 17 September 1951 to 31 December 1952.

2. This Convention shall be open for signature on

behalf of all States Members of the United Nations, and also on behalf of any other State invited to attend the Conference of Plenipotentiaries on the Status of Refugees and Stateless Persons or to which an invitation to sign will have been addressed by the General Assembly. It shall be ratified and the instruments of ratification shall be deposited with the Secretary-General of the United Nations.

3. This Convention shall be open from 28 July 1951 for accession by the States referred to in paragraph 2 of this article. Accession shall be effected by the deposit of an instruments of accession with the Secretary-General of the United Nations.

Article 40. - Territorial application clause

1. Any State may, at the time of signature, ratification or accession, declare that this Convention shall extend to all or any of the territories for the international relations of which it is responsible. Such a declaration shall take effect when the Convention enters into force for the State concerned.

2. At any time thereafter any such extension shall be made by notification addressed to the Secretary-General of the United Nations and shall take effect as from the ninetieth day after the day of receipt by the Secretary-General of the United Nations of this notification, or as from the date of entry into force of the Convention for the State concerned, whichever is the later.

3. With respect to those territories to which this Convention is not extended at the time of signature, ratification or accession, each State concerned shall consider the possibility of taking the necessary steps in order to extend the application of this Convention to such territories, subject, where necessary for constitutional reasons, to the consent of the Governments of such territories.

Article 41. - Federal clause

In the case of a Federal or non-unitary State, the following provisions shall apply:

(a) With respect to those articles of this Convention that come within the legislative jurisdiction of the federal legislative authority, the obligations of the Federal Government shall to this extent be the same as those of parties which are not Federal States;

(b) With respect to those articles of this Convention that come within the legislative jurisdiction of constituent States, provinces or cantons which are not, under the constitutional system of the Federation, bound to take legislative action, the Federal Government shall bring such articles with a favourable recommendation to the notice of the appropriate authorities of States provinces or cantons at the earliest possible moment;

(c) A Federal State Party to this Convention shall, at the request of any other Contracting State transmitted through the Secretary-General of the United nations, supply a statement of the law and practice of the Federation and its constituent units in regard to any particular provision of the Convention showing the extent to which effect has been given to that provision by legislative or other action.

Article 42. - Reservations

1. At the time of signature, ratification or accession, any State may make reservations to articles of the Convention other than to articles 1, 3, 4, 16 (1), 33, 36-46 inclusive.

2. Any State making a reservation in accordance with paragraph 1 of this article may at any time withdraw the reservation by a communication to that effect addressed to the Secretary-General of the United Nations.

Article 43. - Entry into force

1. This Convention shall come into force on the ninetieth day following the day of deposit of the sixth instrument of ratification or accession.

2. For Each State ratifying or acceding to the Convention after the deposit of the sixth instrument of ratification or accession, the Convention shall enter into force on the ninetieth day following the date of deposit by such State of its instrument of ratification or accession.

Article 44. - Denunciation.

1. Any Contracting State may denounce this Convention at any time by a notification addressed to the Secretary-General of the United Nations.

2. Such denunciation shall take effect for the Contracting State concerned one year from the date upon which it is received by the Secretary-General of the United Nations.

3. Any State which has made a declaration or notification under article 40 may, at any time thereafter, by a notification to the Secretary-General of the United Nations, declare that the Convention shall cease to extend to such territory one year after the date of receipt of the notification by the Secretary-General.

Article 45. Revision

1. Any Contracting State may request revision of this Convention at any time by a notification addressed to the Secretary-General of the United Nations.

2. The General Assembly of the United Nations shall recommend the steps, if any, to be taken in respect of such request.

Article 46. - Notifications by the Secretary-General of the United Nations

The Secretary-General of the United nations shall inform all Members of the United Nations and non-member States referred to in article 39:

(a) Of declarations and notifications in accordance with section B of article 1;

(b) Of signatures, ratifications and accession in accordance with article 39;

(c) Of declarations and notifications in accordance with article 40;

(d) Of reservations and withdrawals in accordance with article 42;

(e) Of the date on which this Convention will come into force in accordance with article 43;

(f) Of denunciations and notifications in accordance with article 44;

(g) Of requests for revision in accordance with article 45.

IN FAITH WHEREOF the undersigned, duly authorized, have signed this Convention on behalf of their respective Governments.

DONE at Geneva, this twenty-eighth day of July, one thousand nine hundred and fifty-one, in a single copy, of which the English and French texts are equally authentic and which shall remain deposited in the archives of the United Nations, and certified true copies of which shall be delivered to all Members of the United Nations and to the non-member States referred to in article 39.

6 Protocol Relating to the Status of Refugees

Entry into Force: 4 October 1967, in accordance with article VIII

The States Parties to the present Protocol

Considering that the Convention relating to the Status of Refugees done at Geneva on 28 July 1951 (hereinafter referred to as the Convention) covers only those persons who have become refugees as a result of events occurring before 1 January 1951,

Considering that new refugee situations have arisen since the Convention was adopted and that the refugees concerned may therefore not fall within the scope of the Convention,

Considering that it is desirable that equal status should be enjoyed by all refugees covered by the definition in the Convention irrespective of the dateline 1 January 1951,

Have agreed as follows:

Article I. - General provision

1. The States Parties to the present Protocol undertake to apply articles 2 to 34 inclusive of the Convention to refugees as hereinafter defined.

2. For the purpose of the present Protocol, the term "refugee" shall, except as regards the application of paragraph 3 of this article, mean any person within the

definition of article 1 of the Convention as if the words "As a result of events occurring before 1 January 1951 and..." and the words "...as a result of such events", in article 1 A (2) were omitted.

3. The present Protocol shall be applied by the States Parties hereto without any geographic limitation, save that existing declarations made by States already Parties to the Convention in accordance with article 1 B (1) (a) of the Convention, shall, unless extended under article 1 B (2) thereof, apply also under the present Protocol.

Article II. - Co-operation of the national authorities with the United Nations

1. The States Parties to the present Protocol undertake to co-operate with the Office of the United Nations High Commissioner for Refugees, or any other agency of the United Nations which may succeed it, in the exercise of its functions, and shall in particular facilitate its duty of supervising the application of the provisions of the present Protocol.

2. In order to enable the Office of the High Commissioner or any other agency of the United Nations which may succeed it, to make reports to the competent organs of the United Nations, the States Parties to the present Protocol undertake to provide them with the information and statistical data requested, in the appropriate form, concerning:

(a) The condition of refugees;

(b) The implementation of the present Protocol;

(c) Laws, regulations and decrees which are, or may hereafter be, in force relating to refugees.

Article III. - Information on national legislation

The tates Parties to the present Protocol shall communicate to the Secretary-General of the United Nations the laws and regulations which they may adopt to ensure the application of the present Protocol.

Article IV. - Settlement of disputes

Any dispute between States Parties to the present Protocol which relates to its interpretation or application and which cannot be settled by other means shall be referred to the International Court of Justice at the request of any one of the parties to the dispute.

Article V. - Accession

The present Protocol shall be open for accession on behalf of all States Parties to the Convention and of any other State Member of the United Nations or member of any of the specialized agencies or to which an invitation to accede may have been addressed by the General Assembly of the United Nations. Accession shall be effected by the deposit of an instrument of accession with the Secretary-General of the United Nations.

Article VI. - Federal clause

In the case of a Federal or non-unitary State, the following provisions shall apply:

(a) With respect to those articles of the Convention to be applied in accordance with article I, paragraph 1, of the present Protocol that come within the legislative jurisdiction of the federal legislative authority, the obligations of the Federal Government shall to this extent be the same as those of States Parties which are not Federal States;

(b) With respect to those articles of the Convention to be applied in accordance with article I, paragraph 1, of the present Protocol that come within the legislative jurisdiction of constituent States, provinces or cantons which are not, under the constitutional system of the Federation, bound to take legislative action, the Federal Government shall bring such articles with a favourable recommendation to the notice of the appropriate authorities of States, Provinces or cantons at the earliest possible moment;

(c) A Federal State Party to the present Protocol shall, at the request of any other State Party here to transmitted through the Secretary-General of the United Nations, supply a statement of the law and practice of the Federation and its constituent units in regard to any particular provision of the Convention to be applied in accordance with article I, paragraph 1, of the present Protocol, showing the extent to which effect has been given to that provision by legislative or other action.

Article VII. - Reservations and declarations

1. At the time of accession, any State may make reservations in respect of article IV of the present Protocol and in respect of the application in accordance with article I of the present Protocol of any provisions of the Convention other than those contained in articles 1, 3, 4, 16(1) and 33 thereof, provided that in the case of a State Party to the Convention reservations made under this article shall not extend to refugees in respect of whom the Convention applies.

2. Reservations made by State Parties to the Convention in accordance with article 42 thereof shall, unless withdrawn, be applicable in relation to their obligations under the present Protocol.

3. Any State making a reservation in accordance with paragraph 1 of this article may at any time withdraw such reservation by a communication to that effect addressed to the Secretary-General of the United Nations.

4. Declarations made under article 40, paragraphs 1 and 2, of the Convention by a State Party thereto which accedes to the present Protocol shall be deemed to apply

in respect of the present Protocol, unless upon accession a notification to the contrary is addressed by the State Party concerned to the Secretary-General of the United Nations. The provisions of article 40, paragraph 2 and 3, and of article 44, paragraph 3, of the Convention shall be deemed to apply *mutatis mutandis* to the present protocol.

Article VIII. - Entry into force

1. The present Protocol shall come into force on the day of deposit of the sixth instrument of accession.

2. For each State acceding to the Protocol after the deposit of the sixth instrument of accession, the Protocol shall come into force on the date of deposit by such State of its instrument of accession.

Article IX. - Denunciation

1. Any State Party hereto may denounce this Protocol at any time by a notification addressed to the secretary-General of the United Nations.

2. Such Denunciation shall take effect for the State Party concerned one year from the date on which it is received by the Secretary-General of the United Nations.

Article X. - Notifications by the Secretary-General of the United Nations

The Secretary-General of the United Nations shall inform the States referred to in article V above of the date of entry into force, accessions, reservations and withdrawals of reservations to and denunciations of the present Protocol, and of declarations and notifications relating hereto.

Article XI. - Deposit in the archives of the Secretariat of the United Nations

A copy of the present Protocol, of which the Chinese, English, French Russian and Spanish texts are equally authentic, signed by the President of the General Assembly and by the Secretary-General of the United

Nations, shall be deposited in the archives of the Secretariat of the United Nations. The Secretary-General will transmit certified copies thereof to all States Members of the United Nations and to the other States referred to in article V above.

7 Convention on the Reduction of Statelessness

Entry into force: 13 December 1975, in accordance with article 18

The Contracting States,

Acting in pursuance of resolution 896 (IX), adopted by the General Assembly of the United Nations on 4 December 1954,

Considering it desirable to reduce statelessness by international agreement,

Have agreed as follows:

Article 1

1. A Contracting State shall grant its nationality to a person born in its territory who would otherwise be stateless. Such nationality shall be granted:

(a) At birth, by operation of law, or

(b) Upon an application being law. Subject to the provisions of paragraph 2 of this article, no such application may be rejected.

A Contracting State which provides for the grant of its nationality in accordance with subparagraph (b) of this paragraph may also provide for the grant of its nationality by operation of law at such age and subject to such conditions as may be prescribed by the national law.

2. A Contracting State may make the grant of its nationality in accordance with subparagraph (b) of

paragraph 1 of this article subject to one or more of the following conditions:

(a) That the application is lodged during a period, fixed by the Contracting State, beginning not later than at the age of eighteen years and ending not earlier than at the age of twenty-one years, so, however, that the person concerned shall be allowed at least one year during which he may himself make the application without having to obtain legal authorization to do so;

(b) That the person concerned has habitually resided in the territory of the Contracting State for such period as may be fixed by that State, not exceeding five years immediately preceding the lodging of the application nor ten years in all;

(c) That the person concerned has neither been convicted of an offence against national security nor has been sentenced to imprisonment for a term of five years or more on a criminal charge;

(d) That the person concerned has always been stateless.

3. Notwithstanding the provisions of paragraphs 1 (b) and 2 of this article, a child born in wedlock in the territory of a Contracting State, whose mother has the nationality of that State, shall acquire at birth that nationality if it otherwise would be stateless.

4. A Contracting State shall grant its nationality to a person who would otherwise be stateless and who is unable to acquire the nationality of the Contracting State in whose territory he was born because he has passed the age for lodging his application or has not fulfilled the required residence conditions, if the nationality of one of his parents at the time of the person's birth was that of the Contracting State first above-mentioned. If his parents did not possess the same nationality at the time of his

birth, the question whether the nationality of the person concerned should follow that of the father or that of the mother shall be determined by the national law of such Contracting State. If application for such nationality is required, the application shall be made to the appropriate authority by or on behalf of the applicant in the manner prescribed by the national law. Subject to the provision of paragraph 5 of this article, such application shall not be refused.

5. The Contracting State may make the grant of its nationality in accordance with the provisions of paragraph 4 of this article subject to one or more of the following conditions:

(a) That the application is lodged before the applicant reaches an age, being not less than twenty-three years, fixed by the Contracting State;

(b) That the person concerned has habitually resided in the territory of the Contracting State for such period immediately preceding the lodging of the application, not exceeding three years, as may be fixed by that State;

(c) That the person concerned has always been stateless.

Article 2

A foundling found in the territory of a Contracting State shall, in the absence of proof to the contrary, be considered to have been born within that territory of parents possessing the nationality of that State.

Article 3

For the purpose of determining the obligations of Contracting States under this Convention, birth on a ship or in an aircraft shall be deemed to have taken place in the territory of the State whose flag the ship flies or in the territory of the State in which the aircraft is registered, as the case may be.

Article 4

1. A Contracting State shall grant its nationality to a person, not born in the territory of a Contracting State, who would otherwise be stateless, if the nationality of one of his parents at the time of the person's birth was that of that State. If his parents did not possess the same nationality at the time of his birth, the question whether the nationality of the person concerned should follow that of the father or that of the mother shall be determined by the national law of such Contracting State. Nationality granted in accordance with the provisions of this paragraph shall be granted.

(b) Upon an application being lodged with the appropriate authority, by or on behalf of the person concerned, in the manner prescribed by the national law. Subject to the provision of paragraph 2 of this article, no such application may be rejected.

2. A Contracting State may make the grant of its nationality in accordance with the provisions of paragraph 1 of this article subject to one or more of the following conditions:

(a) That the application is lodged before the applicant reaches an age, being not less than Twenty-three years, fixed by the Contracting State.

(b) That the person concerned has habitually resided in the territory of the Contracting State for such period immediately preceding the lodging of the application, not exceeding three years, as may be fixed by that State;

(c) That the person concerned has not been convicted of an offence against national security;

(d) That the person concerned has always been stateless.

Article 5

1. If the law of a Contracting State entails loss of nationality as a consequence of any change in the personal status of a person such as marriage, termination of marriage, legitimation, recognition or adoption, such loss shall be conditional upon possession or acquisition of another nationality.

2. If, under the law of a Contracting State, a child born out of wedlock loses the nationality of that State in consequence of a recognition of affiliation, he shall be given an opportunity to recover that nationality by written application to the appropriate authority, and the conditions governing such application shall not be more rigorous than those laid down in paragraph 2 of article 1 of this Convention.

Article 6

If the law of a Contracting State provides for loss of its nationality by a person's spouse or children as a consequence of that person losing or being deprived of that nationality, such loss shall be conditional upon their possession or acquisition of another nationality.

Article 7

1. (a) If the law of a Contracting State entails loss or renunciation of nationality, such renunciation shall not result in loss of nationality unless the person concerned possesses or acquires another nationality;

(b) The provisions of subparagraph (a) of this paragraph shall not apply where their application would be inconsistent with the principles stated in articles 13 and 14 of the Universal Declaration of Human Rights approved on 10 December 1948 by the General Assembly of the United Nations.

2. A national of a Contracting State who seeks naturalization in a foreign country shall not lose his nationality unless he acquires or has been accorded

assurance of acquiring the nationality of that foreign country.

3. Subject to the provisions of paragraphs 4 and 5 of this article, a national of a Contracting State shall not lose his nationality, so as to become stateless, on the ground of departure, residence abroad, failure to register or on any similar ground.

4. A naturalized person may lose his nationality on account of residence abroad for a period, not less than seven consecutive years, specified by the law of the Contracting State concerned if he fails to declare to the appropriate authority his intention to retain his nationality.

5. In the case of a national of a Contracting State, born outside its territory, the law of that State may make the retention of its nationality after the expiry of one year from his attaining his majority conditional upon residence at that time in the territory of the State or registration with the appropriate authority.

6. Except in the circumstances mentioned in this article, a person shall not lose the nationality of a Contracting State, if such loss would render him stateless, notwithstanding that such loss is not expressly prohibited by any other provision of this Convention.

Article 8

1. A Contracting State shall not deprive a person of his nationality if such deprivation would render him stateless.

2. Notwithstanding the provisions of paragraph 1 of this article, a person may be deprived of the nationality of a Contracting State:

(a) In the circumstances in which, under paragraphs 4 and 5 of article 7, it is permissible that a person should lose his nationality;

(b) Where the nationality has been obtained by misrepresentation or fraud.

3. Notwithstanding the provisions of paragraph 1 of this article, a Contracting State may retain the right to deprive a person of his nationality, if at the time of signature, ratification or accession it specifies its retention of such right on one or more of the following grounds, being grounds existing in its national law at that time;

(a) That, inconsistently with his duty of loyalty to the Contracting State, the person:

(i) Has, in disregard of an express prohibition by the Contracting State rendered or continued to render services to, or reçeived or continued to receive emoluments from, another State, or

(ii) Has conducted himself in a manner seriously prejudicial to the vital interests of the State;

(b) That the person has taken an oath, or made a formal declaration, of allegiance to another State, or given definite evidence of his determination to repudiate his allegiance to the Contracting State.

4. A Contracting State shall not exercise a power of deprivation permitted by paragraphs 2 or 3 of this article except in accordance with law, which shall provide for the person concerned the right to a fair hearing by a court or other independent body.

Article 9

A Contracting State may not deprive any person or group of persons of their nationality on racial, ethnic, religious or political grounds.

Article 10

1. Every treaty between Contracting States providing for the transfer of territory shall include provisions designed to secure that no person shall become stateless as a result of the transfer. A Contracting State shall use its best endeavours to secure that any such treaty made

by it with a State which is not a Party to this Convention includes such provisions.

2. In the absence of such provisions a Contracting State to which territory is transferred or which otherwise acquires territory shall confer its nationality on such persons as would otherwise become stateless as a result of the transfer or acquisition.

Article 11

The Contracting States shall promote the establishment within the framework of the United Nations, as soon as may be after the deposit of the sixth instrument of ratification or accession, of a body to which a person claiming the benefit of this Convention may apply for the examination of his claim and for assistance in presenting it to the appropriate authority.

Article 12

1. In relation to a Contracting State which does not, in accordance with the provisions of paragraph 1 of article 1 or of article 4 of this Convention, grant its nationality at birth by operation of law, the provisions of paragraph 1 of article 1 or of article 4, as the case may be, shall apply to persons born before as well as to persons born after the entry into force of this Convention.

2. The provisions of paragraph 4 of article 1 of this Convention shall apply to persons born before as well as to persons born after its entry into force.

3. The provisions of article 2 of this Convention shall apply only to foundlings found in the territory of a Contracting State after the entry into force of the Convention for that State.

Article 13

This Convention shall not be construed as affecting any provisions more conducive to the reduction of statelessness which may be contained in the law of any Contracting State now or hereafter in force, or may be contained in any other convention, treaty or agreement now or hereafter in force between two or more Contracting States.

Article 14

Any dispute between Contracting States concerning the interpretation or application of this Convention which cannot be settled by other means shall be submitted to the International Court of Justice at the request of any one of the parties to the dispute.

Article 15

1. This Convention shall apply to all non-governing, trust, colonial and other no-metropolitan territories for the international relations of which any Contracting State is responsible; the Contracting State concerned shall, subject to the provisions of paragraph 2 of this article, at the time of signature, ratification or accession, declare the non-metropolitan territory or territories to which the Convention shall apply ipso facto as a result such signature, ratification or accession.

2. In any case in which, for the purpose of nationality, a non-metropolitan territory is not treated as one with the metropolitan territory, or in any case in which the previous consent of a non-metropolitan territory is required by the constitutional laws or practices of the Contracting State or of the non-metropolitan territory for the application of the Convention to that territory, that Contracting State shall endeavour to secure the needed consent of the non-metropolitan territory within the period of twelve months from the date of signature of the Convention by that Contracting State, and when such consent has been obtained the Contracting State shall notify the Secretary-General of the United Nations. This Convention shall apply to the territory or territories named in such notification from the date of its receipt by the Secretary-General.

3. After the expiry of the twelve-month period mentioned in paragraph 2 of this article, the Contracting States concerned shall inform the Secretary-General of the results of the consultations with those non-metropolitan territories for whose international relations they are responsible and whose consent to the application of this Convention may have been withheld.

Article 16

1. This Convention shall be open for signature at the Headquarters of the United Nations from 30 August 1961 to 31 May 1962.

2. This Convention shall be open for signature on behalf of;

(a) Any State Member of the United Nations;

(b) Any other State invited to attend the United Nations Conference on the Elimination or Reduction of Future Statelessness;

(c) Any State to which an invitation to sign or to accede may be addressed by the General Assembly of the United Nations.

3. This Convention shall be ratified and the instruments of ratification shall be deposited with the Secretary-General of the United Nations.

4. This Convention shall be open for accession by the States referred to in paragraph 2 of this article. Accession shall be effected by the deposit of an instrument of accession with the Secretary-General of the United Nations.

Article 17

1. At the time of signature, ratification or accession any State may make a reservation in respect of articles 11, 14 or 15.

2. No other reservations to this Convention shall be admissible.

Article 18

1. This Convention shall enter into force two years after the date of the deposit of the sixth instrument of ratification or accession.

2. For each State ratifying or acceding to this Convention after the deposit of the sixth instrument of ratification or accession, it shall enter into force on the ninetieth day after the deposit by such State of its instrument of ratification or accession or on the date on which this Convention enters into force in accordance with the provisions of paragraph 1 of this article, whichever is the later.

Article 19

1. Any Contracting State may denounce this Convention at any time by a written notification addressed to the Secretary-General of the United Nations. Such denunciation shall take effect for the Contracting State concerned one year after the date of its receipt by the Secretary-General.

2. In cases where, in accordance with the provisions of article 15, this Convention has become applicable to a non-metropolitan territory of a Contracting State, that State may at any time thereafter, with the Consent of the Territory concerned, give notice to the Secretary-General of the United Nations denouncing this Convention separately in respect to that territory. The denunciation shall take effect one year after the date of the receipt of such notice by the Secretary-General, who shall notify all other Contracting States of such notice and the date of receipt thereof.

Article 20

1. The Secretary-General of the United Nations shall notify all Members of the United Nations and the non-member States referred to in article 16 of the following particulars;

(a) Signatures, ratifications and accessions under article 16;

(b) Reservations under article 17;

(c) The date upon which this Convention enters into force in pursuance of article 18;

(d) Denunciations under article 19.

2. The Secretary-General of the United Nations shall, after the deposit of the sixth instrument of ratification or accession at the latest, bring the the attention of the General Assembly the question of the establishment, in accordance with article 11, of such a body as therein mentioned.

Article 21

This Convention shall be registered by the Secretary-General of the United Nations on the date of its entry into force.

In witness whereof the undersigned Plenipotentiaries have signed this Convention.

Done at new York, this thirtieth day of August, one thousand nine hundred and sixty-one in a single copy of which the Chinese English, French, Russian and Spanish texts are equally authentic and which shall be deposited in the archives of the United Nations, and certified copies of which shall be delivered by the Secretary-General of the United Nations to all members of the United Nations and to the non-member States referred to in article 16 of this Convention.

8 Labour Relations (Public Service) Convention

Adopted on 27 june 1978 by te General Conference of the Internatonal Labour Organisation at its sixth—fourth session.

The General Conference of the International Labour Organisation,

Having been convened at Geneva by the Governing Body of the International Labour Office, and having met in its sixty-fourth session on 7 June 1978, and

Noting the terms of the freedom of Association and Protection of the Right to Organise Convention, 1948, the Right to Organise and Collective Bargaining Convention,1949, and the Workers' Representatives Convention and Recommendation, 1971, and

Recalling that the Right to Organise and Collective Bargaining Convention, 1949, does not cover certain categories of public employees and that the Workers' Representatives Convention and Recommendation, 1971, apply to workers' representatives in the undertaking, and

Noting the considerable expansion of public-service activities in many countries and the need for sound labour relations between public authorities and public enployees' organisations, and

Having regard to the great diversity of political, social and economic systems among Member States and the differences in practice among them (e.g. as to the respective functions of central and local government, of federal, State and provincial authorities, and of state-owned undertakings and various types of autonomous or semi-autonomous public bodies, as well as to the nature of employment relationships), and

Taking into account the particular problems arising as to the scope of, and definitions for the purpose of, any international instrument, owing to the differences in many countries between private and public employment, as well as the difficulties of interpretation which have arisen in respect of the application of relevant provisions of the Right to Organise and Collective Bargaining Convention 1949, to public servants, and the observations of the supervisory bodies of the ILO on a number of occasions that some governments have applied these provisions in a manner which excludes large groups of public employees from coverage by that Convention, and

Having decided upon the adoption of certain proposals with regard to freedom of association and procedures for determining conditions of employment in the public service, which is the fifth item on the agenda of the session, and

Having determined that these proposals shall take the form of an international Convention,

Adopts this twenty-seventh day of June of the year one thousand nine hundred and seventy-eight the following Convention, which may be cited as the Labour Relations (Public Service) Convention, 1978:

Part I

Scope and Definitions

Article 1

1. This Convention applies to all persons employed by public authorities, to the extent that more favourable provisions in other international labour Conventions are not applicable to them.
2. The extent to which the guarantees provided for in

this Convention shall apply to high-level employees whose functions are normally considered as policy-making or managerial, or to employees whose duties are of a highly confidential nature, shall be determined by national laws or regulations.

3. The extent to which the guarantees provided for in this Convention shall apply to the armed forces and the police shall be determined by national laws or regulations.

Article 2

For the purpose of this Convention, the term "public employe" means any person covered by the Convention in accordance with article 1 thereof.

Article 3

For the purpose of this Convention, the term "public employees" organisation" means any organisation, however composed, the purpose of which is to further and defend the interests of public employees.

Part II

Protection of the Right to Organise

Article 4

1. Public employees shall enjoy adequate protection against acts of anti-union discrimination in respect of their employment.
2. Such protection shall apply more particularly in respect of acts calculated to:
   (a) Make the employment of public employees subject to the condition that they shall not join or shall relinquish membership of a public employees' organisation;
   (b) Cause the dismissal of or otherwise prejudice a public employee by reason of membership of a public employees' organisation or because of participation in the normal activities of such an

organisation.

Article 5

1. Public employees' organisations shall enjoy complete independence from public authorities.
2. Public employees' organisations shall enjoy adequate protection against any acts or interference by public authority in their establishment, functioning or administration.
3. In particular, acts which are designed to promote the establishment of public employees' organisations under the domination of a public authority, or to support public employees' organisations by financial or other means, with the object of placing such organisations under the control of a public authority, shall be deemed to constitute acts of interference within the meaning of this article.

Part III

Facilities to be Afforded to Public Employees' Organisations

Article 6

1. Such facilities shall be afforded to the representatives of recognised public employees' organisation as may be appropriate in order to enable them to carry out their functions promptly and efficiently, both during and outside their hours of work.
2. The granting of such facilities shall not impair the efficient operation of he administration or service concerned.
3. The nature and scope of these facilities shall be determined in accordance with the methods referred to in article 7 of this Convention, or by other appropriate means.

Part IV

Procedures for Determining Terms and Conditions of Employment

Article 7

Measures appropriate to national condition shall be taken, where necessary, to encourage and promote the full development and utilisation of machinery for negotiation of terms and conditions of employment between the public authorities concerned and public employees' organisations, or of such other methods as will allow representatives of public employees to participate in the determination of these matters.

Part V

Settlement of Disputes

Article 8

The settlement of disputes arising in connection with the determination of terms and conditions of employment shall be sought, as may be appropriate to national conditions, through negotiation between the parties or through independent and impartial machinery, such as mediation, conciliation and arbitration, established in such a manner as to ensure the confidence of the parties involved.

Part VI

Civil and Political Rights

Article 9

Public employees shall have, as other workers, the civil and political rights which are essential for the normal exercise of freedom of association subject only to the obligations arising from their status and the nature of their functions.

Part VII

Final Provisions

Article 10

The formal ratifications of this Convention shall be

communicated to the Director-General of the International Labour Office for registration.

Article 11

1. This Convention shall be binding only upon those Members of the International Labour Organisation whose ratifications have been registered with the Director-General.
2. It shall come into force twelve months after the date on which the ratifications of two Members have been registered with the Director-General.
3. Thereafter, this Convention shall come into force for any Member twelve months after the date on which its ratification has been registered.

Article 12

1. A Member which has ratified this Convention may denounce it after the expiration of ten years from the date on which the Convention first comes into force, by an act communicated to the Director-General of the International Labour Office for registration. Such denunciation shall not take effect until one year after the date on which it is registered.
2. Each Member which has ratified this Convention and which does not, within the year following the expiration of the period of ten years mentioned in the preceding paragraph, exercise the right of denunciation provided for in this article, will be bound for another period of ten years and, thereafter, may denounce this Convention at the expiration of each period of ten years under the terms provided for in this article.

Article 13

1. The Director-General of the International Labour Office shall notify all Members of the International Labour Organisation of the registration of all ratifications and denunciations communicated to him by the Members of the Organisation.

2. When notifying the Members of the Organisation of the registration of the second ratification communicated to him, the Director-General shall draw the attention of the Members of the Organisation to the date upon which the Convention will come into force.

Article 14

The Director-General of the International Labour Office shall communicate to the Secretary-General of the United Nations for registration in accordance with Article 102 of the Charter of the United Nations full particulars of all ratifications and acts of denunciation registered by him in accordance with the provisions of the preceding articles.

Article 15

At such times as it may consider necessary the Governing Body of the International Labour Office shall present to the General Conference a report on the working of this Convention and shall examine the desirability of placing on the agenda of the Conference the question of its revision in whole or in part.

Article 16

1. Should the Conference adopt a new Convention revising this Convention in whole or in part, then, unless the new Convention otherwise provides:
   (a) The ratification by a Member of the new revising Convention shall ipso jure involve the immediate denunciation of this Convention, notwithstanding the provisions of article 12 above, if and when the new revising Convention shall have come into force;
   (b) As from the date when the new revising Convention comes into force this Convention shall cease to be open to ratification by the Members.

2. This Convention shall in any case remain in force in its actual form and content for those Members which have ratified it but have not ratified the revising Convention.

Article 17

The English and French versions of the text of this Convention are equally authoritative.

9 Forced Labour Convention Concerning Forced Labour

The General Conference of the International Labour Organisation,

Having been convened at Geneva by the Governing Body of the International Labour Office, and having met in its fourteenth session on 10 June 1930, and

Having decided upon the adoption of certain proposals with regard to forced or compulsory labour, which is included in the first item on the agenda of the session, and

Having determined that these proposals shall take the form of an international Convention,

Adopts this twenty-eighth day of June of the year one thousand nine hundred and thirty the following Convention, which may be cited as the Forced Labour Convention, 1930, for ratification by the Members of the International Labour Organisation in accordance with the provisions of the Constitution of the International Labour Organisation:

Article 1

1. Each Member of the International Labour Organisation which ratified this Convention undertakes to suppress the use of forced or compulsory labour in all its forms within the shortest possible period.

2. With a view to this complete suppression, recourse to forced or compulsory labour may be had, during the

transitional period, for public purposes only and as an exceptional measure, subject to the conditions and guarantees hereinafter provided.

3. At the expiration of a period of five years after the coming into force of this Convention, and when the Governing Body of the International Labour Office prepares the report provided for in article 31 below, the said Governing Body shall consider the possibility of the suppression of forced or compulsory labour in all its forms without a further transitional period and the desirability of placing this question on the agenda of the Conference.

Article 2

1. For the purposes of this Convention the term "forced or compulsory labour" shall mean all work or service which is exacted from any person under the menace of any penalty and for which the said person has not offered himself voluntarily.

2. Nevertheless, for the purposes of this Convention the term "forced or compulsory labour" shall not include:

(a) Any work or service exacted in virtue of compulsory military service laws for work of a purely military character:

(b) Any work or service which forms part of thenormal civic obligations of the citizens of a fully self-governing country;

(c) Any work or service exacted from any person as a consequence of a conviction in a court of law, provided that the said work or service is carried out under the supervision and control of a public authority and that the said person is not hired to or placed at the associations;

(d) Any work or service exacted in cases of emergency, that is to say, in the event of war or of a calamity or threatened calamity, such as fire, flood, famine, earthquake, violent epidemic or epizootic diseases, invasion by animal insect or vegetable pests, and in general any circumstance that would endanger the existence or the well-being of the whole or part of the population;

(e) Minor communal services of a kind which, being performed by the members of the community in the direct interest of the said community, can therefore be considered as normal civic obligation incumbent upon the members of the community, provided that the members of the community or their direct representatives shall have the right to be consulted in regard to the need for such services.

Article 3

For the purposes of this Convention the term "competent authority" shall mean either an authority of the metropolitan country or the highest central authority in the territory concerned.

Article 4

1. The competent authority shall not impose or permit the imposition of forced or compulsory labour for the benefit of private individuals, companies or associations.

2. Where such forced or compulsory labour for the benefit of private individuals, companies or associations exists at the date on which a Member's ratification of this Convention is registered by the Director-General of the International Labour Office, the Member shall completely suppress such forced or compulsory labour from the date on which this convention comes into force for that Member.

Article 5

1. No concession granted to private individuals, companies or associations shall involve any form of forced or compulsory labour for the production or the

collection or products which such private individuals, companies or associations utilise or in which they trade.

2. Where concessions exist containing provision involving such forced or compulsory labour, such provisions shall be rescinded as soon as possible, in order to comply with article 1 of this Convention.

Article 6

Officials of the administration, even when they have the duty of encouraging the populations under their charge to engage in some form of labour, shall not put constraint upon the said populations or upon any individual members thereof to work for private individuals, companies or associations.

Article 7

1. Chiefs who do not exercise administrative functions shall not have recourse to forced or compulsory labour.

2. Chiefs who exercise administrative functions may, with the express permission of the competent authority, have recourse to forced or compulsory labour, subject to the provisions of article 10 of this Convention.

3. Chiefs who are duly recognised and who do not receive adequate remuneration in other forms may have the enjoyment of personal services, subject to due regulation and provided that all necessary measures are taken to prevent abuses.

Article 8

1. The responsibility for every decision to have recourse to forced or compulsory labour shall rest with the highest civil authority in the territory concerned.

2. Nevertheless, that authority may delegate powers to the highest local authorities to exact forced or compulsory labour which does not involve the removal of the workers from their place of habitual residence. That authority may also delegate, for such periods and

subject to such conditions as may be laid down in the regulations provided for in article 23 of this Convention, powers to the highest local authorities to exact forced or compulsory labour which involves the removal of the workers from their place of habitual residence for the purpose of facilitating the movement of officials of the administration, when on duty, and for the transport of Government stores.

Article 9

Except as otherwise provided for in article 10 of this Convention, any authority competent to exact forced or compulsory labour shall, before deciding to have recourse to such labour, satisfy itself:

(a) That the work to be done or the service to be rendered is of important direct interest for the community called upon to do the work or render the service;
(b) That the work or service is of present or imminent necessity;
(c) That it has been impossible to obtain voluntary labour for carrying out the work or rendering the service by the offer of rates of wages and conditions of labour not less favourable than those prevailing in the area concerned for similar work or service; and
(d) That the work or service will not lay too heavy a burden upon the present population, having regard to the labour available and its capacity to undertake the work.

Article 10

1. Forced or compulsory labour exacted as a tax and forced or compulsory labour to which recourse is had for the execution of public works by chiefs who exercise administrative functions shall be progressively abolished.

2. Meanwhile, where forced or compulsory labour is

exacted as a tax, and where recourse is had to forced or compulsory labour for the execution of public works by chiefs who exercise administrative functions, the authority concerned shall first satisfy itself:

(a) That the work to be done or the service to be rendered is of important direct interest for the community called upon to do the work or render the service;

(b) That the work or the service is of present or imminent necessity;

(c) That the work or service will not lay too heavy a burden upon the present population, having regard to the labour available and its capacity to undertake the work;

(d) That the work or service will not entail the removal of the workers from their place of habitual residence;

(e) That the execution of the work or the rendering of the service will be directed in accordance with the exigencies of religion, social life and agriculture.

Article 11

1. Only adult able-bodied males who are of an apparent age of not less than 18 and not more than 45 years may be called upon for forced or compulsory labour. Except in respect of the kinds of labour provided for in article 10 of this Convention, the following limitations and conditions shall apply:

(a) Whenever possible prior determination by a medical officer appointed by the administration that the persons concerned are not suffering from any infectious or contagious disease and that they are physically fit for the work required and for the conditions under which it is to be carried out;

(b) Exemption of school teachers and pupils and of officials of the administration in general;

(c) The maintenance in each community of the number of adult able-bodied men indispensable for family and social life;

(d) Respect for conjugal and family ties.

2. For the purpose of subparagraph (c) of the preceding paragraph, the regulations provided for in article 23 of this Convention shall fix the proportion of the resident adult able-bodied males who may be taken at any one time for forced or compulsory labour, provided always that this proportion shall in no case exceed 25 per cent. In fixing this proportion the competent authority shall take account of the density of the population, of its social and physical development, of the seasons, and of the work which must be done by the persons concerned on their own behalf in their locality, and, generally, shall have regard to the economic and social necessities of the normal life of the community concerned.

Article 12

1. The maximum period for which any person may be taken for forced or compulsory labour of all kinds in any one period of twelve months shall not exceed sixty days, including the time spent in going to and from the place of work.

2. Every person from whom forced or compulsory labour is exacted shall be furnished with a certificate indicating the periods of such labour which he has completed.

Article 13

1. The normal working hours of any person from whom forced or compulsory labour is exacted shall be the same as those prevailing in the case of voluntary Labour, and the hours worked in excess of the normal working hours shall be remunerated at the rates prevailing in the case of overtime for voluntary labour.

2. A weekly day of rest shall be granted to all persons from whom forced or compulsory labour of any kind is exacted and this day shall coincide as far as possible with the day fixed by tradition or custom in the territories or regions concerned.

Article 14

1. With the exception of the forced or compulsory labour provided for in article 10 of this Convention, forced or compulsory labour of all kinds shall be remunerated in cash at rates not less than those prevailing for similar kinds of work either in the district in which the labour is employed or in teh district from which the labour recruited, whichever may be the higher.

2. In the case of labour to which recourse is had by chiefs in the exercise of their administrative functions, payment of wages in accordance with the provisions of the preceding paragraph shall be introduced as soon as possible.

3. The wages shall be paid to each worker individually and not to his tribal chief or to any other authority.

4. For the purpose of payment of wages the days spent in travelling to and from the place of work shall be counted as working days.

5. Nothing in this article shall prevent ordinary rations being given as a part of wages, such rations to be at least equivalent in value to the money payment they are taken to represent, but deductions from wages shall not be made either for the payment of taxes or for special food, clothing or accommodation supplied to a worker for the purpose of maintaining him in a fit condition to carry on his work under the special conditions of any employment, or for the supply of tools.

Article 15

1. Any laws or regulations relating to workmen's compensation for accidents or sickness arising out of the employment of the worker and any laws or regulations providing compensation for the dependants of deceased or incapacitated workers which are or shall be in force in the territory concerned shall be equally applicable to persons from whom forced or compulsory labour is exacted and to voluntary workers.

2. In any case it shall be an obligation on any authority employing any worker on forced or compulsory labour to ensure the subsistence of any such worker who, by accident or sickness arising out of his employment, is rendered wholly or partially incapable of providing for himself, and to take measures to ensure the maintenance of any persons actually dependent upon such a worker in the event of his incapacity or decease arising out of his employment.

Article 16

1. Except in cases of special necessity, persons from whom forced or compulsory labour is exacted shall not be transferred to districts where the food and climate differ so considerably from those to which they have been accustomed as to endanger their health.

2. In no case shall the transfer of such workers be permitted unless all measures relating to hygiene and accommodation which are necessary to adapt such workers to the conditions and to safeguard their health can be strictly applied.

3. When such transfer cannot be avoided, measures of gradual habituation to the new conditions of diet and of climate shall be adopted on competent medical advice.

4. In cases where such workers are required to perform regular work to which they are not accustomed, measures shall be taken to ensure their habituation to it, especially as regards progressive training, the hours of

work and the provision of rest intervals, and any increase or amelioration of diet which may be necessary.

Article 17

Before permitting recourse to forced or compulsory labour for works of construction or maintenance which entail the workers remaining at the workplaces for considerable periods, the competent authority shall satisfy itself:

(1) That all necessary measures are taken to safeguard the health of the workers and to guarantee the necessary medical care, and, in particular, (a) that the workers are medically examined before commencing the work and at fixed intervals during the period of service, (b) that there is an adequate medical staff, provided with the dispensaries, infirmaries, hospitals and equipment necessary to meet all requirements, and (c) that the sanitary conditions of the workplaces, the supply of drinking water, food, fuel, and cooking ustensils, and, where necessary, of housing and clothing are satisfactory;

(2) That definite arrangement are made to ensure the subsistence of the families of the workers, in particular by facilitating the remittance, by a safe method, of part of the wages to the family, at the request or with the consent of the workers:

(3) That the journey of the workers to and from the workplaces are made at the expense and under the responsibility of the administration, which shall facilitate such journeys by making the fullest use of all available means of transport;

(4) That, in case of illness or accident causing incapacity to work of a certain duration, the worker is repatriated at the expense of the administration.

(5) the end of his period of forced or compulsory labour is permitted to do so the end of his period of forced or compulsory labour is permitted to do as

without, for a period of two years, losing his right to repatriation free of expense to himself.

Article 18

1. Forced or compulsory labour for the transport of persons or goods, such as the labour of porters or boatmen, shall be abolished within the shortest possible period. Meanwhile the competent authority shall promulgate regulations determining, inter alia, (a) that such labour shall only be employed for the purpose of facilitating the movement of officials of the administration, when on duty, or for the transport of Government stores, or, in cases of very urgent necessity, the transport of persons other than officials, (b) that the workers so employed shall be medically certified to be physically fit, where medical examination is possible, and that where such medical examination is not practicable the person employing such workers shall be held responsible for ensuring that they are physically fit and not suffering from any infectious or contagious diseases, (c) the maximumload which these workers may carry, (D) the maximum distance from their homes to which they may be taken, (e) the maximum number of days per month or other period for which they may be taken, including the days spent in returning to their homes, and (f) the persons entitled to demand this form of forced or compulsory labour and the extent to which they are entitled to demand it.

2. In fixing the maxima referred to under (c), (d) and (e) in the foregoing paragraph, the competent authority shall have regard to all relevant factors, including the physical development of the population from which the workers are recruited, the nature of the country through which they must travel and the climatic conditions.

3. The competent authority shall further provide that the normal daily journey of such workers shall not exceed a distance corresponding to an average working

day of eight hours, it being understood that account shall be taken not only of the weight to be carried and the distance to be covered, but also of the nature of the road, the season and all other relevant factors, and that, where hours of journey in excess of the normal daily journey are exacted, they shall be remunerated at rates higher than the normal rates.

Article 19

1. The competent authority shall only authorise recourse to compulsory cultivation as a method of precaution against famine or a deficiency of food supplies and always under the condition that the food or produce shall remain the property of the individuals or the community producing it.

2. Nothing in this article shall be construed as abrogating the obligation on members of a community, where production is organised on a communal basis by virtue of law or custom and where the procedure or any profit accruing from the sale thereof remain the property of the community, to perform the work demanded by the community by virtue of law or custom.

Article 20

Collective punishment laws under which a community may be punished for crimes committed by any of its members shall not contain provisions for forced or compulsory labour by the community as one of the methods of punishment.

Article 21

Forced or compulsory labour shall not be used for work underground in mines.

Article 22

The annual reports that Members which ratify this Convention agree to make to the International Labour Office, pursuant to the provisions of article 22 of the Constitution of the International Labour Organisation, on the measures they have taken to give effect to the provisions of this Convention, shall contain as full information as possible, in respect of each territory concerned, regarding the extent to which recourse has been had to forced or compulsory labour in that territory, the purposes for which it has been employed, the sickness and death rates, hours of work, methods of payment of wages and rates of wages, and any other relevant information.

Article 23

1. To give effect to the provisions of this Convention the competent authority shall issue complete and precise regulations governing the use of forced or compulsory labour.

2. These regulations shall contain, *inter alia,* rules permitting any person from whom forced or compulsory labour is exacted to forward all complaints relative to the conditions of labour to the authorities and ensuring that such complaints will be examined and taken into consideration.

Article 24

Adequate measures shall in all cases be taken to ensure that the regulations governing the employment of forced or compulsory labour are strictly applied, either by extending the duties of any inspection of forced or compulsory labour or in some other appropriate manner. Measures shall also be taken to ensure that the regulations are brought to the knowledge of person from whom such labour is exacted.

Article 25

The illegal exaction of forced or compulsory labour shall be punishable as a penal offence, and it shall be an obligation on any Member ratifying this Convention to ensure that the penalties imposed by law are really adequate and are strictly enforced.

Article 26

1. Each Member of the International Labour Organisation which ratifies this Convention undertakes to apply it to the territories placed under its sovereignty, jurisdiction, protection, suzerainty, tutelage or authority, so far as it has the right to accept obligations affecting matters of internal jurisdiction; provided that, if such Member may desire to take advantage of the provisions of article 35 of the Constitution of the International Labour Organisation, it shall append to its ratification a declaration stating:

(1) The territories to which it intends to apply the provisions of this Convention without modifications;

(2) The territories to which it intends to apply the provisions of this Convention with modifications, together with details of the said modification;

(3) The territories in respect of which it reserves its decision.

2. The aforesaid declaration shall be deemed to be an integral part of the ratification and shall have the force of ratification. It shall be open to any Member, by a subsequent declaration, to cancel in whole or in part the reservations made, in pursuance of the provisions of subparagraphs (2) and (3) of this article, in the original declaration.

Article 27

The formal ratification of this Convention under the conditions set forth in the Constitution of the International Labour Organisation shall be communicated to the Director-General of the International Labour Office for Registration.

Article 28

1. This Convention shall be binding only upon those Members whose ratifications have been registered with the International Labour Office.

2. It shall come into force twelve months after the date on which the ratifications of two Members of the International Labour Organisation have been registered with the Director-General.

3. Thereafter, this Convention shall come into force for any Member twelve months after the date on which the ratification has been registered.

Article 29

As soon as the ratifications of two Members of the International Labour Organisation have been registered with the International Labour Office, the Director-General of the International Labour Office shall so notify all the Members of the International Labour Organisation. He shall likewise notify them of the registration of ratifications which may be communicated subsequently by other Members of the Organisation.

Article 30

1. A Member which has ratified this Convention may denounce it after the expiration of ten years from the date on which the Convention first comes into force, by an act communicated to the Director-General of the International Labour Office for registration. Such denunciation shall not take effect until one year after the date on which it is registered with the International Labour Office.

2. Each Member which has ratified this Convention and which does not, within the year following the expiration of the period of ten years mentioned in the preceding paragraph, exercise the right of denunciation provided for in this article, will be bound for another period of five years and, thereafter, may denounce this Convention at the expiration of each period of five years under the terms provided for in this article.

Article 31

At the expiration of each period of five years after the

coming into force of this Convention, the Governing Body of the International Labour Office shall present to the General Conference a report on the working of this Convention and shall consider the desirability of placing on the agenda of the Conference the question of its revision in whole or in part.

Article 32

1. Should the Conference adopt a new Convention revising this Convention in whole or in part, the ratification by a Member of the new revising Convention shall ipso jure involve denunciation of this Convention without any requirement of delay, notwithstanding the provisions of article 30 above, if and when the new revising Convention shall have come into force.

2. As from the date of the coming into force of the new revising Convention, the present Convention shall cease to be open to ratification by the Members.

3. Nevertheless, this Convention shall remain in force in its actual form and content for those Members which have ratified it but have not ratified the revising Convention.

Article 33

The French and English texts of this Convention shall both be authentic.

10 Convention for the Suppression of the Traffic in Persons

Preamble

Whereas prostitution and the accompanying even of the traffic in person for the purpose of prostitution are incompatible with the dignity and worth of the human person and endanger the welfare of the individual, the family and the community,

Whereas, with respect to the suppression of the traffic in women and children, the following international instruments are in force:

(1) International Agreement of 18 May 1904 for the Suppression of the White Slave Traffic, as amended by the Protocol approved by the General Assembly of the United Nations on 3 December 1948,

(2) International Convention of 4 May 1910 for the Suppression of the White Slave Traffic, as amended by the above-mentioned Protocol,

(3) International Convention of 30 September 1921 for the Suppression of the Traffic in Women and Children, as amended by the Protocol approved by the General Assembly of the United Nations on 20 October 1947,

(4) International Convention of 11 October 1933 for the Suppression of the Traffic in Women of Full Age, as amended by the aforesaid Protocol,

Whereas the League on Nations in 1937 prepared a

draft Convention extending the scope of the above-mentioned instruments, and

Whereas developments since 1937 make feasible the conclusion of a convention consolidating the above-mentioned instruments and embodying the substance of the 1937 draft Convention as well as desirable alterations therein:

Now therefore

The Contracting parties

Hereby agree as hereinafter provided:

Article 1

The Parties to the present Convention agree to punish any person who, to gratify the passions of another:

(1) Procures, entices or leads away, for purposes of prostitution, another person, even with the consent of that person;

(2) Exploits the prostitution of another person, even with the consent of that person.

Article 2

The Parties to the present Convention further agree to punish any person who:

(1) Keeps or manages, or knowingly finances or takes part in the financing of a brothel;

(2) Knowingly lets or rents a building or other place or any part thereof for the purpose of the prostitution of others.

Article 3

To the extent permitted by domestic law, attempts to commit any of the offences referred to in articles 1 and 2, and acts preparatory to the commission thereof, shall also be punished.

Article 4

To the extent permitted by domestic law, intentional

participation in the acts referred to in articles 1 and 2 above shall also be punishable.

To the extent permitted by domestic law, acts of participation shall be treated as separate offences whenever this is necessary to prevent impunity.

Article 5

In cases where injured persons are entitled under domestic law to be parties to proceedings in respect of any of the offences referred to in the present Convention, aliens shall be so entitled upon the same terms as nationals.

Article 6

Each Party to the present Convention agrees to take all the necessary measures to repeal or abolish any existing law, regulation or administrative provision by virtue of which persons who engage in or are suspected of engaging in prostitution are subject either to special registration or to the possession of a special document or to any exceptional requirements for supervision or notification.

Article 7

Previous convictions pronounced in foreign States for offences referred to in the present Convention shall, to the extent permitted by domestic law, be taken into account for the purpose of:

(1) Establishing recidivism;

(2) Disqualifying the offender from the ????

Article 8

The offences referred to in articles 1 and 2 of the present Convention shall be regarded as extraditable offences in any extradition treaty which has been or may hereafter be concluded between any of the Parties to this Convention.

The Parties to the present Convention which do not

make extradition conditional on the existence of a treaty shall henceforward recognize the offences referred to in articles 1 and 2 of the present Convention as cases for extradition between themselves.

Extradition shall be granted in accordance with the law of the State to which the request is made.

Article 9

In States where the extradition of nationals is not permitted by law, nationals who have returned to their own State after the commission abroad on any of the offences referred to in articles 1 and2 of the present Convention shall be prosecuted in and punished by the courts of their own State.

This provision shall not apply if, in a similar case between the Parties to the present Convention, the extradition of an alien cannot be granted.

Article 10

The provisions of article 9 shall not apply when the person charged with the offence has been tried in a foreign State and, if convicted, has served his sentence or and it remitted or reduced in conformity with the laws of that foreign State.

Article 11

Nothing in the present Convention shall be interpreted as determining the attitude of a party towards the general question of the limits of criminal jurisdiction under international law.

Article 12

The present Convention does not affect the principle that the offences to which it refers shall in each State be defined, prosecuted and punished in conformity with its domestic law.

Article 13

The Parties to the present Convention shall be bound to execute letters of request relating to offences referred to in the Convention in accordance with their domestic law and practice.

The transmission of letters of request shall be effected:

(1) By direct communication between the judicial authorities; or

(2) By direct communication between the Ministers of Justice of the two States, or by direct communication from another competent authority of the State making the request to the Minister of Justice of the State to which the request is made; or

(3) Through the diplomatic or consular representative of the State making the request in the State to which the request is made; this representative shall send the letters of request direct to the competent judicial authority or to the authority indicated by the Government of the State to which the request is made, and shall receive direct from such authority the papers constituting the execution of the letters of request.

In cases 1 and 3 a copy of the letters of request shall always be sent to the superior authority of the State to which application is made.

Unless otherwise agreed, the letters of request shall be drawn up in the language of the authority making the request, provided always that the State to which the request is made may require a translation in its own language, certified correct by the authority making the request.

Each Party to the present Convention shall notify to each of the other Parties to the Convention the method or methods of transmission mentioned above which it will recognize for the letters of request of the latter State.

Until such notification is made by a State, its existing procedure in regard to letters of request shall remain in force.

Execution of letters of request shall not give rise to a claim for reimbursement of charges or expenses of any nature whatever other than expenses of experts.

Nothing in the present article shall be construed as an undertaking on the part of the Parties to the present Convention to adopt in criminal matters any form of methods of proof contrary to their own domestic laws.

Article 14

Each Party to the present Convention shall establish or maintain a service charged with the co-ordination and centralization of the results of the investigation of offences referred to in the present Convention.

Such services should compile all information calculated to facilitate the prevention and punishment of the offences referred to in the present Convention and should be in close contact with the corresponding services in other States.

Article 15

To the extent permitted by domestic law and to the extent to which the authorities responsible for the services referred to in article 14 may judge desirable, they shall furnish to the authorities responsible for the corresponding services in other States the following information:

(1) Particulars of any offences referred to in the present Convention or any attempt to commit such offences;

(2) Particulars of any search for any prosecution, arrest, conviction, refusal of admission or expulsion of persons guilty of any of the offences referred to in the present Convention, the movements of such persons and any other useful information with regard to them.

The information so furnished shall include descriptions of the offenders, their fingerprints, photographs, methods of operation, police records and records of conviction.

Article 16

The Parties to the present Convention agree to take or to encourage, through their public and private educational, health, social economic and other related services, measures for the prevention of prostitution and for the rehabilitation and social adjustment of the victims of prostitution and of the offences referred to in the present Convention.

Article 17

The Parties to the present Convention undertake, in connection with immigration and emigration, to adopt or maintain such measures as are required, in terms of their obligations under the present Convention, to check the traffic in persons of either sex for the purpose of prostitution.

In particular they undertake:

(1) To make such regulations as are necessary for the protection of immigrants or emigrants, and in particular, women and children, both at the place of arrival and departure and while en route;

(2) To arrange for appropriate publicity warning the public of the dangers of the aforesaid traffic;

(3) To take appropriate measures to ensure supervision of railway stations, airports, seaports and en route, and of other public places, in order to prevent international traffic in persons for the purpose of prostitution;

(4) To take appropriate measures in order that the appropriate authorities be informed of the arrival of persons who appear, prima facie, to be the principals and accomplices in or victims of such traffic.

Article 18

The Parties to the present Convention undertake, in

accordance with the conditions laid down by domestic law, to have declarations taken from aliens who are prostitutes, in order to establish their identity and civil status and to discover who has caused them to leave their State. The information obtained shall be communicated to the authorities of the State of origin of the said persons with a view to their eventual repatriation.

Article 19

The Parties to the present Convention undertake, in accordance with the conditions laid down by domestic law and without prejudice to prosecution or other action for violations there under and so far as possible:

(1) Pending the completion of arrangements for the repatriation of destitute victims of international traffic in persons for the purpose of prostitution, to make suitable provisions for their temporary care and maintenance;

(2) To repatriate persons referred to in article 18 who desire to be repatriated or who may be claimed by persons exercising authority over them or whose expulsion is ordered in conformity with the law. Repatriation shall take place only after agreement is reached with the State of destination as to identity and nationality as well as to the place and date of arrival at frontiers. Each Party to the present Convention shall facilitate the passage of such persons through its territory.

Where the persons referred to in the preceding paragraph cannot themselves repay the cost of repatriation and have neither spouse, relatives nor guardian to pay for them, the cost of repatriation as far as the nearest frontier or port of embarkation or airport in the direction of the State of origin shall be borne by the State where they are in residence, and the cost of the remainder of the journey shall be borne by the State of origin.

Article 20

The Parties to the present Convention shall, if they have not already done so take the children, from being exposed to the danger of prostitution.

Article 21

The Parties to the present Convention shall communicate to the Secretary-General of the United Nations such laws and regulations as have already been promulgated in their States, and thereafter annually such laws and regulations as may be promulgated, relating to the subjects of the present Conventions, as well as all measures taken by them concerning the application of the Convention. The information received shall be published periodically by the Secretary-General and sent to all Members of the United Nations and to non-member States to which the present Convention is officially communicated in accordance with article 23.

Article 22

If any dispute shall arise between the Parties to the present Convention relating to its interpretation or application and if such dispute cannot be settled by other means, the dispute shall, at the request of any one of the Parties to the dispute, be referred to the International Court of Justice.

Article 23

The present Convention shall be open on behalf of any Member of the United Nations and also on behalf of any other State to which an invitation has been addressed by the Economic and Social Council.

The present Convention shall be ratified and the instruments of ratification shall be deposited with the Secretary-General of the United Nations.

The States mentioned in the first paragraph which have not signed the Convention may accede to it.

Accession shall be effected by deposit of an instrument of accession with the Secretary-General of the United Nations.

For the purpose of the present Convention the word "State" shall include all the colonies and Trust Territories of a State signatory or acceding to the Convention and all territories for which such State is internationally responsible.

Article 24

The present Convention shall come into force on the ninetieth day following the date of deposit of the second instrument of ratification or accession.

For each State ratifying or acceding to the Convention after the deposit of the second instrument of ratification or accession, the Convention shall enter into force ninety days after the deposit by such State of its instrument of ratification or accession.

Article 25

After the expiration of five years from the entry into force of the present Convention, any Party to the Convention may denounce it by a written notification addressed to the Secretary-General of the United Nations.

Such denunciation shall take effect for the Party making it one year from the date upon which it is received by the Secretary-General of the United Nations.

Article 26

The Secretary-General of the United Nations shall inform all Members of the United Nations and non-member States referred to in article 23:

(a) Of signatures, ratifications and accessions received in accordance with article 23;

(b) Of the date on which the present convention will come into force in accordance with article 24;

(c) Of denunciations received in accordance with article 25.

Article 27

Each Party to the present Convention undertakes to adopt, in accordance with its Constitution, the legislative or other measures necessary to ensure the application of the Convention.

Article 28

The provisions of the present Convention shall supersede in the relations between the Parties thereto the provisions of the international instruments referred to in subparagraphs 1, 2, 3 and 4 of the second paragraph of the Preamble, each of which shall be deemed to be terminated when all the Parties thereto shall have become Parties to the present Convention.

Final Protocol

Nothing in the present Convention shall be deemed to prejudice any legislation which ensures, for the enforcement of the provisions for securing the suppression of the traffic in persons and of the exploitation of others for purposes of prostitution, stricter conditions than those provided by the present Convention.

The provisions of articles 23 to 26 inclusive of the Convention shall apply to the present Protocol.

11 Convention Concerning Indigenous and Tribal Peoples in Independent Countries

The General Conference of the International Labour Organisation,
Having been convened at Geneva by the Governing Body of the International Labour Office, and having met in its seventy-sixth session on 7 June 1989, and

Noting the international standards contained in the Indigenous and Tribal Populations Convention and Recommendation, 1957, and

Recalling the terms of the Universal Declaration of Human Rights, the International Covenant on Economic, Social and Cultural Rights, the International Covnant on Civil and Political Rights, and the many international instruments on the prevention of discrimination, and

Considering that the developments which have taken place in international law since 1957, as well as developments in the situation of indigenous and tribal peoples in all regions of the world, have made it appropriate to adopt new international standards on the subject with a view to removing the assimilationist orientation of the earlier standards, and

Recognising the aspirations of these peoples to exercise control over their own institutions, ways of life and economic development and to maintain and develop their identities, languages and religions, within the framework of the States in which they live, and

Noting that in many parts of the world these peoples

are unable to enjoy their fundamental human rights to the same degree as the rest of the population of the States within which they live, and that their laws, values, customs and perspectives have often been eroded, and

Calling attention to the distinctive contributions of indigenous and tribal peoples to the cultural diversity and social and ecological harmony of humankind and to international co-operation and understanding, and

Noting that the following provisions have been framed with the co-operation of the United Nations, the Food and Agriculture Organization of the United Nations, the United Nations educational, Scientific and Cultural Organization and the World Health Organization, as well as of the Inter-American Indian Institute, at appropriate levels and in their respective fields, and that it is proposed to continue this co-operation in promoting and securing the application of these provisions, and

Having decided upon the adoption of certain proposals with regard to the partial revision of the Indigenous and Tribal Populations Convention, 1957 (No. 107), which is the fourth item on the agenda of the session, and

Having determined that these proposals shall take the form of an international Convention revising the Indigenous and Tribal Populations Convention, 1957,

Adopts this twenty-seventh day of June of the year one thousand nine hundred and eighty-nine the following Convention, which may be cited as the Indigenous and Tribal Peoples Convention, 1989;

Part I

General Policy

Article 1

1. This Convention applies to:

(a) Tribal peoples in independent countries whose social, cultural and economic conditions distinguish them from other sections of the national community, and whose status is regulated wholly or partially by their own customs or traditions or by special laws or regulations;

(b) Peoples in independent countries who are regarded as indigenous on account of their descent from the populations which inhabited the country, or a geographical region to which the country belongs, at the time of conquest or colonisation or the establishment of present State boundaries and who, irrespective of their legal status, retain some or all of their own social, economic, cultural and political institutions.

2. Self-identification as indigenous or tribal shall be regarded as a fundamental criterion for determining the groups to which the provisions of this Convention apply.

3. The use of the term "peoples" in this Convention shall not be construed as having any implications as regards the rights which may attach to the term under international law.

Article 2

1. Governments shall have the responsibility for developing, with the participation of the peoples concerned, co-ordinated and systematic action to protect the rights of these peoples and to guarantee respect for their integrity.

2. Such action shall include measures for:

(a) Ensuring that members of these peoples benefit on an equal footing from the rights and opportunities which national laws and regulations grant to other members of the population;

(b) Promoting the full realisation of the social, economic and cultural rights of these peoples with respect for their social and cultural identity, their customs and traditions and their institutions;

(c) Assisting the members of the peoples concerned to eliminate socio-economic gaps that may exist between indigenous and other members of the national community, in a manner compatible with their aspirations and ways of life.

Article 3

1. Indigenous and tribal peoples shall enjoy the full measure of human rights and fundamental freedoms without hindrance or discrimination. The provisions of the Convention shall be applied without discrimination to male and female members of these peoples.
2. No form of force or coercion shall be used in violation of the human rights and fundamental freedoms of the peoples concerned, including the rights contained in this Convention.

Article 4

1. Special measures shall be adopted as appropriate for safeguarding the persons, institutions, property, labour, cultures and environment of the peoples concerned.
2. Such special measures shall not be contrary to the freely-expressed wishes of the peoples concerned.
3. Enjoyment of the general rights of citizenship, without discrimination, shall not be prejudiced in any way by such special measures.

Article 5

In applying the provisions of this Convention:

(a) The social, cultural, religious and spiritual values and practices of these peoples shall be recognised and protected, and due account shall be taken of the nature of the problems which face them both as groups and as individuals;

(b) The integrity of the values, practices and institutions of these peoples shall be respected;

(c) Policies aimed at mitigating the difficulties experienced by these peoples in facing new conditions of life and work shall be adopted, with the participation and co-operation of the peoples affected.

Article 6

1. In applying the provisions of this Convention, Governments shall:

   (a) Consult the peoples concerned, through appropriate procedures and in particular through their representative institutions, whenever consideration is being given to legislative or administrative measures which may affect them directly;

   (b) Establish means by which these peoples can freely participate, to at least the same extent as other sectors of the population, at all levels of decision-making in elective institutions and administrative and other bodies responsible for policies and programmes which concern them;

   (c) Establish means for the full development of these peoples' own institutions and initiatives, and in appropriate case provide the resources necessary for this purpose.

2. The consultations carried out in application of this Convention shall be undertaken, in good faith and in a form appropriate to the circumstances, with the objective of achieving agreement or consent to the proposed measures.

Article 7

1. The peoples concerned shall have the right to decide their own priorities for the process of development as it affects their lives, beliefs, institutions and spiritual well-being and the lands they occupy or otherwise use, and to exercise control, to the extent possible, over their own economic, social and cultural development. In addition, they shall participate in the formulation, implementation and evaluation of plans and programmes for national and regional development which may affect them directly.
2. The improvement of the conditions of life and work and levels of health and education of the peoples concerned, with their participation and co-operation, shall be a matter of priority in plans for the overall economic development of areas they inhabit. Special projects for development of the areas in question shall also be so designed as to promote such improvement.
3. Governments shall ensure that, whenever appropriate, studies are carried out, in co-operation with the peoples concerned, to assess the social, spiritual, cultural and environmental impact on them of planned development activities. The results of these studies shall be considered as fundamental criteria for the implementation of these activities.
4. Governments shall take measures, in co-operation with the peoples concerned, to protect and preserve the environment of the territories they inhabit.

Article 8

1. In applying national laws and regulations to the peoples concerned, due regard shall be had to their customs or customary laws.
2. These peoples shall have the right to retain their own customs and institutions, where these are not incompatible with fundamental rights defined by the

national legal system and with internationally recognized human rights. Procedures shall be established, whenever necessary, to resolve conflicts which may arise in the application of this principle.

3. The application of paragraphs 1 and 2 of this Article shall not prevent members of these peoples from exercising the rights granted to all citizens and from assuming the corresponding duties.

Article 9

1. To the extent compatible with the national legal system and internationally recognised human rights, the methods customarily practised by the peoples concerned for dealing with offences committed by their members shall be respected.
2. The customs of these peoples in regard to penal matters shall be taken into consideration by the authorities and courts dealing with such cases.

Article 10

1. In imposing penalties laid down by general law on members of these peoples account shall be taken of their economic, social and cultural characteristics.
2. Preference shall be given to methods of punishment other than confinement in prison.

Article 11

The exaction from members of the peoples concerned of compulsory personal services in any form, whether paid or unpaid, shall be prohibited and punishable by law, except in cases prescribed by law for all citizens.

Article 12

The peoples concerned shall be safeguarded against the abuse of their rights and shall be able to take legal proceedings, either individually or through their representative bodies, for the effective protection of these rights. Measures shall be taken to ensure that members of these peoples can understand and be understood in legal proceedings, where necessary through the provision of interpretation or by other effective means.

Part II.

Land

Article 13

1. In applying the provisions of this Part of the Convention governments shall respect the special importance for the cultures and spiritual values of the peoples concerned of their relationship with the lands or territories, or both as applicable, which they occupy or otherwise use, and in particular the collective aspects of this relationship.
2. The use of the term "lands" in Articles 15 and 16 shall include the concept of territories, which covers the total environment of the areas which the peoples concerned occupy otherwise use.

Article 14

1. The rights of ownership and possession of the peoples concerned over the lands which they traditionally occupy shall be recognised. In addition, measures shall be taken in apropriate cases to safeguard the right of the peoples concerned to use lands not exclusively occupied by them, but to which they have traditionally had access for their subsistence and traditional activities. Particular attention shall be paid to the situation of nomadic peoples and shifting cultivators in this respect.
2. Governments shall take steps as necessary to identify the lands which the peoples concerned traditionally occupy, and to guarantee effective protection of their rights of ownership and possession.
3. Adequate procedures shall be established within the national legal system to resolve land claims by the peoples concerned.

Article 15

1. The rights of the peoples concerned to the natural resources pertaining to their lands shall be specially safeguarded. These rights include the right of these peoples to participate in the use, management and conservation of these resources.
2. In cases in which the State retains the ownership of mineral or sub-surface resources or rights to other resources pertaining to lands, governments shall establish or maintain procedures through which they shall consult these peoples, with a view to ascertaining whether and to what degree their interests would be prejudiced, before undertaking or permitting any programmes for the exploration or exploitation of such resources pertaining to their lands. The peoples concerned shall wherever possible participate in the benefits of such activities, and shall receive fair compensation for any damages which they may sustain as a result of such activities.

Article 16

1. Subject to the following paragraphs of this Article, the peoples concerned shall not be removed from the lands which they occupy.
2. Where the relocation of these peoples is considered necessary as an exceptional measure, such relocation shall take place only with their free and informed consent. Where their consent cannot be obtained, such relocation shall take place only following appropriate procedures established by national laws and regulations, including public inquiries where appropriate, which provide the opportunity for effective representation of the peoples concerned.
3. Whenever possible, these peoples shall have the right to return to their traditional lands, as soon as the grounds for relocation cease to exist.

4. When such return is not possible, as determined by agreement or, in the absence of such agreement, through appropriate procedures, these peoples shall be provided in all possible cases with lands of quality and legal status at least equal to that of the lands previously occupied by them, suitable to provide for their present needs and future development. Where the peoples concerned express a preference for compensation in money or in kind, they shall be so compensated under appropriate guarantees.
5. Persons thus relocated shall be fully compensated for any resulting loss or injury.

Article 17

1. Procedures established by the peoples concerned for the transmission of land rights among members of these peoples shall be respected.
2. The peoples concerned shall be consulted whenever consideration is being given to their capacity to alienate their lands or otherwise transmit their rights outside their own community.
3. Persons not belonging to these peoples shall be prevented from taking advantage of their customs or of lack of understanding of the laws on the part of their members to secure the ownership, possession or use of land belonging to them.

Article 18

Adequate penalties shall be established by law for unauthorised intrusion upon, or use of, the lands of the peoples concerned, and governments shall take measures to prevent such offences.

Article 19

National agrarian programmes shall secure to the peoples concerned treatment equivalent to that accorded to other sectors of the population with regard to:

(a) The provision of more land for these peoples when they have not the area necessary for providing the essentials of a normal existence, or for any possible increase in their numbers;

(b) The provision of the means required to promote the development of the lands which these peoples already possess.

Part II. Recruitment and Conditions of Employment

Article 20

1. Governments shall, within the framework of national laws and regulations, and in co-operation with the peoples concerned, adopt special measures to ensure the effective protection with regard to recruitment and conditions of employment of workers belonging to these peoples, to the extent that they are not effectively protected by laws applicable to workers in general.
2. Government shall do everything possible to prevent any discrimination between workers belonging to the peoples concerned and other workers, in particular as regards;
   (a) Admission to employment, including skilled employment, as well as measures for promotion and advancement;
   (b) Equal remuneration for work of equal value;
   (c) Medical and social assistance, occupational safety and health, all social security benefits and any other occupationally related benefits, and housing;
   (d) The right of association and freedom for all lawful trade union activities, and the right to conclude collective agreements with employers or employers' organisation.
3. The measures taken shall include measures to ensure:

(a) That workers belonging to the peoples concerned, including seasonal, casual and migrant workers in agricultural and other employment, as well as those employed by labour contractors, enjoy the protection afforded by national law and practice to other such workers in the same sectors, and that they are fully informed of their rights under labour legislation and of the means of redress available to them;

(b) That workers belonging to these peoples are not subjected to working conditions hazardous to their health, in particular through exposure to pesticides or other toxic substances;

(c) That workers belonging to these peoples are not subjected to coercive recruitment systems, including bonded labour and other forms of debt servitude;

(d) That workers belonging to these peoples enjoy equal opportunities and equal treatment in employment for men and women, and protection from sexual harassment.

4. Particular attention shall be paid to the establishment of adequate labour inspection services in areas where workers belonging to the peoples concerned undertake wage employment, in order to ensure compliance with the provisions of this Part of this Convention.

Part IV. Vocational Training, Handicrafts and Rural Industries

Article 21

Members of the peoples concerned shall enjoy opportunities at least equal to those of other citizens in respect of vocational training measures.

Article 22

1. Measures shall be taken to promote the voluntary participation of members of the peoples concerned in

vocational training programmes of general application.

2. Whenever existing programmes of vocational training of general application do not meet the special needs of the peoples concerned, governments shall, with the participation of these peoples, ensure the provision of special training programmes and facilities.
3. Any special training programmes shall be based on the economic environment, social and cultural conditions and practical needs of the peoples concerned. Any studies made in this connection shall be carried out in co-operation with these peoples, who shall be consulted on the organisation and operation of such programmes. Where feasible, these peoples shall progressively assume responsibility for the organisation and operation of such special training programmes, if they so decide.

Article 23

1. Handicrafts, rural and community-based industries, and subsistence economy and traditional activities of the peoples concerned, such as hunting, fishing, trapping and gathering, shall be recognised as important factors in the maintenance of their cultures and in their economic self-reliance and development. Governments shall, with the participation of these peoples and whenever appropriate, ensure that these activities are strengthened and promoted.
2. Upon the request of the peoples concerned, appropriate technical and financial assistance shall be provided wherever possible, taking into account the traditional technologies and cultural characteristic of these peoples, as well as the importance of sustainable and equitable development.

Part V. Social Security and Health

Article 24
Social security schemes shall be extended progressively to cover the peoples concerned, and applied without discrimination against them.

Article 25
1. Governments shall ensure that adequate health services are made available to the peoples concerned, or shall provide them with resources to allow them to design and deliver such services under their own responsibility and control, so that they may enjoy the highest attainable standard of physical and mental health.
2. Health services shall, to the extent possible, be community-based. These services shall be planned and administered in co-operation with the peoples concerned and take into account their economic, geographic, social and cultural conditions as well as their traditional preventive care, healing practices and medicines.
3. The health care system shall give preference to the training and employment of local community health workers, and focus on primary health care while maintaining strong links with other levels of health care services.
4. The provision of such health services shall be co-ordinated with other social, economic and cultural measures in the country.

Part VI. Education and Means of Communication

Article 26
Measures shall be taken to ensure that members of the peoples concerned have the opportunity to acquire education at all levels on at least an equal footing with the rest of the national community.

Article 27

1. Education programmes and services for the peoples concerned shall be developed and implemented in co-operation with them to address their special needs, and shall incorporate their histories, their knowledge and technologies, their value systems and their further social, economic and cultural aspirations.
2. The competent authority shall ensure the training of members of these peoples and their involvement in the formulation and implementation of education programmes, with a view to the progressive transfer of responsibility for the conduct of these programmes to these peoples as appropriate.
3. In addition, governments shall recognise the right of these peoples to establish their own educational institutions and facilities, provided that such institutions meet minimum standards established by the competent authority in consultation with these peoples. Appropriate resources shall be provided for this purpose.

Article 28

1. Children belonging to the peoples concerned shall, wherever practicable, be taught to read and write in their own Indigenous language or in the language most commonly used by the group to which they belong. When this is not practicable, the competent authorities shall undertake consultations with these peoples with a view to the adoption of measures to achieve this objective.
2. Adequate measures shall be taken to ensure that these peoples have the opportunity to attain fluency in the national language or in one of the official languages of the country.
3. Measures shall be taken to preserve and promote the development and practice of the indigenous language of the peoples concerned.

Article 29

The imparting of general knowledge and skills that will help children belonging to the peoples concerned to participate fully and on an equal footing in their own community and in the national community shall be an aim of education for these peoples.

Article 30

1. Governments shall adopt measures appropriate to the traditions and cultures of the peoples concerned, to make known to them their rights and duties, especially in regard to labour, economic opportunities, education and health matters, social welfare and their rights deriving from this Convention.
2. If necessary, this shall be done by means of written translations and through the use of mass communications in the languages of these peoples.

Article 31

Educational measures shall be taken among all sections of the national community, and particularly among those that are in most direct contact with the peoples concerned, with the object of eliminating prejudices that they may harbour in respect of these peoples. To this end, efforts shall be made to ensure that history textbooks and other educational materials provide a fair, accurate and informative portrayal of the societies and cultures of these peoples.

Part VII. Contracts and Co-Operation Across Borders

Article 32

Governments shall take appropriate measures, including by means of international agreements, to facilitate contacts and co-operation between indigenous and tribal peoples across borders, including activities in the economic, social, cultural, spiritual and environmental fields.

Part VIII. Administration

Article 33

1. The governmental authority responsible for the matters covered in this Convention shall ensure that agencies or other appropriate mechanisms exist to administer the programmes affecting the peoples concerned, and shall ensure that they have the means necessary for the proper fulfilment of the functions assigned to them.
2. These programmes shall include:
   (a) The planning, coordination, execution and evaluation, in co-operation with the peoples concerned, of the measures provided for in this Convention;
   (b) The proposing of legislative and other measures to the competent authorities and supervision of the application of the measures taken, in co-operation with the peoples concerned.

Part IX. General Provisions

Article 34

The nature and scope of the measures to be taken to give effect to this Convention shall be determined in a flexible manner, having regard to the conditions characteristic of each country.

Article 35

The application of the provisions of this Convention shall not adversely affect rights and benefits of the peoples concerned pursuant to other Conventions and Recommendations, international instruments, treaties, or national laws, awards, custom or agreements.

Part X. Final Provisions

Article 36

This Convention revises the Indigenous and Tribal Populations Convention, 1957.

Article 37

The formal ratifications of this Convention shall be communicated to the Director-General of the International Office for registration.

Article 38

1. This Convention shall be binding only upon those Members of the International Labour Organisation whose ratifications have been registered with the Director-General.
2. It shall come into force twelve months after the date on which the ratifications of two Members have been registered with the Director-General.
3. Thereafter, this Convention shall come into force for any Member twelve months after the date on which its ratification has been registered.

Article 39

1. A Member which has ratified this Convention may denounce it after the expiration of ten years from the date on which the Convention first comes into force, by an act communicated to the Director-General of the International Labour Office for registration. Such denunciation shall not take effect until one year after the date on which it is registered.
2. Each Member which has ratified this Convention and which does not, within the year following the expiration of the period of ten years mentioned in the preceding paragraph, exercise the right of denunciation provided of in this Article, will be bound for another period of ten years and, thereafter, may denounce this Convention at the expiration of each period of ten years under the terms provided for in this Article.

Article 40

1. The Director-General of the International Labour Office shall notify all Members of the International

labour Organisation of the registration of all ratifications and denunciation communicated to him by the Members of the Organisation.

2. When notifying the Members of the Organisation of the registration of the second ratification communicated to him the Director-General shall draw the attention of the Members of the Organisation to the date upon which the Convention will come into force.

Article 41

The Director-General of the International Labour Office shall communicate to the Secretary-General of the United Nations for registration in accordance with Article 102 of the Charter of the United Nations full particulars of all ratifications and acts of denunciation registered by him in accordance with the provisions of the preceding Articles.

Article 42

At such times as it may consider necessary the Governing Body of the International Labour Office shall present to the General Conference a report on the working of this Convention and shall examine the desirability of placing on the agenda of the Conference the question of its revision in whole or in part.

Article 43

1. Should the Conference adopt a new Convention revising this Convention in whole or in part, then, unless the new Convention otherwise provides:
   (a) The ratification by a Member of the new revising Convention shall ipso jure involve the immediate denunciation of this Convention, notwithstanding the provisions of Article 39 above, if and when the new revising Convention shall have come into force;
   (b) As from the date when the new revising

Convention comes into force this Convention shall cease to be open to ratification by the Members.

2. This Convention shall in any case remain in force in its actual form and content for those Members which have ratified it but have not ratified the revising Convention.

Article 44

The English and French versions of the text of this Convention are equally authoritative.

12 Standard Minimum Rules for the Treatment of Prisoners

Preliminary Observations

1. The following rules are not intended to describe in detail a model system of penal institutions. They seek only, on the basis of the general consensus of contemporary thought and the essential elements of the most adequate systems of today, to set out what is generally accepted as being good principle and practice in the treatment of prisoners and the management of institutions.

2. In view of the great variety of legal, social, economic and geographical conditions of the world, it is evident that not all of the rules are capable of application in all places and at all times. They should, however, serve to stimulate a constant endeavour to overcome practical difficulties in the way of their application, in the knowledge that they represent, as a whole, the minimum conditions which are accepted as suitable by the United Nations.

3. On the other hand, the rules cover a field in which thought is constantly developing. They are not intended to preclude experiment and practices, provided these are in harmony with the principles and seek to further the purposes which derive from the text of the rules as a whole. It will always be justifiable for the central prison administration to authorize departures from the rules in this spirit.

4. (1) Part I of the rules covers the general management of institutions and is applicable to all categories of prisoners, criminal or civil, untried or, convicted, including prisoners subject to "security measures" or corrective measures ordered by the judge.

(2) Part II contains rules applicable only to the special categories dealt with in each section. Nevertheless, the rules under section A, applicable to prisoners under sentence, shall be equally applicable to categories of prisoners dealt with in sections B, C and D, provided they do not conflict with the rules governing those categories and are for their benefit.

5. (1) The rules do not seek to regulate the management of institutions set aside for young persons such as Borstal institutions or correctional schools, but in general part I would be equally applicable in such institutions.

(2) The categories of young prisoners should include at least all young persons who come within the jurisdiction of juvenile courts. As a rule, such young persons should not be sentenced to imprisonment.

Part I: Rules of General Applications

Basic principle

6. (1) The following rules shall be applied impartially. There shall be no discrimination on grounds of race, colour, sex, language, religion, political or other opinion, national or social origin, property, birth or other status.

(2) On the other hand, it is necessary to respect the religious beliefs and moral precepts cf the group to which a prisoner belongs.

Register

7. (1) In every place where persons are imprisoned there shall be kept a bound registration book with numbered pages in which shall be entered in respect of each prisoner received.

(a) Information concerning his identity;

(b) The reasons for his commitment and the authority therefor;

(c) The day and hour of his admission and release.

(2) No person shall be received in an institution without a valid commitment order of which the details shall have been previously entered in the register.

Separation of categories

8. The different categories of prisoners shall be kept in separate institutions or parts of institutions taking account of their sex, age, criminal record, the legal reason for their detention and the necessities of their treatment. Thus,

(a) Men and women shall so far as possible be detained in separate institutions; in an institution which received both men and women the whole of the premises allocated to women shall be entirely separate;

(b) Untried prisoners shall be kept separate from convicted prisoners;

(c) Persons imprisoned for debt and other civil prisoners shall be kept separate from persons imprisoned by reason of a criminal offence;

(d) Young prisoners shall be kept separate from adults.

Accommodation

9. (1) Where sleeping accommodation is in individual cells or rooms each prisoner shall occupy by night a cell or room by himself. If for special reasons, such as temporary overcrowding, it becomes necessary for the central prison administration to make an exception to this rule, it is not desirable to have two prisoners in a cell or room.

(2) Where dormitories are used, they shall be occupied by prisoners carefully selected as being suitable to associate with one another in those conditions. There shall be regular supervisions by night, in keeping with the nature of the institution.

10. All accommodation provided for the use of prisoners and in particular all sleeping accommodation shall meet all requirements of health, due regard being paid to climatic conditions and particularly to cubic content of air, minimum floor space, lighting, heating and ventilation.

11. In all places where prisoners are required to live or work,

(a) The windows shall be large enough to enable the prisoners to read or work by natural light, and shall be so constructed that they can allow the entrance of fresh air whether or not there is artificiel ventilation;

(b) Artifical light shall be provided sufficient for the prisoners to read or work without injury to eyesight.

12. The sanitary installations shall be adequate to enable every prisoner to comply with the needs of nature when necessary and in a clean and decent manner.

13. Adequate bathing and shower installation shall be provided so that every prisoner may be enabled and required to have a bath or shower, at a temperature suitable to the climate, as frequently as necessary for general hygiene according to season and geographical region, but at least once a week in a temperate climate.

14. All parts of an institution regularly used by prisoners shall be properly maintained and kept scrupulously clean at all times.

Personal hygiene

15. Prisoners shall be required to keep their persons

clean, an to this end they shall be provided with water and with such toilet articles as are necessary for health and cleanliness.

16. In order that prisoners may maintain a good appearance compatible with their self-respect, facilities shall be provided for the proper care of the hair and beard and men shall be enabled to shave regularly.

Clothing and bedding

17. (1) Every prisoner who is not allowed to wear his own clothing shall be provided with an outfit of clothing suitable for the climate and adequate to keep him in good health. Such clothing shall in no manner be degrading or humiliating.

(2) All clothing shall be clean and kept in proper condition. Underclothing shall be changed and washed as often as necessary for the maintenance of hygiene.

(3) In exceptional circumstances, whenever a prisoner is removed outside the institution for an authorized purpose, he shall be allowed to wear his own clothing or other inconspicuous clothing.

18. If prisoners are allowed to wear their own clothing, arrangements shall be made on their admission to the institution to ensure that it shall be clean and fit for use.

19. Every prisoner shall in accordance with local or national standards, be provided with a separate bed, and with separate and sufficient bedding which shall be clean when issued, kept in good order and changed often enough to ensure its cleanliness.

Food

20. (1) Every prisoner shall be provided by the administration at the usual hours with food of nutritional value adequate for health and strength, of wholesome quality and well prepared and served.

(2) Drinking water shall be available to every prisoner whenever he needs it.

Exercise and sport

21. (1) Every prisoner who is not employed in outdoor work shall have at least one hour of suitable exercise in the open air daily if the weather permits.

(2) Young prisoners, and others of suitable age and physique, shall receive physical and recreational training during the period of exercise. To this end space, installations and equipment should be provided.

Medical services

22. (1) At every institution there shall be available the services of at least one qualified medical officer who should have some knowledge of psychiatry. The medical services should be organized in close relationship to the general health administration of the community or nation. They shall include a psychiatric service for the diagnosis and, in proper cases, the treatment of states of mental abnormality.

(2) Sick prisoners who require specialist treatment shall be transferred to specialized institutions or to civil hospitals. Where hospital facilities are provided in an institution, their equipment, furnishings and pharmaceutical supplies shall be proper for the medical care and treatment of sick prisoners, and there shall be a staff of suitable trained officers.

(3) The services of a qualified dental officer shall be available to every prisoner.

23. (1) In women's institutions there shall be special accommodation for all necessary pre-natal and post-natal care and treatment. Arrangements shall be made wherever practicable for children to be born in a hospital outside the institution. A child is born in prison, this fact shall not be mentioned in the birth certificate.

(2) Where nursing infants are allowed to remain in the institution with their mothers, provision shall be made for a nursery staffed by qualified person, where the infants shall be placed when they are not in the care of their mothers.

24. The medical officer shall see and examine every prisoner as soon as possible after his admission and thereafter as necessary, with a view particularly to the discovery of physical or mental illness and the taking of all necessary measures; the segregation of prisoners suspected of infectious or contagious conditions; the noting of physical or mental defects which might hamper rehabilitation, and the determination of the physical capacity of every prisoner for work.

25. (1) The medical officer shall have the care of the physical and mental health of the prisoners and should daily see all sick prisoners, all who complain of illness, and any prisoner to whom his attention is specially directed.

(2) The medical officer shall report to the director whenever he considers that a prisoner's physical or mental health has been or will be injuriously affected by continued imprisonment or by any condition of imprisonment.

26. (1) The medical officer shall regularly inspect and advise the director upon:

(a) The quantity, quality, preparation and service of food;

(b) The hygiene and cleanliness of the institution and the prisoners;

(c) The sanitation, heating, lighting and ventilation of the institution;

(d) The suitability and cleanliness of the prisoners' clothing and bedding;

(e) the observance of the rules concerning physical education and sports, in caes where there is no technical personnel in charge of these activities.

(2) The director shall take into consideration the reports and advice that the medical officer submits according to rules 25C2) and 26 and, in case he concurs with the recommendations made, shall take immediate steps to give effect to those recommendations; if they are not within his competence or if he does not concur with them, he shall immediately submit his own report and the advice of the medical officer to higher authority.

Discipline and punishment

27. Discipline and order shall be maintained with firmness, but with no more restriction than is necessary for safe custody and well-ordered community life.

28. (1) No prisoner shall be employed, in the service of the institution, in any disciplinary capacity.

(2) This rule shall not, however, impede the proper functioning of systems based on self-government, under which specified social, educational or sports activities or responsibilities are entrusted, under supervision, to prisoners who are formed into groups for the purpose of treatment.

29. The following shall always be determined by the law or by the regulation of the competent administrative authority:

(a) Conduct constituting a disciplinary offence;

(b) The types and duration of punishment which may be inflicted;

(c) The authority competent to impose such punishment.

30. (1) No prisoner shall be punished except in accordance with the terms of such law or regulation, and never twice for the same offence.

(2) No prisoner shall be punished unless he has been informed of the offence alleged against him and given a proper opportunity of presenting his defence. The competent authority shall conduct a thorough examination of the case.

(3) Where necessary and practicable the prisoner shall be allowed to make his defence through an interpreter.

31. Corporal punishment, punishment by placing in a dark cell, and all cruel, inhuman or degrading punishments shall be completely prohibited as punishments for disciplinary offences.

32. (1) Punishment by close confinement or reduction of diet shall never be inflicted unless the medical officer has examined the prisoner and certified in writing that he is fit to sustain it.

(2) the same shall apply to any other punishment that may be prejudicial to the physical or mental health of a prisoner. In no case may such punishment be contrary to or depart from the principle stated in rule 31.

(3) The medical officer shall visit daily prisoners undergoing such punishments and shall advise the director if he considers the termination or alteration of the punishment necessary on grounds of physical or mental health.

Instruments of restraint

33. Instruments of restraint, such as handcuffs, chains, irons an straitjackets, shall never be applied as a punishments. Furthermore, chains or irons shall not be used as restraints. Other instruments of restraint shall not be used except in the following circumstances:

(a) As a precaution against escape during a transfer, provided that they shall be removed when the prisoner appears before a judicial or administrative authority;

(b) On medical grounds by direction of the medical officer;

(c) By order of the director, if other methods of control fail, in order to prevent a prisoner from injuring himself or others or from damaging property; in such instances the director shall at once consult the medical officer and report to the higher administrative authority.

34. The patterns and manner of use of instruments of restraint shall be decided by the central prison administration. Such instruments must not be applied for any longer time than is strictly necessary.

Information to and complaints by prisoners

35. (1) Every prisoner on admission shall be provided with written information about the regulations governing the treatment of prisoners of his category, the disciplinary requirements of the institution, the authorized methods of seeking information and making complaints, and all such other matters as are necessary to enable him to understand both his rights and his obligations and to adapt himself to the life of the institution.

(2) If a prisoner is illiterate, the aforesaid information shall be conveyed to him orally.

36. (1) Every prisoner shall have the opportunity each week day of making requests or complaints to the director of the institution or the officer authorized to represent him.

(2) It shall be possible to make requests or complaints to the inspector of prisons during his inspection. The prisoner shall have the opportunity to talk to the inspector or to any other inspecting officer without the director or other members of the staff being present.

(3) Every prisoner shall be allowed to make a request or complaint, without censorship as to substance but in

proper form, of the central prison administration, the judicial authority or other proper authorities through approved channels.

(4) Unless it is evidently frivolous or groundless, every request or complaint shall be promptly dealt with and replied to without undue delay.

Contact with the outside world

37. Prisoners shall be allowed under necessary supervision to communicate with their family and reputable friends at regular intervals, both by correspondence and by receiving visits.

38. (1) Prisoners who are foreign nationals shall be allowed reasonable facilities to communicate with the diplomatic and consular representatives of the State to which they belong.

(2) Prisoners who are nationals of States without diplomatic or consular representation in the country and refugees or stateless persons shall be allowed similar facilities to communicate with the diplomatic representative of the State which takes charge of their interests or any national or international authority whose task it is to protect such persons.

39. Prisoners shall be kept informed regularly of the more important items of news by the reading of newspapers, periodicals or special institutional publications, by hearing wireless transmissions, by lectures or by any similar means as authorized or controlled by the administration.

Books

40. Every institution shall have a library for the use of all categories of prisoners, adequately stocked with both recreational and instructional books, and prisoners shall be encouraged to make full use of it.

Religion

41. (1) If the institution contains a sufficient number of prisoners of the same religion, a qualified representative of that religion shall be appointed or approved. If the number of prisoners justifies it and conditions permit, the arrangement should be on a full-time basis.

(2) A qualified representative appointed or approved under paragraph (1) shall be allowed to hold regular services and to pay pastoral visits in private to prisoners of his religion at proper times.

(3) Access to a qualified representative of any religion shall not be refused to any prisoner. On the other hand, if any prisoner should object to a visit to any religious representative, his attitude shall be fully respected.

42. So far as practicable, every prisoner shall be allowed to satisfy the needs of his religious life by attending the services provided in the institution and having in his possession the books of religious observance and instruction of his denomination.

Retention of prisoners' property

43. (1) All money, valuables, clothing and other effects belonging to a prisoner which under the regulations of the institution he is not allowed to retain shall on his admission to the institution be placed in safe custody. An inventory thereof shall be signed by the prisoner. Steps shall be taken to keep them in good condition.

(2) On the release of the prisoner all such articles and money shall be returned to him except in so far as he has been authorized to spend money or send any such property out of the institution, or it has been found necessary on hygienic grounds to destroy any article of clothing. The prisoner shall sign a receipt for the articles and money returned to him.

(3) Any money or effects received for a prisoner from outside shall be treated in the same way.

(4) If a prisoner brings in any drugs or medicine, the medical officer shall decide what use shall be made of them.

Notification of death, illness, transfer, etc.

44. (1) Upon the death or serious illness of, or serious injury to a prisoner, or his removal to an institution for the treatment of mental affections, the director shall at once inform the spouse, if the prisoner is married, or the nearest relative and shall in any event inform any other person previously designated by the prisoner.

(2) A prisoner shall be informed at once of the death or serious illness of any near relative. In case of the critical illness of a near relative, the prisoner should be authorized, whenever circumstances allow, to go to his bedside either under escort or alone.

(3) Every prisoner shall have the right to inform at once his family of his imprisonment or his transfer to another institution.

Removal of prisoners

45. (1) When the prisoners are being removed to or from an institution, they shall be exposed to public view as little as possible, and proper safeguards shall be adopted to protect them from insult, curiosity and publicity in any form.

(2) The transport of prisoners in conveyances with inadequate ventilation or light, or in any way which would subject them to unnecessary physical hardship, shall be prohibited.

(3) The transport of prisoners shall be carried out at the expense of the administration and equal conditions shall obtain for all of them.

Institutional personnel

46. (1) The prison administration, shall provide for the careful selection of every grade of the personnel, since it is on their integrity, humanity, professional capacity and personal suitability for the work that the proper administration of the institution depends.

(2) The prison administration shall constantly seek to awaken and maintain in the minds both of the personnel and of the public the conviction that this work is a social service of great importance, and to this end all appropriate means of informing the public should be used.

(3) To secure the foregoing ends, personnel shall be appointed on a full-time basis as professional prison officers and have civil service status with security of tenure subject only to good conduct, efficiency and physical fitness. Salaries shall be adequate to attract and retain suitable men and women; employment benefits and conditions of services shall be favourable in view of the exacting nature of the work.

47. (1) The personnel shall possess an adequate standard of education and intelligence.

(2) Before entering on duty, the personnel shall be given a course of training in their general and specific duties and be required to pass theoretical and practical tests.

(3) After entering on duty and during their career, the personnel shall maintain and improve their knowledge and professional capacity by attending courses of in-service training to be organized at suitable intervals.

48. All members of the personnel shall at all times so conduct themselves and perform their duties as to influence the prisoners for good by their example and to command their respect.

49. (1) So far as possible, the personnel shall include a sufficient number of specialist such as psychiatrists, psychologists, social workers, teachers and trade instructors.

(2) The services of social workers, teachers and trade instructors shall be secured on a permanent basis, without thereby excluding part-time or voluntary workers.

50. (1) The director of an institution should be adequately qualified for his task by character, administrative ability, suitable training and experience.

(2) He shall devote his entire time to his official duties and shall not be appointed on a part-time basis.

(3) He shall reside on the premises of the institution or in its immediate vicinity.

(4) When two or more institutions are under the authority of one director, he shall visit each of them at frequent intervals. A responsible resident official shall be in charge of each of these institutions.

51. (1) The director, his deputy, and the majority of the other personnel of the institution shall be able to speak the language of the greatest number of prisoners, or a language understood by the greatest number of them.

(2) Whenever necessary, the services of an interpreter shall be used.

52. (1) In institutions which are large enough to require the services of one or more full-time medical officers, at least one of them shall reside on the premises of the institution or in its immediate vicinity.

(2) In other institutions the medical officer shall visit daily and shall reside near enough to be able to attend without delay in cases of urgency.

53. (1) In an institution for both men and women, the

part of the institution set aside for women shall be under the authority of a responsible woman officer who shall have the custody of the keys of all that part of the institution.

(2) No male member of the staff shall enter the part of the institution set aside for women unless accompanied by a woman officer.

(3) Women prisoners shall be attended and supervised only by women officers. This does not, however, preclude male members of the staff, particularly doctors and teachers, from carrying out their professional duties in institutions or parts of institutions set aside for women.

54. (1) Officers of the institutions shall not, in their relations with the prisoners, use force except in self-defence or in cases of attempted escape, or active or passive physical resistance to an order based on law or regulations. Officers who have recourse to force must use no more than is strictly necessary and must report the incident immediately to the director of the institution.

(2) Prison officers shall be given special physical training to enable them to restrain aggressive prisoners.

(3) Except in special circumstances, staff performing duties which bring them into direct contact with prisoners should not be armed. Furthermore, staff should in no circumstances be provided with arms unless they have been trained in their use.

Inspection

55. There shall be a regular inspection of penal institution and services by qualified and experienced inspectors appointed by a competent authority. Their task shall be in particular to ensure that these institutions are administered in accordance with existing laws and regulations and with a view to bringing about the objectives of penal and correctional services.

Part II: Rules Applicable to Special Categories

A. Prisoners Under Sentence

Guiding principles

56. The guiding principles hereafter are intended to show the spirit in which penal institutions should be administered and the purpose at which they should aim, in accordance with the declaration made under Preliminary Observation 1 of the present text.

57. Imprisonment and other measures which result in cutting off an offender from the outside world are afflictive by the very fact of taking from the person the right of self-determination by depriving him of his liberty. Therefore the prison system shall not, except as incidental to justifiable segregation or the maintenance of discipline, aggravate the suffering inherent in such a situation.

58. The purpose and justification of a sentence of imprisonment or a similar measure deprivative of liberty is ultimately to protect society against crime. This end can only be achieved if the period of imprisonment is used to ensure, so far as possible, that upon his return to society the offender is not only willing but able to lead a law-abiding and self-supporting life.

59. To this end, the institution should utilize all the remedial, educational, moral, spiritual and other forces and forms of assistance which are appropriate and available, and should seek to apply them according to the individual treatment needs of the prisoners.

60. (1) The regime of the institution should seek to minimize any differences between prison life and life at liberty which tend to lessen the responsibility of the prisoners or the respect due to their dignity as human beings.

(2) Before the completion of the sentence, it is desirable that the necessary steps be taken to ensure for

the prisoner a gradual return to life in society. This aim may be achieved, depending on the case, by a pre-release regime organized in the same institution or in another appropriate institution, or by release on trial under some kind of supervision which must not be entrusted to the police but should be combined with effective social aid.

61. The treatment of prisoners should emphasize not their exclusion from the community, but their continuing part in it. Community agencies should, therefore, be enlisted wherever possible to assist the staff of the institution in the task of social rehabilitation of the prisoners. There should be in connection with every institution social workers charged with the duty of maintaining and improving all desirable relations of a prisoner with his family and with valuable social agencies. Steps should be taken to safeguard, to the maximum extent compatible with the law and the sentence, the rights relating to civil interests, social security rights and other social benefits of prisoners.

62. The medical services of the institution shall seek to detect and shall treat any physical or mental illnesses or defects which may hamper a prisoner's rehabilitation. All necessary medical, surgical and psychiatric services shall be provided to that end.

63. (1) The fulfilment of these principles requires individualization of treatment and for this purpose a flexible system of classifying prisoners in groups; it is therefore desirable that such groups should be distributed in separate institutions suitable for the treatment of each group.

(2) These institutions need not provide the same degree of security for every group. It is desirable to provide varying degrees of security according to the needs of different groups. Open institutions, by the very fact that they provide no physical security against escape but rely on the self-discipline of the inmates, provide the

conditions most favourable to rehabilitation for carefully selected prisoners.

(3) It is desirable that the number of prisoners in closed institutions should not be so large that the individualization of treatment is hindered. In some countries it is considered that the population of such institutions should not exceed five hundred. In open institutions the population should be as small as possible.

(4) On the other hand, it is undesirable to maintain prisons which are so small that proper facilities cannot be provided.

64. The duty of society does not end with a prisoner's release. There should, therefore, be governmental or private agencies capable of lending the released prisoner efficient after—care directed towards the lessening of prejudice against him and towards his social rehabilitation.

Treatment

65. The treatment of persons sentenced to imprisonment or a similar measure shall have as its purpose, so far as the length of the sentence permits, to establish in them the will to lead law-abiding and self-supporting lives after their release and to fit them to do so. The treatment shall be such as will encourage their self-respect and develop their sense of responsibility.

66. (1) To these ends, all appropriate means shall be used, including religious care in the countries where this is possible, education, vocational guidance and training, social casework, employment counselling physical development and strengthening of moral character, in accordance with the individual needs of each prisoner, taking account of his social and criminal history, his physical and mental capacities and aptitudes, his personal temperament, the length of his sentence and his prospects after release.

(2) For every prisoner with a sentence of suitable length, the director shall receive, as soon as possible after his admission, full reports on all the matters referred to in the foregoing paragraph. Such reports shall always include a report by a medical officer, wherever possible qualified in psychiatry, on the physical and mental condition of the prisoner.

(3) The reports and other relevant documents shall be placed in an individual file. This file shall be kept up to date and classified in such a way that it can be consulted by the responsible personnel whenever the need arises.

Classification and individualization

67. The purpose of classification shall be:

(a) To separate from others those prisoners who by reason of their criminal records or bad characters, are likely to exercise a bad influence;

(b) To divide the prisoners into classes in order to facilitate their treatment with a view of their social rehabilitation.

68. So far as possible separate institutions or separate sections of an institution shall be used for the treatment of the different classes of prisoners.

69. As soon as possible after admission and after a study of the personality of each prisoner with a sentence of suitable length, a programme of treatment shall be prepared for him in the light of the knowledge obtained about his individual needs, his capacities and dispositions.

Privileges

70. Systems of privileges appropriate for the different classes of prisoners and the different methods of treatment shall be established at every institution, in order to encourage good conduct, develop a sense of responsibility and secure the interest and co-operation of the prisoners in their treatment.

Work

71. (1) Prison labour must not be of an afflictive nature.

(2) All prisoners under sentence shall be required to work, subject to their physical and mental fitness as determined by the medical officer.

(3) Sufficient work of a useful nature shall be provided to keep prisoners actively employed for a normal working day.

(4) So far as possible the work provided shall be such as will maintain or increase the prisoner's ability to earn an honest living after release.

(5) Vocational training in useful trades shall be provided for prisoners able to profit thereby and especially for young prisoners.

(6) Within the limits compatible with proper vocational selection and with the requirements of institutional administration and discipline, the prisoners shall be able to choose the type of work they wish to perform.

72. (1) The organization and methods of work in the institutions shall resemble as closely as possible those of similar work outside institution, so as to prepare prisoners for the conditions of normal occupational life.

(2) The interests of the prisoners and of their vocational training, however must not be subordinated to the purpose of making a financial profit from an industry in the institution.

73. (1) Preferably institutional industries and farms should be operated directly by the administration and not by private contractors.

(2) Where prisoners are employed in work not controlled by the administration, they shall always be under the supervision of the institution's personnel. Unless the work is for other departments of the

government the full normal wages for such work shall be paid to the administration by the persons to whom the labour is supplied, account being taken to the output of the prisoners.

74. (1) The precautions laid down to protect the safety and health of free workmen shall be equally observed in institutions.

(2) Provision shall be made to indemnify prisoners against industrial injury, including occupational disease, on terms not less favourable than those extended by law to free workmen.

75. (1) The maximum daily and weekly working hours of the prisoners shall be fixed by law or by administrative regulation, taking into account local rules or custom in regard to the employment of free workmen.

(2) The hours so fixed shall leave one last day a week and sufficient time for education and other activities required as part of the treatment and rehabilitation of the prisoners.

76. (1) There shall be a system of equitable remuneration of the work of prisoners.

(2) Under the system prisoners shall be allowed to spend at least a part of their earnings on approved articles for their own use and to send a part of their earnings to their family.

(3) The system should also provide that a part of the earnings should be set aside by the administration so as to constitute a savings fund to be handed over to the prisoner on his release.

Education and recreation

77. (1) Provision shall be made for the further education of all prisoners capable of profiting thereby, including religious instruction in the countries where this is possible. The education of illiterates and young

prisoners shall be compulsory and special attention shall be paid to it by the administration.

(2) So far as practicable, the education of prisoners shall be integrated with the educational system of the country so that after their release they may continue their education without difficulty.

78. Recreational and cultural activities shall be provided in all institutions for the benefit of the mental and physical health of prisoners.

Social relations and after-care

79. Special attention shall be paid to the maintenance and improvement of such relations between a prisoner and his family as are desirable in the best interest of both.

80. From the beginning of a prisoner's sentence consideration shall be given to his future after release and he shall be encouraged and assisted to maintain or establish such relations with persons or agencies outside the institution as may promote the best interest of his family and his own social rehabilitation.

81. (1) Services and agencies, governmental or otherwise, which assist released prisoners to re-establish themselves in society shall ensure, so far as is possible and necessary, that released prisoners by provided with appropriate documents and identification papers, have suitable homes and work to go to, are suitably and adequately clothed having regard to the climate and season, and have sufficient means to reach their destination and maintain themselves in the period immediately following their release.

(2) The approved representatives of such agencies shall have all necessary access to the institution and to prisoners and shall be taken into consultation as to the future of a prisoner from the beginning of his sentence.

(3) It is desirable that the activities of such agencies shall be centralized or co-ordinated as far as possible in order to secure the best use of their efforts.

B. Insane and Mentally Abnormal Prisoners

82. (1) Persons who are found to be insane shall not be detained in prisons and arrangements shall be made to remove them to mental institutions as soon as possible.

(2) Prisoners who suffer from other mental diseases or abnormalities shall be observed and treated in specialized institutions under medical management.

(3) During their stay in a prison, such prisoners shall be placed under the special supervision of a medical officer.

(4) The medical or psychiatric service of the penal institutions shall provide for the psychiatric treatment of all other prisoners who are in need of such treatment.

83. It is desirable that steps should be taken, by arrangement with the appropriate agencies, to ensure if necessary the continuation of psychiatric treatment after release and the provision of social-psychiatric after-care.

C. Prisoners under arrest or awaiting trial

84. (1) persons arrested or imprisoned by reason of a criminal charge against them, who are detained either in police custody or in prison custody jail but have not yet been tried and sentenced, will be referred to as "untried prisoners" hereinafter in these rules.

(2) Unconvicted prisoners are presumed to be innocent and shall be treated as such.

(3) Without prejudice to legal rules for the protection of individual liberty or prescribing the procedure to be observed in respect of untried prisoners, these prisoners shall benefit by a special regime which is described in the following rules in its essential requirements only.

85. (1) Untried prisoners shall be kept separate from convicted prisoners.

(2) Young untried prisoners shall be kept separate from adults and shall in principle be detained in separate institutions.

86. Untried prisoners shall sleep singly in separate rooms, with the reservation of different local custom in respect of the climate.

87. Within the limits compatible with the good order of the institution, untried prisoners may, if they so desire, have their food procured at their own expense from the outside, either through the administration or through their family or friends. Otherwise, the administration shall provide their food.

88. (1) An untried prisoner shall be allowed to wear his own clothing if it is clean and suitable.

(2) If he wears prison dress, it shall be different from that supplied to convicted prisoners.

89. An untried prisoner shall always be offered opportunity to work, but shall not be required to work. If he chooses to work, he shall be paid for it.

90. An untried prisoner shall be allowed to procure at his own expense or at the expense of a third party such books, newspapers, writing materials and other means of occupation as are compatible with the interests of the administration of justice and the security and good order of the institution.

91. An untried prisoner shall be allowed to be visited and treated by his own doctor or dentist if there is reasonable ground for his application and he is able to pay any expenses incurred.

92. An untried prisoner shall be allowed to inform immediately his family of his detention and shall be given all reasonable facilities for communicating with his

family and friends, and for receiving visits from them, subject only to restrictions and supervision as are necessary in the interests of the administration of justice and of the security and good order of the institution..

93. For the purposes of his defence, an untried prisoner shall be allowed to apply for from legal aid where such aid is available, and to receive visits free his legal adviser with a view to his defence and to prepare and hand to him confidential instructions. For these purposes, he shall if he so desires be supplied with writing material. Interviews between the prisoner and his legal adviser may be within sight but not within the hearing of a police or institution official.

D. Civil Prisoners

94. In countries where the law permits imprisonment for debt, or by order of a court under any other non-criminal process, persons so imprisoned shall not be subjected to any greater restriction or severity than is necessary to ensure safe custody and good order. Their treatment shall be not less favourable than that of untried prisoners, with that reservation, however, that they may possibly be required to work.

E. Persons arrested or detained without charge

95. Without prejudice to the provisions of article 9 of the International Government on Civil and Political Rights, persons arrested or imprisoned without charge shall be accorded the same protection as that accorded under part I and part II , section C. Relevant provisions of part II, section A, shall likewise be applicable where their application may be conducive to the benefit of this special group of persons in custody, provided that no measures shall be been taken implying that re-education or rehabilitation is in any way appropriate to persons not convicted of any criminal offence.

13 Eradication of Hunger and Manlnutrition

The World Food Conference,

Convened by the General Assembly of the United Nations and entrusted with developing ways and means whereby the international community, as a whole, could take specific action to resolve the world food problem within the broader context of development and international economic co-operation,

Adopts the following Declaration:

Recognizing that:

(a) The grave food crisis that is afflicting the peoples of the developing countries where most of the world's hungry and ill-nourished live and where more than two thirds of the world's population produce about one third of the world's food—an imbalance which threatens to increase in the next 10 years—is not only fraught with grave economic and social implications, but also acutely jeopardizes the most fundamental principles and values associated with the right to life and human dignity as enshrined in the Universal Declaration of Human Rights;

(b) The elimination of hunger and malnutrition, included as one of the objectives in the United Nations Declaration on Social Progress and Development, and the elimination of the causes that determine this situation are the common objectives of all nations;

(c) The situation of the peoples afflicted by hunger and malnutrition arises from their historical circumstances, especially social inequalities, including in many cases alien and colonial domination, foreign occupation, racial discrimination, apartheid and neo-colonialism in all its forms, which continue to be among the greatest obstacles to the full emancipation and progress of the developing countries and all the peoples involved;

(d) This situation has been aggravated in recent years by a series of crises to which the world economy has been subjected, such as the deterioration in the international monetary system, the inflationary increase in import costs, the heavy burdens imposed by external debt on the balance of payments of many developing countries, a rising food demand partly due to demographic pressure, speculation, and a shortage of, and increased costs for, essential agricultural inputs;

(e) These phenomena should be considered within the framework of the on-going negotiations on the Charter of Economic Rights and Duties of States, and the General Assembly of the United Nations should be urged unanimously to agree upon, and to adopt, a Charter that will be an effective instrument for the establishment of new international economic relations based on principles of equity and justice;

(f) All countries, big or small, rich or poor, are equal. All countries have the full right to participate in the decisions on the food problem;

(g) The well-being of the peoples of the world largely depends on the adequate production and distribution of food as well as the establishment of a world food security system which would ensure adequate availability of, and reasonable prices for, food at all times, irrespective of periodic fluctuations and vagaries of weather and free of political and economic pressures, and should thus facilitate, amongst other things, the development process of developing countries;

(h) Peace and justice encompass an economic dimension helping the solution of the world economic problems, the liquidation of underdevelopment, offering a lasting and definitive solution of the food problem for all peoples and guaranteeing to all countries the right to implement freely and effectively their development programmes. To this effect, it is necessary to eliminate threats and resort to force and to promote peaceful co-operation between States to the fullest extent possible, to apply the principles of noninterference in the internal affairs of other States, full equality of rights and respect of national independence and sovereignty, as well as to encourage the peaceful co-operation between all States, irrespective of their political, social and economic systems. The further improvement of international relations will create better conditions for international co-operation in all fields which should make possible large financial and material resources to be used, *inter alia*, for developing agricultural production and substantially improving world food security;

(i) For a lasting solution of the food problem all efforts should be made to eliminate the widening gaps which today separate developed and developing countries and to bring about a new international economic order. It should be possible for all countries to participate actively and effectively in the new international economic relations by the establishment of suitable international systems, where appropriate, capable of producing adequate action in order to establish just and equitable relations in international economic co-operation;

(j) Developing countries reaffirm their belief that the primary responsibility for ensuring their own rapid development rests with themselves. They declare, therefore, their readiness to continue to intensify their individual and collective efforts with a view to expanding their mutual co-operation in the field of agricultural development and food production, including the eradication of hunger and malnutrition;

(k) Since, for various reasons, many developing countries are not yet always able to meet their own food needs, urgent and effective international action should be taken to assist them, free of political presures,

Consistent with the aims and objectives of the Declaration on the Establishment of a New International Economic Order and the Programme of Actiort adopted by the General Assembly at its sixth special session,

The Conference consequently solemnly proclaims:

1. Every man, woman and child has the inalienable right to be free from hunger and malnutrition in order to develop fully and maintain their physical and mental faculties. Society today already possesses sufficient resources, organizational ability and technology and hence the competence to achieve this objective. Accordingly, the eradication of hunger is a common objective of all the countries of the international community, especially of the developed countries and others in a position to help.

2. It is a fundamental responsibility of Govern-ments to work together for higher food production and a more equitable and efficient distribution of food between countries and within countries. Governments should initiate immediately a greater concerned attack on chronic malnutrition and deficiency diseases among the vulnerable and lower income groups. In order to ensure adequate nutrition for all, Governments should formulate appropriate food and nutrition policies integrated in overall socio-economic and agricultural development plans based on adequate knowledge of available as well

as potential food resources. The importance of human milk in this connection should be stressed on nutritional grounds.

3. Food problems must be tackled during the preparation and implementation of national plans and programmes for economic and social development, with emphasis on their humanitarian aspects.

4. It is a responsibility of each State concerned, in accordance with its sovereign judgement internal legislation, to remove the obstacles to food production and to provide proper incentives to agricultural producers. Of prime importance for the attainment of these objectives are effective measures of socio-economic transformation by agrarian, tax, credit and investment policy reform and the reorganization of rural structures, such as the reform of the conditions of ownership, the encouragement of producer and consumer co-operatives, the mobilization of the full potential of human resources, both male and female, in the developing countries for an integrated rural development and the involvement of small farmers, fishermen and landless workers in attaining the required food production and employment targets. Moreover, it is necessary to recognize the key role of women in agricultural production and rural economy in many countries, and to ensure that appropriate education, extension programmes and financial facilities are made available to women on equal terms with men.

5. Marine and inland water resources are today becoming more important than ever as a source of food and economic prosperity. Accordingly, action should be taken to promote a rational exploitation of these resources, preferably for direct consumption, in order to contribute to meeting the food requirements of all peoples.

6. The efforts to increase food production should be complemented by every endeavour to prevent wastage of food in all its forms.

7. To give impetus to food production in developing countries and in particular in the least developed and most seriously affected among them urgent and effective international action should be taken, by the developed countries and other countries in a position to do so, to provide them with sustained additional technical and financial assistance on favourable terms and in a volume sufficient to their needs on the basis of bilateral and multilateral arrangements. This assistance must be free of conditions inconsistent with the sovereignty of the receiving States.

8. All countries, and primarily the highly industrialized countries should promote the advancement of food production technology and should make all efforts to promote the transfer, adaptation and dissemination of appropriate food production technology for the benefit of the developing countries and, to that end, they should *inter alia* make all efforts to disseminate the results of their research work to Governments and scientific institutions of developing countries in order to enable them to promote a sustained agricultural development.

9. To assure the proper conservation of natural resources being utilized of which might be utilized, for food production, all countries must collaborate in order to facilitate the preservation of the environment, including the marine environment.

10. All developed countries and others able to do so should collaborate technically and financially with the developing countries in their efforts to expand land and water resources for agricultural production and to assure a rapid increase in the availability, at fair costs, of agricultural inputs such as fertilizers and other chemicals,

high-quality seeds, credit and technology co-operation among developing countries, in this connection, is also important.

11. All States should strive to the utmost to readjust, where appropriate, their agricultural policies to give priority to food production, recognizing, in this connection the interrelationship between the world food problem and international trade. In the determination of attitudes towards farm support programmes for domestic food production, developed countries should take into account, as far as possible, the interest of the food-exporting developing countries, in order to avoid detrimental effect on their exports. Moreover, all countries should co-operate to devise effective steps to deal with the problem of stabilizing world markets and promoting equitable and remunerative prices, where appropriate through international arrangements, to improve access to markets through reduction or elimination of tariff and non-tariff barriers on the products of interest to the developing countries, to substantially increase the export earnings of these countries, to contribute to the diversification of their exports, and apply to them, in the multilateral trade negotiations, the principles as agreed upon in the Tokyo Declaration, including the concept of non-reciprocity and more favourable treatment.

12. As it is the common responsibility of the entire international community to ensure the availability at all times of adequate world supplies of basic food-stuffs by way of appropriate reserves, including emergency reserves, all countries should co-operate in the establishment of an effective system of world food security by:

Participating in and supporting the operation of the Global Information and Early Warning System on Food and Agriculture;

Adhering to the objectives, policies and guidelines of the proposed International Undertaking on World Food Security as endorsed by the World Food conference;

Earmarking, where possible, stocks or funds for meeting international emergency food requirements as envisaged in the proposed International Undertaking on World Food Security and developing international guidelines to provide for the co-ordination and the utilization of such stocks;

Co-operating in the provision of food aid for meeting emergency and nutritional needs as well as for stimulating rural employment through development projects.

All donor countries should accept and implement the concept of forward planning of food aid and make all efforts to provide commodities and/or financial assistance that will ensure adequate quantities of grains and other food commodities.

Time is short. Urgent and sustained action is vital. The Conference, therefore, calls upon all people expressing their will as individuals, and through their governments, and non-governmental organizations, to work together to bring about the end of the age-old scourge of hunger.

The Conference affirms:

The determination of the participating State to make full use of the United Nations system in the implementation of this Declaration and the other decision adopted by the Conference.

14 Discrimination (Employment and Occupation) Convention

The General Conference of the International Labour Organisation,

Having been convened at Geneva by the Governing Body of the International Labour Office, and having met in its forty-second session on 4 June 1958, and

Having decided upon the adoption of certain proposals with regard to discrimination in the field of employment and occupation, which is the fourth item on the agenda of the session, and

Having determined that these proposals shall take the form of an international Convention, and

Considering that the Declaration of Philadelphia affirms that all human beings, irrespective of race, creed or sex, have the right to pursue both their material well-being and their spiritual development in conditions of freedom and dignity, of economic security and equal opportunity, and

Considering further that discrimination constitutes a violation of rights enunciated by the Universal Declaration of Human Rights,

Adopts this twenty-fifth day of June of the year one thousand nine hundred and fifty-eight the following Convention, which may be cited as the Discrimination (Employment and Occupation), 1958:

Article 1

1. For the purpose of this Convention the term "discrimination" includes:

(a) Any distinction, exclusion or preference made on the basis of race, colour, sex, religion, political opinion, national extraction or social origin, which has the effect of nullifying or impairing equality of opportunity or treatment in employment or occupation;

(b) Such other distinction, exclusion or preference which has the effect of nullifying or impairing equality of opportunity or treatment in employment or occupation as may be determined by the Member concerned after consultation with representative employers' and workers' organisations, where such exist, and with other appropriate bodies.

2. Any distinction, exclusion or preference in respect of a particular job based on the inherent requirements thereof shall not be deemed to be discrimination.

3. For the purpose of this Convention the terms "employment" and "occupation" include access to vocational training, access to employment and to particular occupations, and terms and conditions of employment.

Article 2

Each Member for which this Convention is in force undertakes to declare and pursue a national policy designed to promote, by methods appropriate to national conditions and practice equality of opportunity and treatment in respect of employment and occupation, with a view to eliminating any discrimination respect thereof.

Article 3

Each Member for which this Convention is in force undertakes, by methods appropriate to national conditions and practice:

(a) To seek the co-operation of employers' and workers' organisations and other appropriate bodies in promoting the acceptance and observance of this policy;

(b) To enact such legislation and to promote such educational programmes as may be calculated to secure the acceptance and observance of the policy;

(c) To repeal any statutory provisions and modify any administrative instructions or practices which are inconsistent with the policy;

(d) To pursue the policy in respect of employment under the direct control of a national authority;

(e) To ensure observance of the policy in activities of vocational guidance, vocational training and placement services under the direction of a national authority;

(f) To indicate in its annual reports on the application of the Convention the action taken in pursuance of the policy and the results secured by such action.

Article 4

Any measures affecting an individual who is justifiably suspected of, or engaged in, activities prejudicial to the security of the State shall not be deemed to be discrimination, provided that the individual concerned shall have the right to appeal to a competent body established in accordance with national practice.

Article 5

1. Special measures of protection or assistance provided in other Conventions or Recommendations adopted by the International Labour Conference shall not be deemed to be discrimination.

2. Any Member may, after consultation with representative employers' and workers' organisations, where such exist, determine that other special measures designed to meet the particular requirements of persons who, for reasons such as sex, age, disablement, family

responsibilities or social or cultural status, are generally recognised to require special protection or assistance, shall not be deemed to be discrimination.

Article 6

Each Member which ratifies this Convention Undertakes to apply it to non-metropolitan territories in accordance with the provisions of the constitution of the International Labour Organisation.

Article 7

The formal ratifications of this Convention shall be communicated to the Director-General of the International Labour Office for registration.

Article 8

1. This Convention shall be binding only upon those Members of the International Labour Organisation whose ratifications have been registered with the Director-General.

2. It shall come into force twelve months after the date on which the ratifications of two Members have been registered with the Director-General.

3. Thereafter, this Convention shall come into force for any Member twelve months after the date on which its ratification has been registered.

Article 9

1. A Member which has ratified this Convention may denounce it after the expiration of ten years from the date on which the Convention first comes into force, by an act communicated to the Director-General of the International Labour Office for registration. Such denunciation shall not take effect until one year after the date on which it is registered.

2. Each Member which has ratified this Convention and which does not, within the year following the expiration of the period of ten years mentioned in the preceding paragraph, exercise the right of denunciation

provided for in this article, will be bound for another period of ten years and, thereafter, may denounce this Convention at the expiration of each period of ten years under the terms provided for in this article.

Article 10

1. The Director-General of the International Labour Office shall notify all Members of the International Labour Organisation of the registration of all ratifications and denunciations communicated to him by the Members of the Organisation.

2. When notifying the Members of the Organisation of the registration of the second ratification communicated to him, the Director-General shall draw the attention of the Members of the Organisation to the date upon which the Convention will come into force.

Article 11

The Director-General of the International Labour Office shall communicate to the Secretary-General of the United Nations for registration in accordance with Article 102 of the Charter of the United Nations full particulars of all ratifications and acts of denunciation registered by him in accordance with the provisions of the preceding articles.

Article 12

At such times as it may consider necessary the Governing Body of the International Labour Office shall present to the General Conference a report on the working of this Convention and shall examine the desirability of placing on the agenda of the Conference the question of its revision in whole or in part.

Article 13

1. Should the Conference adopt a new Convention revising this Convention in whole or in part, then, unless the new Convention otherwise provides:

(a) The ratification by a Member of the new revising Convention shall ipso jure involve the immediate denunciation of this convention, notwithstanding the provisions of article 9 above, if and when the new revising Convention shall have come into force;

(b) As from the date when the new revising Convention comes into force this Convention shall cease to be open to ratification by the Members.

2. This Convention shall in any case remain in force in its actual form and content for those Members which have ratified it but have not ratified the revising Convention.

Article 14

The English and French versions of the text of this Convention are equally authoritative.

The foregoing is the authentic text of the Convention duly adopted by the General Conference of the International Labour Organisation during its forty-second session which was held at Geneva and declared closed the twenty-sixth day of June 1958.

IN FAITH WHEREOF we have appended our signatures this fifth day of July 1958.

15 Promotion of Human Rights and to Countering Racialism, Apartheid and Incitement to War

Preamble

The General Conference,

Recalling that by virtue of its Constitution the purpose of UNESCO is to "contribute to peace and security by promoting collaboration among the nations through education, science and culture in order to further universal respect for justice, for the rule of law and for the human rights and fundamental freedoms" (Art. I 1), and that to realize this purpose the Organization will strive "to promote the free flow of ideas by word and image" (Art. I, 2),

Further recalling that under the Constitution the Member States of UNESCO, "believing in full and equal opportunities for education for all, in the unrestricted pursuit of objective truth, and in the free exchange of ideas and knowledge, are agreed and determined to develop and to increase the means of communication between their peoples and to employ these means for the purposes of mutual understanding and a truer and more perfect knowledge of each other's lives" (sixth preambular paragraph),

Recalling the purposes and principles of the United Nations, as specified in its Charter,

Recalling the Universal Declaration of Human Rights, adopted by the General Assembly of the United Nations in 1948 and particularly article 19 thereof, which provides that "everyone has the right to freedom of opinion and expression; this right includes freedom to hold opinions without interference and to seek, receive and impart information and ideas through any media and regardless of frontiers"; and the International Covenant on Civil and Political Rights, adopted by the General Assembly of the United Nations in 1966, article 19 of which proclaims the same principles and article 20 of which condemns incitement to war, the advocacy of national, racial or religious hatred and any form of discrimination, hostility or violence,

Recalling article 4 of the International Convention on the Elimination of All Forms of Racial Discrimination, adopted by the General Assembly of the United Nations in 1965, and the International Convention on the Suppression and Punishment of the Crime of Apartheid, adopted by the General Assembly of the United Nations in 1973, whereby the States acceding to these Conventions undertook to adopt immediate and positive measures designed to eradicate all incitement to, or acts of, racial discrimination, and agreed to prevent any encouragement of the crime of apartheid and similar segregationist policies or their manifestations,

Recalling the Declaration on the Promotion among Youth of the Ideals of Peace, Mutual Respect and Understanding between Peoples, adopted by the General Assembly of the United Nations in 1965,

Recalling the declarations and resolutions adopted by the various organs of the United Nations concerning the establishment of a new international economic order and the role UNESCO is called upon to play in this respect,

Recalling the Declaration of the Principles of International Cultural Co-operation, adopted by the General Conference of UNESCO in 1966,

Recalling resolution 59 (I) of the General Assembly of the United Nations, adopted in 1946 and declaring:

Freedom of information is a fundamental human right and is the touchstone of all the freedoms to which the United Nations is consecrated:

Freedom of information requires as an indispensable element the willingness and capacity to employ its privileges without abuse. It requires as a basic discipline the moral obligation to seek the facts without prejudice and to spread knowledge without malicious intent:

Recalling resolution 110 (II) of the General Assembly of the United Nations, adopted in 1947, condemning all forms of propaganda which are designed or likely to provoke or encourage any threat to the peace, breach of the peace, or act of aggression,

Recalling resolution 127 (II), also adopted by the General Assembly in 1947, which invites Member States to take measures, within the limits of constitutional procedures, to combat the diffusion of false or distorted reports likely to injure friendly relations between States, as well as the other resolutions of the General Assembly concerning the mass media and their contribution to strengthening peace, trust and friendly relations among States,

Recalling resolution 9.12 adopted by the General Conference of UNESCO in 1968, reiterating UNESCO's objective to helpd to eradicate colonialism and racialism, and resolution 12.1 adopted by the General Conference in 1976, which proclaims that colonialism, neocolonialism and racialism in all its forms and manifestations are incompatible with the fundamental aims of UNESCO,

Recalling resolution 4.301 adopted in 1970 by the General Conference of UNESCO on the contribution of the information media to furthering international understanding and co-operation in the interests of peace and human welfare, and to countering propaganda on behalf of war, racialism, apartheid and hatred among nations, and aware of the fundamental contribution that mass media can make to the realizations of these objectives,

Recalling the Declaration on Race and Racial Prejudice adopted by the General Conference of UNESCO at its twentieth session,

Conscious of the complexity of the problems of information in modern society, of the diversity of solutions which have been offered to them, as evidenced in particular by the consideration given to them within UNESCO, and of the legitimate desire of all parties concerned that their aspirations, points of view and cultural identity be taken into due consideration,

Conscious of the aspirations of the developing countries for the establishment of a new, more just and more effective world information and communi-cation order,

Proclaims on this twenty-eighth day of November 1978 this Declaration of Fundamental Principles concerning the Contribution of the Mass Media to Strengthening Peace and International Under-standing, to the Promotion of Human Rights and to Countering Racialism, Apartheid and Incitement to War.

Article I

The strengthening of peace and international understanding, the promotion of human rights and the countering of racialism, apartheid and incitement to war demand a free flow and a wider and better balanced dissemination of information. To this end, the mass media have a leading contribution to make. This contribution will be the more effective to the extent that the information reflects the different aspects of the subject dealt with.

Article II

1. The exercise of freedom of opinion, expression and information, recognized as an integral part of human rights and fundamental freedoms, is a vital factor in the strengthening of peace and international understanding.

2. Access by the public to information should be guaranteed by the diversity of the sources and means of information available to it, thus enabling each individual to check the accuracy of facts and to appraise events objectively. To this end, journalists must have freedom to report and the fullest possible facilities of access to information. Similarly, it is important that the mass media be responsive to concerns of peoples and individuals, thus promoting the participation of the public in the elaboration of information.

3. With a view to the strengthening of peace and international understanding, to promoting human rights and to countering racialism, apartheid and incitement to war, the mass media throughout the world, by reason of their role, contribute to promoting human rights, in particular by giving expression to oppressed peoples who struggle against colonialism, neocolonialism, foreign occupation and all forms of racial discrimination and oppression and who are unable to make their voices heard within their own territories.

4. If the mass media are to be in a position to promote the principles of this Declaration in their activities, it is essential that journalists and other agents of the mass media, in their own country or abroad, be assured of protection guaranteeing them the best conditions for the exercise of their profession.

Article III

1. The mass media have an important contribution to make to the strengthening of peace and international understanding and in countering racialism, apartheid and incitement to war.

2. In countering aggressive war, racialism apartheid and other violations of human rights which are inter alia spawned by prejudice and ignorance, the mass media, by disseminating information on the aims, aspirations cultures and needs of all peoples, contribute to eliminate ignorance and misunderstanding between peoples, to make nationals of a country sensitive to the needs and desires of others, to ensure the respect of the rights and dignity of all nations, all peoples and all individuals without distinction of race, sex, language, religion or nationality and to draw attention to the great evils which afflict humanity, such as poverty, malnutrition and diseases, thereby promoting the formulation by States of the policis best able to promote the reduction of international tension and the peaceful and equitable settlement of international disputes.

Article IV

The mass media have an essential part to play in the education of young people in spirit of peace, justice, freedom, mutual respect and understanding in order to promote human rights, equality of rights as between all human beings and alll nations, and economic and social progress. Equally, they have an important role to play in making known the views and aspirations of the younger generation.

Article V

In order to respect freedom of opinion, expression and information and in order that information may reflect all points of view, it is important that the points of view presented by those who consider that the information published or disseminated about them has seriously prejudiced their effort to strengthen peace and international understanding, to promote human rights or to counter racialism, apartheid and incitement to war be disseminated.

Article VI

For the establishment of lasting peace and to the economic and political independence of the developing countries, it is necessary to correct the inequalities in the flow of information to and from developing countries, and between those countries. To this end, it is essential that their mass media should have conditions and resources enabling them to gain strength and expand, and to co-operate both among themselves and with the mass media in developed countries.

Article VII

By disseminating more widely all of the information concerning the universally accepted objectives and principles which are the bases of the resolutions adopted by the different organs of the United Nations, the mass media contribute effectively to the strengthening of peace and international understanding, to the promotion of human rights, and to the establishment of a more just and equitable international economic order.

Article VIII

Professional organizations, and people who participate in the professional training of journalists and other agents of the mass media and who assist them in performing their functions in a responsible manner should attach special importance to the principles of this Declaration when drawing up and ensuring application of their codes of ethics.

Article IX

In the spirit of this Declaration, it is for the international community to contribute to the creation of the conditions for a free flow and wider and more balanced dissemination of information, and of the conditions of the protection, in the exercise of their functions, of journalists and other agents of the mass media. UNESCO is well placed to make a valuable contribution in this respect.

Article X

1. With due respect for constitutional provisions designed to guarantee freedom of information and for the applicable international instruments and agreements, it is indispensable to create and maintain throughout the world the conditions which make it possible for the organizations and persons professionally involved in the dissemination of information to achieve the objectives of this Declaration.

2 It is important that a free flow and wider and better balanced dissemination of information be encouraged.

3. To this end, it is necessary that States facilitate the procurement by the mass media in the developing countries of adequate conditions and resources enabling them to gain strength and expand, and that they support co-operation by the latter both among themselves and with the mass media in developed countries.

4. Similarly, on a basis of equality of rights, mutual advantage and respect for the diversity of the cultures which go to make up the common heritage of mankind, it is essential that bilateral and multilateral exchanges of information among all States, and in particular between those which have different economic and social systems, be encouraged and developed.

Article XI

For this declaration to be fully effective it is necessary, with due respect for the legislative and administrative provisions and the other obligations of Member States, to guarantee the existence of favourable conditions for the operation of the mass media, in conformity with the provisions of the Universal Declaration of Human Rights and with the corresponding principles proclaimed in the International Covenant on Civil and Political Rights adopted by the General Assembly of the United Nations in 1966.

16 The Need for an Agenda for Development

Introduction

1. The purpose of the present note is to provide information on progress in the implementation of General Assembly resolution 47/181 of 22 December 1992, in which the Assembly requested the Secretary-General, in consultation with Member States, to prepare an agenda for development for submission to it at its forty-eighth session.

2. Accordingly, the note provides information on the replies received from Member States in response to the Secretary-General's note verbale of 20 May 1993, eliciting views on an Agenda for Development. It also contains initial indications, in the light of these replies, as well as consultations within the Secretariat and with the organizations of the United Nations system, including at the recent session of the Administrative Committee on Coordination on 28 and 29 October 1993, as to some of the approaches and broad themes which the Secretary-General would propose to pursue in an Agenda for Development. It is hoped that this information will facilitate an open and wide-ranging debate in the meetings of the current session of the General Assembly to be devoted to this subject. The views expressed in the debate will be drawn upon in pursuing ongoing work in the preparation of the

report on an Agenda for Development requested by the Assembly.

3. As far as the timetable for the issuance of the report is concerned, in the note verbale referred to above, the Secretary-General indicated that the complexity of the issues to be addressed in an Agenda for Development required a longer time-frame for its elaboration than that envisaged in General Assembly resolution 47/181. This view was generally shared by Member States in their replies to the note verbale. It is therefore the intention of the Secretary-General to issue the report requested in General Assembly resolution 47/181 in the early months of 1994. In that light, it is proposed, for the Assembly's consideration, that an item on the subject be included in the agendas of the Economic and Social Council in 1994 and of the forty-ninth session of the Assembly.

Replies Received from Member States

4. As at 16 November 1993, the following Member States had responded to the Secretary-General's note verbale of 20 May 1993; Austria, Bangladesh, Brazil, Canada, China, Cuba, Denmark (on behalf of the European Community), Finland (on behalf of the Nordic countries), Ghana, Japan, Mexico, Morocco, Panama, Poland, United Kingdom of Great Britain and Northern Ireland, United States of America and Zimbabwe.

5. Many of the replies refer to peace and development as the major twin themes of international cooperation. They note the opportunity provided by an Agenda for Development to redress what is seen as a risk of marginalization of the United Nations system in the economic and social sphere, and of a widening gap between the objectives set out in an Agenda for Peace and the ability of the system to

advance the goals of sustained and sustainable development.

6. An overriding objective of an Agenda for Development should thus be, in the view of many respondents, the enhancement of international cooperation for the sustained growth of the world economy and, in particular, the revitalization of growth and development of the developing countries.

7. Many replies state that an Agenda for Development should address the root causes of instability, which are often directly linked to poverty and underdevelopment. At the same time, the view is expressed that, despite its indisputable links with peace, security and stability, an agenda for development to overcome poverty and social exclusion and enhance the well-being of people deserves to be dealt with in its own right. While the importance of human rights and democratization are generally recognized, different views are expressed, and emphasis placed, on their relationship with economic and social development.

8. Most responses agree that an Agenda for Development (a) should be an instrument for integrating new areas of consensus for action into an overall framework, drawing or relevant intergovernmental agreements, declarations and programmes of action, and (b) should provide a substantive basis to strengthen coordination of activities within the United Nations system.

A. Agenda for Development as an instrument for integrating new areas of consensus

9. Replies point to far-reaching changes taking place and trends emerging, which make it imperative for the international community to give renewed

attention to the definition of development as a global issue and its place in the international agenda, and to review and reassess approaches to development at all levels.

10. In the same context, replies point to the growing globalization of the world economy and the increasing evidence of interdependence among countries and issue in the economic, social and environmental fields. They also highlight the gravity of the problems facing developing countries as well as the close interrelationships between sustained and sustainable development.

11. In the face of these changes and trends, areas of growing consensus are emerging. In this connection, replies highlight the integrative approach to ecological and economic issues developed at the United Nations Conference on Environment and Development. They also refer to the growing consensus around the concept of people-centred development, which guarantees equity and sustainability. Forthcoming conferences and summits on population, women and social development should serve to expand these areas of consensus.

12. Many respondents view the main potential contribution of an Agenda for Development as helping to restore development cooperation as a central global concern, while promoting new, more comprehensive and effective approaches to development. It would do so by building on objectives and commitments adopted in the General Assembly and other international forums, assessing progress achieved and proposing ways and means of overcoming obstacles encountered, furthering emerging new areas of international consensus, and integrating them in the international framework.

13. The hope is expressed in many replies that, as part of a process of renewal and consensus building, an Agenda for Development should promote new partnerships among Governments, based on the recognition of sovereign equality, mutual interest and shared responsibility, as well as between Governments, the United Nations and other actors in development. In this connection, a further expansion of the development dialogue to include community organizations and non-governmental organizations, at both the national and international levels, is seen as increasingly essential to arrive at sound development strategies, based on popular participation and the needs of the people.

14. Replies propose various priority objectives to be addressed. Among them:

    (a) Mobilizing new and additional financial resources, taking into account, *inter alia,* the light of the urgent needs of the least developed countries, as well as of the economies in transition;

    (b) Promoting the fulfilment of commitments in the areas of trade, money and finance and macroeconomic policy coordination, and ensuring fuller participation of developing countries in international economic cooperation;

    (c) Emphasizing investments in people;

    (d) Advancing economic growth to foster long-term social progress, including income distribution;

    (e) Alleviating demographic pressures;

    (f) Promoting the participation of women in development.

B. Agenda for Development as an instrument for enhancing coordination within the United Nations system

15. Noting that the economic and social sectors of the United Nations suffer from an unclear identity, insufficient visibility and credibility, and excessive fragmentation, a number of replies see an Agenda for Development as an important vehicle for better defining the purposes, goals and role of the United Nations in development, in a way which would enhance both the effectiveness of its own interventions and its ability to develop well-defined positions contributing to improved coordination within the United Nations system as a whole.

16. Some countries draw attention to what they see as the three main functions of the United Nations:
    (a) A universal meeting place where all Members can raise issues for discussion and, hopefully, resolution;
    (b) An instrument for analysis and information gathering and for the elaboration of and monitoring of adherence to international norms;
    (c) A network of institutions entrusted with development as well as relief tasks in support of Member States.

17. Some replies also provide suggestions as to specific areas on which United Nations activities should focus. Among them:
    (a) Introducing strengthened mechanisms for macroeconomic policy surveillance and monitoring;
    (b) Overseeing issues relating to trade investments and commodities, including technology transfers and the fostering of greater technological cooperation among countries; addressing the emergence of new trade relationships, including trade-blocs and their impact on international trade;

(c) Helping reconcile market-oriented approaches to development with social protection, welfare and equity considerations;

(d) Addressing the role of foreign direct investments and transnational corporations in development;

(e) Advancing the sustainable development agenda;

(f) Assisting countries emerging from crisis situations in the rehabilitation phase and in setting their development agendas;

(g) Playing an advocacy role in the area of human capacity-building and furthering human resource development in developing countries, including as a means for their effective participation in international economic and trade relations;

(h) Building-up global databases in support of enhanced policy planning capacities in developing countries.

18. Replies reflect the expectation that, by promoting a more comprehensive and effective approach to development and a refocusing of the United Nations role and contribution, an Agenda for Development will, in turn, further the objective of greater coherence in the development activities of the system as a whole. Relationships and the fostering of closer cooperation, between the United Nations and the Bretton Woods institutions are highlighted in many replies as a key issue in this respect. In the same context, the role of the multilateral financial institutions in mobilizing resources for use in social development projects is stressed. The need for improved coordination in the work of agencies concerned, respectively, with development financing and environmental issues is likewise highlighted.

19. In general, the fostering of a greater "unity of purpose" within the United Nations and the system as a whole, in both the policy and operational spheres, is viewed as a crucial objective of an Agenda for Development.

Some Approaches and Themes to be Pursued in an Agenda for Development

20. In the light of the views put forward by Member States in different forums, and in response to the Secretary-General's note verbale, and taking into account ongoing discussions with programmes and agencies of the United Nations system, the Secretary-General wishes to offer some initial reflections on possible approaches to an Agenda for Development, and on some of the broad themes to be addressed in that report.

21. An Agenda for Development should not attempt to provide new macroeconomic theory or seek to present an exhaustive analysis of the world economy. The most useful contribution which, in the Secretary-General's view, can be made at this stage through that report is to offer the international community an open working Agenda, which would be the beginning of a process rather than its end. In this perspective, its effectiveness should be judged, in the first instance, by the quality of the debate it generates and the follow-up given to it, through a process of discussion and consensus building, and the testing of new approaches.

22. In the post-colonial period, much of the impetus for development cooperation came from the bipolar competition. Today, that rationale has gone. The evidence, so far, is that the imperative of human solidarity does not have the mobilizing power of the cold war. Development appears to be slipping down the international agenda and risks to be increasingly

marginalized in the face of short-term imperatives. An Agenda for Development should seek a reversal of these trends at all levels and help restore development to its rightful place at the top of the world agenda.

23. Economic growth is the mainspring of development. An acceleration of the rate of growth is a condition for expanding the resource base of the developing countries, and hence for economic, technological and social transformation.

24. In the continuum of the work of the United Nations for peace and development, preventive diplomacy seeks to avoid the break down of conditions of peace. At the other end of the continuum, post-conflict peace-building must involve efforts to identify and support structures which build trust and well-being among peoples. The promotion of economic and social development is crucial at both ends of the continuum.

25. Traditional approaches to development have failed to transform poor countries and countries in post-conflict situations. They have not succeeded in achieving growth in most developing countries and, more importantly, have failed to reduce poverty and to set the stage for sustainable progress.. The assumption of conditions of peace, on which development strategies have traditionally been built, is in stark contrast with the actual situation prevailing in a growing number of countries in Africa, as well as elsewhere.

26. An Agenda for Development would thus complement an Agenda for Peace, by addressing the deeper foundations of global peace and security in the economic, social and environmental spheres.

27. One of the contributions of an Agenda for

Development should be to bring out the new face of the world economy, stressing the globalization of economic flows, and taking stock of the increased interdependence among nations and issues.

28. Greater interdependence among nations, facilitated by liberalization and deregulation and driven by technological innovation, means that economic problems must, now more than ever before, be seen in a global perspective. The distinction between national and international economic policies is fading. Financial and trade flows and international cooperation in the area of technology need to be re-examined in this context.

29. Growing levels of interdependence also require a rethinking of the overall content of development cooperation. It is frequently equated with the concessional elements injected into the trade, finance and technology flows between developed and developing countries. These elements remain important. In this context, the consequences and impact of a premature reduction in the availability of official development assistance should not be underestimated. For many developing countries, however, trade, debt and private flows are equally, if not more, crucial. Development cooperation today must mean the integration of developing countries concerns into all discussions of global trade, finance and technology cooperation.

30. During the past decade, only a few developing countries have been successful in expanding their exports and achieving self-reliance. For most of them the full potential for enhancing export earnings through gains from trade liberalization has not yet been realized. Protectionism is still high and reduces the capacity of developing countries to generate additional financial resources for development

through higher export earnings. A major factor inhibiting investment in export supply capabilities is uncertainty as to whether current access levels will be liberalized, curtailed or remain unchanged.

31. Technology, whether embodied in physical capital or in the knowledge processed by human beings, is a powerful engine for growth. Technology is also fundamental and the key element in the process of globalization. A sustained development process will not take place unless countries participate in the progress made possible by the rapid advances in science and technology that have characterized the global economy in recent years and will continue in the future. Technology has to be developed, deployed and shared, not just for promoting growth, but also for environmental management and poverty alleviation. Access to technology will be one of the determining factors for growth in the world economy. As the world becomes increasingly integrated, the comparative advantage of all nations is likely to rest on the skill, education and technical competence of their labour force.

32. Development must thus be seen as a shared concern of all nations, rich and poor, whatever their orientations. In addressing development as a key global issue, commonalities as well as the specificity of conditions and requirements must be fully borne in mind. One important commonality relates to the place of developing countries in the international economic system and their capacity to affect decisions which have sometimes a profound impact on opportunities for their economic and social development. There are, at the same time, specificities which must be clarified and addressed, if development support actions are to have the necessary impact and meet the specific requirements of the countries concerned.

33. An important illustration in this respect is the particular problems being faced by countries in transition. This situation is common to a large number of countries, not only in Eastern Europe but also in Africa, Asia and Latin America, where the move to a more market-oriented system is being undertaken, with all the promise, but also all the difficulties, which this process implies.
34. A second illustration relates to the requirements of countries emerging from natural disasters. No geographical area is exempt. The challenge of effective international relief in such situations and of proceedings from relief to rehabilitation and the resumption of development will need to be addressed in an Agenda for Development.
35. A third example relates to the support requirements of countries which are in the midst of a conflict, be it the result of a civil war or an international conflict. The challenge of pursing development efforts in such situations is a reality with which the United Nations is increasingly faced and which will have to be taken into account in an Agenda for Development.
36. A fourth illustration relates to the requirements of countries which are recovering from a conflict. Their special development needs are also not accounted for in traditional development theory and will need to be brought out in an Agenda for Development.
37. The need to pursue a more holistic view of development, fully encompassing economic as well as social dimensions, and the importance of taking into account the specificities of particular requirements and situations, should not preclude the identification of areas of concentration and priority themes for United Nations actions. Ways of enhancing the role of the General Assembly and the

Economic and Social Council in promoting policy development at the national and regional levels and harmonizing policies at the international level in relation to these themes will need to be examined. The contribution of special conferences should be reviewed in the same context.

38. An assessment of development assistance policies and of the role of the United Nations in supporting the development of national capacities should equally, form an important part of this debate, as should the contribution of the United Nations in promoting the role of the private sector and the development of entrepreneurship.

39. The search for more effective approaches to development and a sharpening of the role of the United Nations in development, should, in turn, provide the basis for an examination of ways of enhancing inter-agency coordination, including closer cooperation with the Bretton Woods institutions. In the same perspective, an Agenda for Development should include a discussion of the regional dimension of development, including the role of the regional commissions and relations with regional organizations outside the United Nations system.

40. The title of the report which the Secretary-General is to submit to the General Assembly will be *An Agenda for Development*. The use of the indefinite article is significant. The contribution of each and every State, in the further elaboration of the Agenda will be vital. The presentation by the Secretary-General of an "open", "working" Agenda should be the beginning of a new process of dialogue where all States can contribute to the determination of their common future, and it should serve to generate a renewed debate among Member States as to the

development themes and priorities to be addressed by the United Nations. This should, in turn, lead to a new sense of cohesion among all parts of the system.

41. The Secretary-General invites the views of the Member States of the approach.

17 An Agenda for Development

Preface

1. The General Assembly, in its resolution 47/181 of 22 with Member States, a report on an agenda for development. In an effort to gather the widest range of views about the topic of development, I asked for submissions from all Member States, as well as the agencies and programmes of the United Nations system, and encouraged ideas from public and private sources on a worldwide basis. Contributions received in the course of this process have been drawn upon in preparing the present report.

2. As requested in paragraph 5 of General Assembly resolution 48/166 of 21 December 1993, I will present my conclusions and recommendations on an agenda for development during the forty-ninth session of the Assembly, taking into account the debate at the substantive session of 1994 of the Economic and Social Council, as well as the views expressed during the discussions to be promoted by the President of the General Assembly.

I. Introduction: why an Agenda for Development?

3. Development is a fundamental human right. Development is the most secure basis for peace.

4. Taking stock of these principles, and in keeping with my strong personal commitment to development and the recognized needs of the United Nations at this

point in history, the idea of an agenda for development took shape.

5. The concept of development, and decades of effort to reduce poverty, illiteracy, disease and mortality rates, are great achievements of this century. But development as a common cause is in danger of fading from the forefront of our agenda. The competition for influence during the cold war stimulated interest in development. The motives were not always altruistic, but countries seeking to develop could benefit from that interest. Today, the competition to bring development to the poorest countries has ended. Many donors have grown weary of the task. Many of the poor are dispirited. Development is in crisis.

6. The poorest nations fall farther behind. Nations in transition from command to open economies face immense hardships. Nations that have achieved prosperity see their success accompanied by a new array of problems social environmental, cultural and economic, and many are consequently reluctant even to pursue their assistance policies at former levels.

7. The current situation calls for wider intellectual understanding, deeper moral commitment and more effective policy measures. Without them, a half century of considerable progress could be undermined. Worse, all peoples of the world will live on a deteriorating planet, and will increasingly lose the ability to shape their destiny in a coherent way.

8. Specific suggestions and detailed proposals for development have been produced in great quantity and are deserving of serious study. the United Nations system has produced a wealth of studies and reports on various aspects of development; they are an invaluable resource.

9. Building upon these efforts, the present report

seeks to revitalize the vision of development and stimulate an intensified discussion of all its aspect.

10. The Charter of the United Nations makes possible a maturing elaboration of the crucial idea of development, but it has been left to us in the last decades of the twentieth century to try to bring the concept of development to fulfilment.

11. Concerns have been expressed that the United Nations puts greater emphasis on peace-keeping than on issues of development. These fears are not borne out by the regular budgets or the numbers of staff members engaged in peace and in development. Yet with growing requests for funds for peace-keeping, some Member States find it difficult to increase their contributions to the developmental activities of the United Nations. Without development, however, there is no prospect for lasting peace.

12. While national Governments bear the major responsibility for development, the United Nations has been entrusted with important mandates for assisting in this task. The involvement of the United Nations in development spans five development decades and encompasses the full range of global problems of an economic, social, cultural and humanitarian character. It operates in all categories and at every level of development.

13. This agenda, therefore, is grounded in unique United Nations experience. Section II sets forth the five major and interlinked dimensions of development. Section III notes the multiplicity of actors in development and the process by which the United Nations can help to link these actors to the different dimensions of development. Annex I to the present report shows the scale of the United Nations involvement in development. In discussing the involvement of the United Nation in development, I have primarily limited myself to the

United Nations itself, including its funds and programmes. The work of the specialized agencies of the United Nations system, essential as it is, is not the focus of the present document.

14. In the light of the new vision of development that is emerging, an alternative to the United Nations in development simply does not exist. The United nations is a forum where the voices of all States, great and small, can be heard with equal clarity, and where non-State actors can make their views known to the widest audience. there is still time to move forward together, but greater urgency is necessary. With each passing day's delay, the work grows more costly and difficult.

15. While there is war, no State is securely at peace. While there is want, no people can achieve lasting development.

II. The dimensions of development

A. Peace as the foundation

16. Traditional approaches to development presuppose that it takes place under conditions of peace. Yet that is rarely the case. The absence of peace is a pervasive reality in many parts of the world. Most peoples must strive to achieve their development against a background of past, present or threatened conflict. Many carry the burden of recent devastation and continuing ethnic strife. None can avoid the realities of a world of ongoing arms proliferation, regional war, and the possibility of a return to potentially antagonistic spheres of influence. To the categorization of countries by level of development should be added the categorization of countries in conflict. Because the United Nations is active at the forefront of humanitarian aid, refugee assistance, and the range of peace operations, it is deeply and inextricably involved in peace as a fundamental dimension of development.

17. Development cannot proceed easily in societies where military concerns are at or near the centre of life. Societies whose economic effort is given in substantial part to military production inevitably diminish the prospects of their people for development. The absence of peace often leads societies to devote a higher percentage of their budget to the military than to development needs in health, education and housing. Preparation for war absorbs inordinate resources and impedes the development of social institutions.

18. The lack of development contributes to international tension and to a perceived need for military power. This in turn heightens tensions. Societies caught in this cycle find it difficult to avoid involvement in confrontation, conflict or all-out warfare.

19. While in some nations service in the military is the most reliable path to an education and to the acquisition of job skills for civilian life, there are also cases in which military production may disseminate advanced technologies of eventual use for civilian purposes. But national budgets which focus directly on development better serve the cause of peace and human security.

20. Situations of conflict require a development strategy different from that obtaining under peaceful conditions. The characteristics of development will differ according to the nature of the situation. Development in the context of international war does not involve the same problems as development during guerrilla warfare, or development when governmental institutions are under military control.

21. Although development activities yield their best results in conditions of peace, they should start prior to the end of hostilities. Emergency relief and development should not be regarded as alternatives; one provides a starting point and a foundation for the other. Relief

requirements must be met in a way which, from the outset, provides a foundation for lasting development. Camps for refugees and displaced persons must be more than mere holding grounds for victims. Vaccination campaigns, literacy drives and special attention to the conditions of women are important at these times. All can lay the groundwork for community development even while emergency relief is being provided. Capacity-building steps should not await the formal termination of hostilities, but must begin to be performed alongside urgent wartime services, conflict, terrible as it is, can provide opportunities for major reform and its consolidation. The ideals of democracy, respect for human rights and measures for social justice can begin to take form at this stage.

22. Peace-building means action to identify and support structures which will tend to strengthen and solidify peace in order to avoid a relapse into conflict. As preventive diplomacy aims to prevent the outbreak of a conflict, peace-building starts during the course of a conflict to prevent its recurrence. Only sustained, cooperative work on the underlying economic, social, cultural and humanitarian problems can place an achieved peace on a durable foundation. Unless there is reconstruction and development in the aftermath of conflict, there can be little expectation that peace will endure.

23. Peace-building is a matter for countries at all stages of development. For counties emerging from conflict, peace-building offers the chance to establish new institutions, social, political and judicial, that can give impetus to development. Land reform and other measures of social justice can be undertaken. Countries in transition can use peace-building measures as a chance to put their national systems on the path of sustainable development. Countries high on the scale of wealth and

power must hasten the process of partial demobilization and defence conversion. Decisions made at this stage can have an immense impact on the course of their societies and the international community for future generations.

24. The most immediate task for peace-building is to alleviate the effects of war on the population. Food aid, support for health and hygiene systems, the clearance of mines and logistical support to essential organizations in the field represent the first peace-building task.

25. At this stage too, it is essential that efforts to address immediate needs are undertaken in ways that promote, rather than compromise, long-term development objectives. As food is provided there must be concentration on restoring food production capacities. In conjunction with the delivery of relief supplies, attention should be given to road construction, restoration and improvement of port facilities and establishment of regional stocks and distribution centres.

26. Mine clearance is a unique post-conflict undertaking. The world is awakening to the reality that the proliferation of land-mines poses a major obstacle to development and must be halted. Because they remain in the ground long after hostilities have ended. Killing and maiming indiscriminately, mines effectively prevent the use of large tracts of land, while imposing a huge burden on families and the health infrastructures of post-conflict countries. In many cases, the removal of land-mines and unexploded ordnance is a prerequisite for all the post-conflict peace-building activities. Techniques applicable under conditions prevalent in most countries are slow and painstaking. Mine clearance has to be conducted for a great many years and therefore must be managed and undertaken by nationals. Capacity needs to be established to undertake, monitor and assess mine clearance and to maintian national standards in accordance with international guidelines.

27. The reintegration of combatants is difficult, but it is critically important to stability in the post-conflict period. In many conflicts, soldiers have been recruited at a very young age. As a result, the capacity of former combatants to return to peacetime society and make a living is severely compromised, thereby undermining society's prospects for development.

28. Effective reintegration of combatants is also essential to the sustainability of peace. Credit and small-enterprise programmes are vital if ex-combatants are to find productive employment. Basic education for re-entry into civilian society, special vocational programmes, on-the-job training, and education in agricultural techniques and management skills are key to post-conflict peace-building. to a certain extent, some technical skills learned by soldiers can be important to national reconstruction.

29. As conflict typically takes a heavy toll on the mechanisms of governance, post-conflict efforts must pay special attention to their repair. Key institutions of civil society, judicial systems, for example, may need to be reinforced or even created anew. This means assistance for a variety of governmental activities, such as a fair system for generating public sector revenue, a legislative basis for the protection of human rights, and rules for the operation of private enterprise.

30. Pulling up the roots of conflict goes beyond immediate post-conflict requirements and the repair of war-torn societies. The underlying conditions that led to conflict must be addressed. As the causes of conflict are varied, so must be the means of addressing them. Peace-building means fostering a culture of peace. Land reform, water-sharing schemes, common economic enterprise zones, joint tourism projects and cultural exchanges can make a major difference. Restoring employment growth will be a strong inducement to the young to abandon the vocation of war.

31. Reduction of military expenditure is a vital link in the chain between development and peace. Although worldwide military expenditures continue to consume too large a share of productive resources and capacity, progress has been made in recent years. Worldwide, between 1978 and 1992 a cumulative peace dividend of $500 billion was realized; $425 billion in industrial and transitional countries and $75 billion in developing countries. Little of this peace dividend appears to have been channelled into development.

32. While figures for exports of weapons show substantial declines in real terms in the early years of this decade, major concerns persist. Imported stocks of conventional weapons from countries rapidly reducing their military establishments are finding their way to third countries. relatively unsophisticated weapons such as mortars, machine-guns and rocket launchers, even in the hands of those with rudimentary military training, have caused immense death and destruction. Paradoxically, those expressing great concern over the rising stocks of arms worldwide are also the source of that phenomenon. The five permanent members of the Security councils account for 86 per cent of the arms supplies now flowing to the countries of the world.

33. Imports of armaments are often purchased at the expense of capital or consumer goods. Reducing military expenditures makes more funds available to finance development, satisfy consumer demands and meet basic social welfare needs. A decrease in military outlays may support budgetary reform and promote macroeconomic stability. National efforts can be reoriented away from military priorities towards more productive and peaceful objectives. Global tensions and rivalries can be reduced. The overall impact on development is potentially profound.

34. The armed forces absorb some of the most talented members of society, whose training costs are considerably above the social average and whose energies are directed to the operation of increasingly sophisticated military hardware. Armament production utilizes industrial skills and capacity that could be put to other uses.

35. Among many of the countries in transition, procurement of new weapons systems has collapsed and most military expenditure is now for personnel costs, including pensions. Whole communities which were dependent on defence industries are now threatened, unless they can adapt themselves to changing requirements. Fears of further increases in unemployment are slowing reductions in the size of armed forces, while military industries are being kept solvent by massive subsidies to the detriment of overall macroeconomic goals.

36. Demilitarization has also produced painful strains among the industrialized market economies, though less severe than those in countries in transition. Particular localities and firms have been severely affected, but he market mechanism has made it easier for resources to be absorbed in other sectors of the economy. Alternative employment has often been difficult to find for many workers however, and retraining remains sporadic.

37. These problems, however, should not deter countries from promoting the transition towards smaller militaries. The reduction of military spending not only frees up public expenditures for social purposes, but also allows credit to flow to needed economic investments. Over the longer term, these transitions will prove worthwhile, even if they are painful in the short term.

38. While it had been hoped that the end of the cold war would lead to a dramatic fall in military spending, progress has been difficult to achieve in an atmosphere

increasingly marked by ethnic strife and economic insecurity. Relief at the end of the bipolar arms race is being supplanted by alarm over the prospect of several regional build-ups of both conventional arms and weapons of mass destruction. In a number of countries, especially in the Middle East and Asia, military expenditure has continued to increase. Fear of confrontation over shared resources, domestic instability and fear of heavily armed neighbours have all been factors. In some instances, the diminished possibility of super-Power intervention has increased the explosiveness of regional antagonisms. The lucrative aspect of the arms trade should also be taken into account. In this context, I support calls for a worldwide ban on the production and transfer of land-mines and their components.

39. Arms control and disarmament reduce the threat of destruction, economic decline and tensions that lead to war. A world of lower military expenditures, reduced military establishments, smaller stocks of weapons and less environmental destruction by military-related activities is not only desirable in itself, but propitious for development.

40. Today, even remote conflicts can pose security and developmental concerns far beyond a State's borders. This new recognition gives international peace and security a wider meaning, calls for measures that can further development even during conflict, and indicates that development, when successfully pursued, is another way to define peace.

B. The economy as the engine of progress

41. Economic growth is the engine of development as a whole. Without economic growth, there can be no sustained increase in household or government consumption, in private or public capital formation, in health, welfare and security levels. By whatever social processes distributional choices are made, the capacity to

make them is severely limited in poor societies and is enhanced by economic growth. Progress in the other aspects of development discussed in this report, peace, the environment, society and democracy, will have a positive effect on economic growth.

42. Accelerating the rate of economic growth is a condition for expanding the resource base and hence for economic, technological and social transformation. While economic growth does not ensure that benefits will be equitably distributed or that the physical environment will be protected, without economic growth the material resources for tackling environmental degradation will not exist, nor will it be possible to pursue social programmes effectively in the long term. the advantage of economic growth is that it increases the range of human choice.

43. It is not sufficient, however, to pursue economic growth for its own sake. It is important that growth be sustained and sustainable. Growth should promote full employment and poverty reduction, and should seek improved patterns of income distribution through greater equality of opportunity.

44. If poverty persists or increases and there is neglect of the human condition, political and social strains will endanger stability over time. The reduction of poverty requires development in which access to the benefits of economic progress are as widely available as possible, and not concentrated excessively in certain localities, sectors or groups of the population.

45. Improved education, health and shelter, together with an increase in meaningful employment opportunities, will contribute directly to reducing poverty and its consequences. Apart from being desirable goals in themselves, education, health and shelter are all essential to a productive workforce and hence to economic growth. The elimination of hunger and malnutrition should be targets in their own right.

46. For sustained growth to take place, two conditions are necessary; a supportive national environment, and a favourable international climate. Without appropriate national policies, no amount of assistance, bilateral or multilateral, will lead to sustained growth. On the contrary, assistance given in this way can reinforce dependence on the outside world. Without a favourable international climate, domestic policy reform will be difficult to achieve, threatening the success of reforms and increasing the hardships suffered by the population.

47. Successful national economic experiences must be based on pragmatic policies. The need to take advantage of the efficiency of markets must be tempered by recognition of the need for Governments to act where markets cannot provide all the answers.

48. Governments can no longer be assumed to the paramount economic agents. They nevertheless retain the responsibility to provide a regulatory framework for the effective operation of a competitive market system. Governments have to intervene where appropriate: to invest in infrastructure, to facilitate the development of productive sectors, to provide an enabling environment for the promotion of private enterprise, to ensure that proper social safety nets are in place, to invest in human capital and to protect the environment. Governments provide the framework in which individuals can plan their long-term prospects.

49. There are no definite prescriptions for a division of roles. Public and private expenditures are not invariably substitutes for one another. The relationship between them is frequently of a complementary rather than a competitive character. Government policies for the promotion of a sound macroeconomic framework are essential for sustained economic growth. Such macroeconomic policies, however, must rest upon solid micro-economic foundations which provide for the

efficient allocation of scarce resources. Should markets fail to perform their functions, or fail to address essential welfare considerations, there is scope for government intervention. However, government policies and programmes are subject to failure as well; in such circumstances an empowered private sector can be essential.

50. Finding the right blend of government direction of the economy and encouragement of private initiative is perhaps the most pressing challenge of economic development. This is not only a problem for developing or transitional economies. In the search for the difficult path which lies between dirigisme and laissez-faire, all countries are involved. Major market economies, with recurrent recession and persistent high rates of unemployment, are also facing this challenge.

51. Increasing interdependence among nations has accelerated the transmission of both positive growth impulses and negative shocks. As a result, economic problems, even at he national level,k now have to be seen in their global context. The distinction between national and international economic policies is fading. No nation, however successful, can insulate itself from the demographic, environmental, economic, social and military problems which exist in the the world. The effects of deprivation, disease and strife in one part of the globe are felt everywhere. They will not be successfully managed until global development is under way.

52. All countries are part of an international economic system, but while many countries remain imperfectly integrated into it, others are excessively vulnerable to its instability. Development is hampered by external debt problems, the decrease in external resource flows,sharply declining terms of trade and mounting barriers to market access. Inadequate technological cooperation has prevented many countries from improving the efficiency

of resource use, thus adversely affecting their international competitiveness and further inhibiting their integration into the world economy.

53. The expansion of international trade is essential to economic growth and is an integral part of he economic dimension of development. The benefits of increased commerce and trade are not in doubt: lower transaction costs, greater economic opportunities and enhanced international confidence, trust and security.

54. Difficult access to the world trading system is an enormous obstacle to development. At present, that system often discriminates against the developing world by limiting its advantage in low labour costs, while the price of many primary commodities had tended to decline.

55. The internationalization of economic activity, the increasing reliance on market forces, the widespread recognition that private initiative is a potent force for economic growth, and the massive efforts undertaken towards trade liberalization by developing and transitional countries call for an open and transparent trading system in which rules and disciplines are respected by all. When countries find that they have a distinct comparative advantage in one particular economic activity and invest accordingly, they should not be confronted later with new protectionist measures when their investment is beginning to yield fruit and their product penetrates other markets.

56. But economic interdependence is rapidly becoming far more than a matter of trade and finance. There are also strong trends towards greater openness in the movement of funds, people and ideas around the world. This has encouraged Governments to create a national environment that attract outside investment.

57. The pursuit of globally responsible

macroeconomic policies by those countries whose economic strength shapes the international economic environment is essential to all development efforts. The role of the major economic environment is essential to all development efforts. The role of the major economies in world finance remains preponderant. Their policies on interest rates, inflation and exchange rate stability are particularly significant. Exchange rate volatility compounds the debt problem through its effect on interest rates, foreign exchange earnings and reserves, and debt servicing. the policies the major economies follow in their domestic affairs will be of decisive importance in a world increasingly characterized by global capital markets.

58. Effective international cooperation for development cannot succeed unless the major economies make it their own objective. No mechanism exists by which the major economics can be induced to make globally beneficial structural change in their own economies, or to adopt more globally responsible economic, fiscal and monetary policies.

59. At present, economic policy coordination among the major economies centres on the Group of Seven industrialized countries. Repeated efforts by the developing world, such as the current attempt to create a Group of Seven-Group of Fifteen (Summit Level Group for South-South Consultation and Cooperation) connection, have failed. With the recognition that growth in the major industrialized countries is no longer the sole engine of global development, change is warranted so that the processes of economic policy coordination become more broad-based.

60. The mechanisms for integrating responsible economic policies at the international level and growth at the national level are not yet fully developed. Leading the list of priorities are adequate measures to reduce the

crippling burden of international debt, policies to discourage tendencies towards protectionism, and ensuring that the developing world shares in the benefits of the new World Trade Organization regime.

61. The lack of financial resources necessary for economic development is exacerbated by the debt crisis, which makes an already difficult situation such worse. In the last decade, indebted developing countries have had to transfer on average between 2 and 3 per cent of their gross domestic product (GDP) abroad; in some instances transfers have amounted to 6 per cent or more of GDP. Perversely, some developing countries have now become net exporters of financial resources.

62. The debt problem has many facets. Large amounts are owed to commercial banks by some countries. Many low-income countries owe large amounts to official bilateral and multilateral creditors. efforts have been made to restructure commercial debt and, in certain cases, forgive bilateral official debt. But not enough has been done to alleviate the burden of multilateral debt or to assist countries that, despite a large debt-servicing burden, are not in default.

63. No single formula for generating economic growth exist, but, half a century after the emergence of development as an independent field inquiry, certain basic conditions are recognized as essential. Foremost among these is the need to take a strategic decision for development. The State must have the politicalwill to act.

18 An Agenda for Development
Recommendations

1. In accordance with General Assembly resolution 47.181 of 22 December 1992, I circulated on 6 May 1994 a report on an Agenda for Development (UN document A/48/935) to elicit the views of all Member States, the agencies and programmes of the United Nations system, as well as a wide range of public and private sources.

2. That report was available at the World Hearings on Development organized by the President of the General Assembly in June 1994, and was discussed at the substantive session of the Economic and Social Council in July 1994. Additional comments were received from a wide variety of sources. I have considered all contributions with great care. Most recently, I have had the benefit of statements presented during the general debate of the forty-ninth session of the General Assembly, many of which addressed an agenda for development.

3. As requested in paragraph 5 of General Assembly resolution 48/166 of 21 December 1993, I am now submitting to the General Assembly at its forty-ninth session my recommendations, to follow up on my report on an Agenda for Development of 6 May 1994, taking into account the discussions during the substantive session of 1994 of the Economic and Social Council, as well as the views presented during the Hearings conducted by the President of the General Assembly and summarized under his own responsibility (UN document

A/49/320, annex). In doing so, I have been mindful of the requests regarding the contents of the Agenda contained in the operative paragraph of general Assembly resolution 47/181. A summary of the recommendations appears in the annex to the present report.

I. Introduction

4. The general recommendations that have emerged can be simply stated, but they are fundamentally important. Firstly, development should be recognized as the foremost and most far-reaching task of our time. Recognition of this imperative, commitment to achieving development, and continual, cooperative and effective action towards it are crucial for humanity's common future. It is urgent for Governments, intergovernmental institutions and the United Nations to review their priorities with the goal of elevating dramatically the attention and support given to development.

5. Secondly, development must be seen in its many dimensions. My report on an Agenda for Development of 6 May 1994 identified five dimensions of development: peace, the economy, environmental protection, social justice and democracy. The importance of these dimensions has been understood and supported by Member States. For most people and most countries, economic growth is the *sine qua non* of development. Economic growth is not an option; it is an imperative. But it is a means to an end. New development approaches should not only generate economic growth, they should make its benefits equitably available. They should enable people to participate in decisions affecting their lives. They should provide job-led growth. They must replenish the natural heritage on which all life depends. They must be based upon a comprehensive vision of development.

6 At its core, development must be about

improvement of human well-being; removal of hunger, disease and ignorance; and productive employment for all. Its first goal must be to end poverty and satisfy the priority needs of all people in a way that can be productively sustained over future generations.

7. Thirdly, the emerging consensus on the priority and dimensions of development should find expression in a new framework for international cooperation. The enterprise we call international cooperation for development is needed now more than ever, but it must be revitalized in order to escape fully its Cold War past and contribute fully to the realization of development goals.

8. Fourthly, within this new framework for development cooperation, the United Nations must play a major role in both policy leadership and operations. Comments on the May 1994 report on an agenda for development have not only strengthened understanding of the dimensions of development. They have also revealed strong support for a revitalized role of the Organization and for measures to enhance the coherence and relevance of the United Nations system in development.

9. The development mission and responsibilities of the United Nations stem directly from the Charter of the United Nations and the fundamental nature of the United Nations as an international political entity and moral force; from the inseparability of peace-keeping, humanitarian and development objectives; from the contribution of development to the universal goals of peace, freedom, social justice and environmental quality - goals for which the United Nations stands and for which it works daily around the world; and from the strengths of the programmes that have developed over its 50-year life. The United Nations cannot be a strong force for peace unless it is also a strong force for development.

10. It is time for the United Nations to realize its original mandate in the social and economic fields, to make the comprehensive pursuit of development the centre of its action, and, in this new context, to assist Member States in their efforts to realize their diverse development goals.

11. The United Nations system - the United Nations itself, the specialized agencies, and the Bretton Woods institutions — has much to bring to the development process. But the system will realize its potential only if its intergovernmental processes are strengthened and made more coherent and if the various development assistance components integrate their complementary mandates into coherent and coordinated support for countries' aspirations. There is also great room for improvement in the Organization's operations, including the linkages among peace-keeping, humanitarian assistance and development.

12. The general recommendations that have emerged from the process of forging an Agenda for Development have brought to the fore three key objectives: to strengthen and revitalize international development cooperation generally to build a stronger, more effective and coherent multilateral system in support of development; and to enhance the effectiveness of the development work of the Organization itself - its departments, regional commissions, funds and programmes - in partnership with the United Nations system as a whole.

13. The recommendations presented in the following paragraphs are addressed and organized according to these three objectives, with a special focus in each case on what the United Nations can and should do. No real improvements will be possible unless the Member States are convinced of the need for, and unless nations and peoples everywhere share the fruits of, the proposed

changes. Member States are challenged to grasp this opportunity and make the United Nations system a far more effective instrument of multilateralism.

Recommendations for revitalizing international development cooperation

14. A new framework for international development cooperation requires mutually supporting actions at the national and international level.

A. National policies for development

15. Development can succeed only if it is driven by national priorities and dedicated to the improvement of the well-being of the country and its people. National capacities to plan, manage and implement development programmes must be built both in government and in civil society.

16. While the individual State is no longer the sole actor in development, each State bears primary responsibility for its own development. Whether expressed as a responsibility of States or as a right of peoples, development requires competent governmental leadership, coherent national policies and strong popular commitment.

17. A strong partnership between government and civil society is an important presquisite for sustainable development.

18. Governments have a special responsibility to protect poor and marginalized peoples and to seek policies which offer them avenues towards productive involvement in their societies and economies.

19. Non-State actors, including grass-roots people's movements supported. These organizations of civil society give a voice to the people, and should be recognized and included in new development models.

20. The importance of private business should not be underestimated. As part of the partnership, strong

private enterprise sectors, the use of market forces and market-based mechanisms, and the cultivation of entrepreneurship should be encouraged. Governments should ensure that social and environmental costs are accurately reflected in prices, and lead to macroeconomic stability.

21. Government, civil and social action must be taken to fight corruption and protect consumers, investors, workers and the environment through appropriate regulations.

B. International setting

22. A favourable, growth-oriented international setting for development is vital. External macroeconomic forces - trade, debt management, direct investment, capital flows and access to technology-must support development objectives. International cooperation for development must include partnerships with the business community, national and international.

23. The equitable integration of the poorest and least-endowed countries into the world economy is a major requirement. The marginalization of these countries is perceptible and must be reversed.

24. It is distressing that the official development assistance target of 0.7 per cent of gross national product, which was adopted in 1970 and reaffirmed as recently as 1992 at the United Nations Conference on Environment and Development (UNCED), was achieved in 1993 by only four countries: Denmark, the Netherlands, Norway and Sweden. Development assistance must be brought closer to the agreed targets, and its diversion to non-development priorities must be reversed. New agreements should be reached on plausible interim goals for steady increases in official development assistance. A larger share should be allocated to the development work of the United Nations.

25. There is an urgent need to increase the overall level of development assistance and to ensure that funding for peace-keeping, humanitarian emergencies and the global environment is provided from new and additional resources and not from development assistance.

26. The international community must find a solution for an issue that has bedevilled development efforts for two decades: debt. Debt problems are acute among the poorest countries, particularly those in Africa.

27. Reforming countries in debt crisis require an adequate and permanent reduction in the stock of debt that will restore private sector confidence at home and abroad and facilitate their recovery, growth and development. The debts of the least developed and poorest countries should be canceled outright. Recycling debt to finance economic, social and environmental project should be considered.

28. Developing nations must be provided equitable access to expanding global opportunities in trade, technology, investment and information. The fruits of the technological and informatics revolution must be more evenly available if present international economic disparities are not be deepen further and weaken the foundations of global progress.

29. Countries in transition to a market economy face special problems stemming from the need for rapid but sensitive transformation in fundamental economic organization, lack of competitiveness in international markets, economic depression and other factors. These countries should be supported by additional resources from the international community.

30. Regional economic cooperation should be recognized as an important component of many countries' development strategies. Regional integration

schemes, from loose associations to free trade agreements, provide a rich experience upon which new policy initiatives can draw. Economic and technical cooperation among developing countries with similar challenges and experiences should be encouraged.

31. Economic progress and human well-being in many parts of the world are threatened by unchecked population growth and environmental deterioration. Programmes to address these issues, including the programme of Action recently forged at the International Conference on Population and Development in Cairo and the agreements reached at UNCED in Rio de Janeiro, must be given high priority as an integral part of comprehensive development.

32. The rapid application of new technology and changes in consumption are needed to check extravagant consumption of natural and environmental resources.

33. Excessive military spending and its consequences are deeply inimical to development goals. A unique opportunity is now available for further progress on reducing military expenditures, phasing out most forms of military assistance and subsidies to arms exporters, and effectively curtailing indiscriminate international trafficking in arms. Greater transparency of military spending is needed. The United Nations Register of Conventional Arms must be strengthened. More extensive comparative analysis of military and social budgets must be undertaken. Land-mines are a major obstacle to development, shattering lives and removing land from productive use. An outright world-wide ban on the production and transfer of land-mines and their components should be declared. The holding of world hearings on the connection between disarmament and development conducted by the President of the General Assembly should be seriously considered.

34. As the success of the International Conference on

Population and Development at Cairo demonstrates, a powerful international development agenda is emerging on an ongoing basis through the work of a continuum of United Nations conferences and summits. Effective and realistic mechanisms must be made available to implement goals established at these conferences.

35. A common framework should be developed to follow up major United Nations conferences, past and future. Goals and targets in the economic and social development field endorsed by past international conferences and summits should be synthesized, costed, prioritized and placed in a reasonable time perspective for implementation.

36. The fiftieth session of the General Assembly provides an appropriate opportunity for focusing the attention of the international community on forging a new framework for development cooperation between industrialized and developing countries, in which common interests and mutual needs provide the basic rationale for a new partnership.

37. In this regard, an international conference on the financing of development should be considered by the Assembly. Such a conference could be convened in close consultation with the Bretton Woods institutions, the regional development banks and the Development Assistance Committee of the Organization for Economic Cooperation and Development.

III. Recommendations for an effective multilateral development system

38. With increasing global interdependence, the need for multilateral cooperation will inevitably expand. A strong and effective multilateral system with the United Nations at its centre is an essential prerequisite for successful multilateral cooperation on development and international economic policy and operations.

39. The responsibility for building a new framework for development cooperation is widely shared. But the role of the United Nations is unique and indispensable. As the world Organization based on the principle of universality, and with an unmatched global network at all levels, the United Nations can promote awareness, build consensus, inform policy in every dimension affecting development, and help to rationalize and harmonize the multiplicity of public and private efforts worldwide in the cause of development. Enhancing the role of the General Assembly and the Economic and Social Council, and strengthening linkages between the Organization and the Bretton Woods institutions on the one hand, and the sectoral and technical agencies on the other, are crucial requirements to these ends.

A. General Assembly

40. In the context of the ongoing intergovernmental reform process on the restructuring and revitalization of the United Nations in the economic, social and related fields, the General Assembly must play a major role to focus the attention of the international community on forging a new framework for development cooperation.

41. The General Assembly should identify critical issues for international cooperation and policy development and serve as a forum for regular identification of gaps and inconsistencies, as well as emerging problems that are likely to fall between the purviews of more narrowly focused institutions in the fields of development, trade and finance. The Assembly should focus on the development of norms, standard and rules of the game required to manage global interdependence in a rapidly changing international environment and promote an integrated approach to economic and social development. The roles of the Seconds and Third Committees could be reviewed from this perspective.

42. The early part of General Assembly sessions, with high-level representatives present, could be used to organize a focused dialogue on these issues in the plenary sessions. Consideration could be given to convening, every few years, special sessions of the Assembly on major aspects of international cooperation for development.

B. Economic and Social Council

43. Key to the ongoing effort to strengthen the United Nations as the centre of an effective multilateral development system is the revitalization of the Economic and Social Council to fulfil the role envisaged for it under the Charter.

44. Firstly, the Council should deliberate and decide upon the full range of development issues in accordance with that role, mindful of the Relationship Agreements with and mandates of the specialized agencies and the Bretton Woods institutions. The Council should bring the specialized agencies into a closer working relationship with the United Nations and perform the functions specified in the Charter under Chapter IV, on the General Assembly; Chapter IX, on international economic and social cooperation; and Chapter X, on the Council itself.

45. Secondly, the Council should serve as an international development assistance review committee, providing a regular opportunity for both donors and recipients to discuss and assess aid programmes and policies. As part of this role, the Council should function as a unifying governing entity to which the existing governing bodies of the United Nations funds and programmes would relate on major policy matters. It would also provide intergovernmental oversight of the relevant United Nations departments with responsibilities for operational activities for development.

46. Thirdly, the Council should identify potential or

emerging humanitarian emergencies and provide policy guidelines in developing coordinated initiatives to address such situations.

47. These responsibilities and functions of the Council could be reinforced by an expanded bureau, meeting inter-sessionally to focus the work of the Council and facilitate agreement on issues for endorsement by the Council. To preserve efficiency while retaining representativeness, the expanded bureau should be limited in membership. Its working methods should provide for maximum flexibility so as to ensure timely responses. The entire Council, at a high level, would meet at specific times of the year to provide general policy guidance and to review the work of the expanded bureau.

48. To support the General Assembly and the Economic and Social Council in providing effective leadership in development, a council of international development advisers should be considered. This council would issue an independent annual or biennial report, analyes key issues concerning the global economy and their impact on development, and inform international opinion.

C. Bretton Woods institutions

49. Strengthening the links with the Bretton Woods institutions was one of the dominant themes during the recent debate in the Economic and Social Council high-level session and in the World Hearings on Development. Enhancing the relationship between the United Nations and the Bretton Woods institutions is one of the mandates contained in the original General Assembly resolution 47/181 calling for an Agenda for Development.

50. There are many fields in which the ongoing dialogue and substantive partnerships between the

Bretton Woods institutions and the United Nations may be strengthened. In particular, with the expansion of the World Bank lending into social, environmental and other sectors which require capacity building, decentralized planning and execution, small loans and more participatory development involving all institutions of civil society, there should be greater scope for collaboration with United Nations programmes and agencies working in these areas.

51. Similarly, the World Bank could utilize and support United Nations programmes in delivering grant-based technical assistance, particularly "free standing" technical assistance unrelated to specific capital investment projects.

52. There are successful examples of country-level collaboration between the Bretton Wood institutions and the United Nations programmes in these and other areas, which should be employed as models for replication.

53. Cooperation between the Bretton Woods institutions and the United Nations could be pursued through joint initiatives in, among others, the following fields: poverty reduction strategies, including small enterprise development and micro-credit availability; improvements in the productivity of the resources sector and sustainable energy development; preventive development and post-conflict peace-building and reconstruction; socially and environmentally responsible structural adjustment programmes; and capacity-building and improved public sector management.

54. An issue that has attracted considerable attention in the Economic and Social Council discussions and in the World Hearings on Development is the policy conditionality for structural adjustment loans designed by the World Bank and the International Monetary Fund (IMF). There is little disagreement on the need for structural adjustment and economic reform. There is,

however, controversy over the policy content 9of structural adjustment programmes and concern that such programmes are, in and of themselves, insufficient.

55. The Organization and the Bretton Woods institutions should work together with concerned countries on the components of the policy dialogue and other complementary and compensating initiatives that must accompany structural adjustment programmes. There is considerable scope for such collaboration in the aid consortia, consultative groups and round tables organized under multilateral auspices, particularly by the World Bank and the United Nations Development Programme (UNDP). Special attention also needs to be given to making the country policy dialogue more transparent and relevant by building governments' capacities to lead the dialogue process and in clearly detailing policy options in country documents prepared by the World Bank/IMF and the United Nations development system. The United Nations resident coordinator should be involved with such policy dialogues. Efforts now under way to promote greater complementarity between country strategy notes and policy framework papers should be pursued.

56. The revival of the United Nations/Bretton Woods Liaison Committee could also be explored with the aim of enhancing substantive consultation. In additions, the Secretary-General should convey, as appropriate, the concerns of the United Nations system as a whole to the Joint Committee on Development of the Board of Governors of the IMF and the World Bank.

D. Sectoral and technical agencies

57. The diversity represented in the agencies of the United Nations system can be a great source of strength if the variety of constituencies and expertise which they represent is harnessed in support of comprehensive, sustainable development.

58. The contribution which the sectoral and technical agencies have been making to the preparation for, and follow-up to, major global conferences-encompassing intergovernmental policy inputs, specialized secretariat expertise, and the promotion of contributions from different sectors of civil society-represents a model which should be applied progressively to all aspects of the development work of the Organization. Initiatives for joint action, such as the new inter-agency programme on the human immunodeficiency virus/ acquired immunodeficiency syndrome (HIV/AIDS), should similarly be expanded to other areas.

59. Technical contributions from these agencies, particularly the smaller technical agencies concerned with various aspects of infrastructure development, should be integrated more fully in economic and social plans and priorities promoted by the United Nations system.

60. Maintaining the integrity and comprehensive nature of the United Nations system should be a major, constant concern of the international community. In this context, the desirability of bringing new organizations such as the World Trade Organization, endowed with wide international responsibilities in fields of international economic and social cooperation, into relationship with the United Nations, deserves priority attention.

61. In line with the objectives that have guided the recent restructuring of the inter-secretariat coordination machinery, members of the Administrative Committee on Coordination, under the Chairmanship of the Secretary-General, will pursue further measures to strengthen the contribution of that Committee to enhancing the coherence and impact of the work of the system. As part of this effort, it is intended to make greater use of small task forces at the executive head level focusing on critical development issued, and to develop joint programmes

based on common policies for implementation at the country level.

IV. Recommendations for more efficient and effective United nations development activities

62. The development activities of the Organization span a wide range: long-term social, economic and political development; post-crisis reconstruction and rehabilitation; and issues such as population, the status of women, child survival, the environment, drug central, and housing and urban management. Confidence in the United Nations depends to a large extent on the efficiency and effectiveness of these programmes.

63. The fundamental reason for improving United Nations development assistance efforts is not because these efforts are failing but because they are succeeding. The demand for the services that the United Nations provides far outstrips its capacity. In other words, the need to build on past successes, to take full advantage of proven capabilities and to respond to new demands and new opportunities, is the most compelling reason for strengthening United Nations operational activities for development.

64. Further measures to improve and strengthen governance, management, funding, the division of labour and the allocation of responsibilities, coordination and staffing, must build upon the reform initiatives undertaken to date. These include the series of changes in United Nations operations set in motion by General Assembly resolutions 44/211 of 22 December 1989 and 47/199 of 22 December 1992, in the context of its triennial policy reviews of operational activities for development, as well as by other restructuring and revitalization efforts. Enhancing coordination and effectiveness within the United Nations itself can go a long way to foster coherence in the system as a whole.

A. Assets and strengths

65. Efforts to make United Nations operational activities more efficient and effective must begin with careful identification of those areas where the United Nations has special assets and strengths in support of development.

66. The United Nations provides a unique forum for raising public consciousness, providing information, defining the international development agenda and building the consensus needed for action. Once forged, consensus is translated into international norms and agreements, integrated into national development priorities and supported through United Nations operational activities.

67. The neutrality of the United Nations means that it does not represent any particular national or commercial interest. The United Nations can therefore develop special relationships of trust with the countries it supports in their development efforts. It can provide stable, long-term capacity-building assistance free of short-term political or economic objectives.

68. The United Nations has an unmatched global network of regional commissions and country offices. The resulting delivery capacity of the United Nations is uniquely strong. Because of its universal presence, the United nations can operate effectively at both the country and the intercountry and regional levels.

69.The United Nations emphasizes bottom-up, country-driven programming of development assistance resources, without conditionalities. Coupled with the participation of developing countries in United Nations governance, this ensures that United Nations development initiatives derive from national priorities and are dedicated to the progress of the countries involved and their peoples.

70. The United Nations has a comprehensive mandate, spanning social, economic and political issues. Working in partnership with the specialized agencies, the United Nations has expertise across virtually the full range of development interests. This breadth further enhances delivery capacity.

71. United Nations programmes focus on the neediest countries and on the neediest people within those countries. The United Nations has special strengths and experience in addressing social aspects of development and integrating social and economic dimensions, working with Governments, grass-roots people's movements and other non-governmental organizations.

72. The United Nations is able to mobilize, deliver and coordinate humanitarian assistance. It can promote reconstruction, reintegration and other development in post-emergency situations. It can link peace-keeping, refugee assistance, relief efforts and development. It provides an ideal base for support for early warning and preventive development initiatives. In this area, as in others, the United Nations organizations have established close working relationships with non-governmental organizations at all levels.

B. Common goals

73. Where is a shared vision and common purpose, coordination and integration in the Organizations's operational activities will follow. Through international conferences and in other ways, the United nations and its Member States are seeking to articulate and promote a shared vision of development that is human-centred, equitable, and socially and environmentally sustainable. Through this process, common goals are emerging that can serve to galvanize the energies and focus the efforts of the United Nations funds and programmes, together with their agency partners.

74. A major goal in this regard is the empowerment of women. with the emerging consensus on the priority and dimensions of development has come a deeper understanding that in virtually every dimension of development - whether political, social, economic, environmental or security related - the role of women is central. Policies and institutions that suppress the real potential of half of the earth's people must be reformed. The empowerment of women must be recognized and utilized as a powerful tool for liberating the full creative energies of a society. The visibility, coordination, programming and accountability of the United Nations in gender-related development issues must be improved.

75. The outcome of the International conference on Population and Development, the adoption of the Declaration on the Elimination of Violence against Women by the General Assembly at its fortyeighth session, and the decision of the Commission on Human Rights to create the position of the Special Rapporteur on violence against women are major recent achievements for the protection of women's human rights. At the Fourth World conference on Women, further international agreement on measures to promote the advancement of women should be reached. Implementation of such agreements should proceed in a coordinated way and be fully integrated in overall development efforts.

76 Three other common goals are outlined in the paragraphs that follow: poverty eradication, preventive and curative development, and African development. Member States are urged go support United Nations leadership in these areas. Other key goals that can unity the development work of the United nations funds and programmes range from support for programme country priorities in food security, full employment and education for all, to protecting and regenerating the natural resource base for sustained production.

77. All countries should agree on a global compact to eliminate poverty over a specified period of time.

78. Upcoming conferences, especially the World Summit for Social Development and the fourth World Conference on Women, can define clear, ambitious and monitorable objectives in the area of poverty eradication, supported by operational strategies adapted to each country's situation. The United Nations should play a direct role in this effort to seek to mobilize action on these objectives by the entire international community.

79 The critical elements for a poverty eradication initiative such as basic social services, employment generation, food security, drug and transnational crime control, and access to credit, technology, training and markets-should be integrated into comprehensive operational package.

80 Recent years have witnessed phenomenal growth in the Organization's activities in peace-keeping, refugee assistance and other humanitarian relief. These activities must be complemented by new development initiatives for preventive and curative development.

81 Preventive development is a necessary complement to preventive diplomacy. The United Nations should build state-of-the-art capabilities to act preventively for development, anticipating and responding to crises, natural and man-made, before they occur. As proposed earlier, this should be a new main focus of the work of the Economic and social Council.

82 A global watch system should be considered to provide early detection of impending humanitarian emergencies and guidelines for preventive action for consideration by the Economic and Social Council. This system would access, build upon and seek to strengthen existing capabilities.

83 A new focus on curative development is required.

When the time comes to heal the wounds of a society, demobilize soldiers and reintegrate refugees and internally displaced persons, timely, postconflict peace-building and development including reconstruction and rehabilitation-are essential.

84 Special initiatives to give added momentum to development efforts in Africa are urgently required. Of the 47 least developed countries in the world, 33 are in Africa. Africa accounts for just 2 per cent of world trade and only 1.4 per cent of world exports. Economic growth is hampered by external debt problems, by the decrease in external resource flows, by sharply declining terms of trade and by mounting barriers to market access. Desertification poses a severe obstacle to development. And across the continent, the persistence of poverty and widespread unemployment have undermined social confidence and social stability, fuelling conflict and unrest.

85 In the light of Economic and Social Council resolution 1994/38 of 29 July 1994 on the United Nations New Agenda for the Development of Africa in the 1990s, and as suggested in the most recent meeting of the Administrative Committee on Coordination, consideration is being given to setting up a task force of that Committee to identify major inter-agency initiatives to be taken in support of Africa. The task force would focus on the development of country-level cooperation around specific goals and issues and define the required policy options to galvanize international support for African economic recovery and development.

C. Operational coordination

86 The various development entities comprising the United Nations have their own organizational cultures, public name recognition and constituencies, and resource mobilization capacities. Moreover, a certain amount of organizational diversity and pluralism can be

healthy. Efforts to enhance operational coordination within the United Nations should endeavour to achieve the benefits of a unified system, while preserving the strenght of the current approach.

87 Such efforts should be aimed at the following objectives, among others: building a more integrated, efficient and effective framework through which the United Nations can better assist countries in realizing their development objectives, including clearer and more complementary definition of the roles and missions of the various components; eliminating duplication and fragmentation; strengthening leadership and cooperation at country, regional and headquarters levels; strengthening United Nations capabilities in the coordination and delivery of humanitarian assistance, the linking of emergency relief and development, and the promotion of preventive and curative development; mobilizing analytical and normative capacities and strengthening the role of the Organization in interrelated areas such as trade and access to technology, in support of operational activites; defining the appropriate level-country, region or headquarters-for activity on various issues; integrating the regional commissions with the development work of the Organization as a whole; strengthening the resident coordinator and country-driven approaches; streamlining the delivery capacity of the United Nations through common premises, the programme approach and common programming cycles; and achieving more rapid and aggressive implementation of General Assembly resolutions 44/211 and 47/199, including the country strategy note and other tools, for a more integrated United Nations response to country priorities.

88 In pursuit of these objectives, I intend to convene frequent meetings of all senior officials in the economic and social sector, with the support of the Administrator

of UNDP, as a main instrument to improve overall programme coordination and policy coherence within the Organization. The outcome of the work of a strengthened Joint consultative Group on Policy, focusing on country-level coordination and related issues, should constitute an important input into these senior official meetings

89 When operational activities for development are undertaken within the context of a peace-keeping mission, which is placed under the command of a special representative, all elements of the United Nations system at all levels that are active in the theatre of operations must come under the command and direction of the special representative. It must be recognized that the special representative has not only a political but also an essential coordinating role in this regard.

D. Financing for the future

90 Although better operational coordination and a top-calibre international civil service are essential, the effectiveness of the United Nations operational activites for development will ultimately depend upon financial resources. The most significant difficulty facing the United Nations entities engaged n development work is that they are unable, owing to resource constraints, to mount assistance efforts on a scale commensurate with the challenges they help Member States address.

91 The United Nations is in financial crisis. Reliance on voluntary contributions alone, in light of the expanded development mandate of the Organization, is no longer feasible. To deal with this, a number of principles and proposals have been put forward. It has been recognized that more resources are needed, that mandates and the resources provided for them must be in a sound relationship, and that predictability in funding is essential so that operations are not undermined in the midst of performance. It has been suggested that a system of assessed, negotiated and voluntary

contributions provides the most logical and appropriate means of financing the United Nations as it permits governments to maintain proper control over the United Nations' budget and its agenda. It has further been suggested that the Organization should review its voluntarily funded programmes, especially those that are financed through trust funds to eliminate unnecessary and duplicative expenditures. Other measures that may be considered include a fee on speculative international financial transactions, a levy on fossil fuel use (or its resulting pollution) in all countries, earmarking a small portion of the anticipated decline in world military expenditures, utilizing some of the resources that could be released through the elimination of unnecessary subsidirs, and utilizing resources generated form a stamp tax on international travel and travel documents.

V. Conclusion

92 The battle for people-centred and sustainable development will be won or lost not in the corridors of governments, but in every hamlet and home, in every village and town, in the daily enterprise of every member of the global community and every institution of civil society. The Charter of the United Nations begins with a pledge by "We the Peoples....". It is the people, on whose behalf we all act, who are the true custodians of the emerging new vision of development. It is for them that we must work to achieve a new framework for development cooperation and the revitalization of the United Nations system.

19 Agenda 21

Preamble

Humanity stands at a defining moment in history. We are confronted with a perpetuation of disparities between and within nations, a worsening of poverty, hunger, ill health and illiteracy, and the continuing deterioration of the ecosystems on which we depend for our well-being. However, integration of environment and development concerns and greater attention to them will lead to the fulfilment of basic needs, improved living standards for all, better protected and manages ecosystems and a safer, more prosperous future. No nation can achieve this on its own; but together we can in a global partnership for sustainable development.

This global partnership must build on the premises of General Assembly resolution 44/228 of 22 December 1989, which was adopted when the nations of world called for the United Nations Conference on Environment and Development, and on the acceptance of the need to take a balanced and integrated approach to environment and development questions.

Agenda 21 addresses the pressing problems of today and also aims at preparing the world for the challenges of the next century. It reflects a global consensus and political commitment at the highest level on development and environment cooperation. Its successfully implementation is first and foremost the responsibility of

Governments. National strategies, plans, policies and processes are crucial in achieving this. International cooperation should support and supplement such national efforts. In this context, the United Nations system has a key role to play. Other international, regional and subregional organizations are also called upon to contribute to this effort. The broadest public participation and the active involvement of the non-governmental organizations and other groups should also be encouraged.

The development and environmental objectives of Agenda 21 will require a substantial flow of new and additional financial resources to developing countries, in order to cover the incremental costs for the actions they have to undertake to deal with global environmental problems and to accelerate sustainable development. Financial resources are also required for strengthening the capacity of international institutions for the implementation of Agenda 21. An indicative order-of-magnitude assessment of costs is included in each of the programme areas. This assessment will need to be examined and refined by the relevant implementing agencies and organizations.

In the implementation of the relevant programme areas identified in Agenda 21, special attention should be given to the particular circumstances facing the economies in transition. It must also be recognised that these countries are facing unprecedented challenges in transforming their economies, in some cases in the midst of considerable social and political tension".

The programme areas that constitute Agenda 21 are described in terms of the basic for action, objective, activities and means of implementation. Agenda 21 is a dynamic programme. It will be carried out by the various actors according to the different situations, capacities and priorities of countries and regions in full respect of all the principles contained in the Rio Declaration on Environment and Development. It could evolve over time in the light of changing needs and circumstances. Throughout Agenda 21 the term 'environmentally sound' means 'environmentally safe & sound', in particular when applied to the terms 'energy resources', supplies', 'energy systems', or technology/technologies.

Combating Poverty Programme Area

Basis for action

Poverty is a complex multidimensional problem with origins in both the national and international domains. No uniform solution can be found for global application. Rather, country-specific programmes to tackle poverty and international eforts supporting national efforts, as well as the parallel process of creating a supportive international environment, are crucial for a solution to this problem. The eradication of poverty and hunger, greater equity in income distribution and human resource development remain major challenges everywhere. the struggle against poverty is the shared responsibility of all countries.

While managing resources sustainably, an environmental policy that focuses mainly on the conservation and protection of resources must take due account of those who depend on the resources for their livelihoods. Otherwise it could have an adverse impact both on poverty and on chances for long-term success in resource and environmental conservation. Equally, a development policy that focuses mainly on increasing the production of goods without addressing the sustainability of the resources on which production is based will sooner or later run into declining productivity, which could also have an adverse impact on poverty. A specific anti-poverty strategy is therefore on of the basic conditions for ensuring sustainable development. An effective strategy for tackling the problems of poverty, development and environment simultaneously should begin by focusing on resources, production and people and should cover demographic issues, enhanced health care and education, the rights of women, the role of youth and of indigenous people and local communities and democratic participation process in association with improved governance.

Integral to such action is, together with international support, the promotion of economic growth in developing countries that is both sustained and sustainable and direct action in eradicating poverty by strengthening employment and income-generating programmes.

Objectives

The long-term objective of enabling all people to achieve sustainable livelihoods should provide an integrating factor that allows policies to address issues of development, sustainable resource management and poverty eradication simultaneously. The objectives of this programme area are:

(a) To provide all persons urgently with the opportunity to earn a sustainable livelihood;

(b) To implement policies and strategies that promote adequate levels of funding and focus on integrated human development policies, including income generation, increased local control of resources, local institution-strengthening and capacity-building and greater involvement of non-governmental organizations and local levels of government as delivery mechanisms;

(c) To develop for all poverty-stricken areas integrated strategies and programmes of sound and sustainable management of environment, resource mobilization, poverty eradication and alleviation, employment and income generation;

(d) To create a focus in national development plans and budgets on investment in human capital, with special policies and programmes directed rural areas, the urban poor, women and children.

Activities

Activities that will contribute to the integrated promotion of sustainable livelihood and environmental protection cover a variety of sectoral interventions involving a range of actors, from local to global, and are essential at every level, especially the community and local levels. Enabling actions will be necessary at the national and international levels, taking full account of regional and subregional conditions to support a locally driven and country-specific approach. In general design, the programmes should:

(a) Focus on the empowerment of local and community groups through the principle of delegating authority, accountability and resources to the most appropriate level to ensure that the programme will be geographically and ecologically specific.

(b) Contain immediate measures to enable those groups to alleviate poverty and to develop sustainability;

(c) Contain a long-term strategy aimed at establishing the best possible conditions for sustainable local, regional and national development that would eliminate poverty and reduce the inequalities between various population groups. It should assist the most disadvantaged groups - in particular, women, children and youth within those groups - refugees. The groups will include poor smallholders, pastoralists, artisans, fishing communities, landless people, indigenous communities, migrants and the urban informal sector.

The focus here is on specific cross-cutting measures - in particular, in the areas of basic education, primary/maternal health care, and the advancement of women.

(a) Empowering communities

Sustainable development must be achieved at every level of society. Peoples' organizations, women's groups and non-governmental organizations are important sources of innovation and action at the local level and have a strong interest and proven ability to promote sustainable livelihoods. Governments, in cooperation with appropriate international and non-governmental organization, should support a community-driven approach to sustainability, which would include, inter alia:

(a) Empowering women through full participation in decision-making;

(b) Respecting the cultural integrity and the rights of indigenous people and their communities;

(c) Promoting or establishing grass-roots mechanisms to allow for the sharing of experience and knowledge between communities;

(d) Giving communities a large measure of participation in the sustainable management and protection of the local natural resources in order to enhance their productive capacity;

(e) Establishing a network of community-based learning centres for capacity-building and sustainable development.

(b) Management related activities

Governments, with the assistance of and in cooperation with appropriate international, non-governmental and local community organizations, should establish measures that will directly or indirectly;

(a) Generate remunerative employment and productive occupational opportunities compatible with country-specific factor endowments, on a scale sufficient to take care of prospective increases in the labour force and to cover backlogs;

(b) With international support, where necessary, develop adequate infrastructure, marketing system, technology systems, credit systems and the like and the human resources needed to support the above actions and to achieve a widening of options for resource-poor people. High priority should be given to basic education and professional training;

(c) Provide substantial increases in economically efficient resource productivity and measures to ensure that the local population benefits in adequate measure from resource use;

(d) Empower community organization and people to enable them to achieve sustainable livelihoods;

(e) Set up an effective primary health care and maternal health care system accessible to all;

(f) Consider strengthening/developing legal frameworks for land management, access to land resources and land ownership-in particular, for women-and for the protection of tenants;

(g) Rehabilitate degraded resources, to the extent practicable, and introduce policy measures to promote sustainable use of resources for basic human needs;

(h) Establish new community-based mechanisms and strengthen existing mechanisms to enable communities to gain sustained access to resources needed by the poor to overcome their poverty;

(i) Implement mechanisms for popular participations-particularly poor people, especially women—in local community groups, to promote sustainable development;

(j) Implement, as a matter of urgency, in accordance with country-specific conditions and legal systems, measures to ensure that women and men have the same right to decide freely and responsibly on the number and spacing of their children and have access to the information, education and means, as appropriate, to enable them to exercise this right in keeping with their freedom, dignity and personally held values, taking into account ethical and cultural considerations. Governments should take active steps to implement programmes to establish and strengthen preventive and curative health facilities, which include women—centred, women managed, safe and effective reproductive health care and affordable, accessible services, as appropriate, for the responsible planning of family size, in keeping with freedom, dignity and personally held values, taking into account ethical and cultural consderations. Programmes should focus on providing comprehensive health care, including pre-natal care, education and information on health and responsible parenthood and should provide the opportunity for all women breast-feed fully, at least during the first four months post-partum. Programmes should fully support women's productive and reproductive roles and well-being, with special attention to the need for providing equal and improved health care for all children and the need to reduce the risk of maternal and child mortality and sickness;

(k) Adopt integrated policies aiming at sustainability in the management of urban centres;

(l) Undertake activities aimed at the promotion of security and, where appropriate, food self-sufficiency within the context of sustainable agriculture;

(m) Support research on and integration of traditional methods of production that have been shown to be environmentally sustainable;

(n) Actively seek to recognize and integrate informal-sector activities into the economy by removing regulation and hindrances that discriminate against activities in those sectors;

(o) Consider making available lines of credit and other facilities for the informal sector and improved access to land for the landless poor so that they can acquire the means of production and reliable access to natural resources. In many instances special considerations for women are required. Strict feasibility appraisals are needed for borrowers to avoid debt crises;

(p) Provide the poor with access to fresh water and sanitation;

(q) Provide the poor with access to primary education.

(c) Data, information and evaluation

Governments should improve the collection of information on target groups and target areas in order to facilitate and design of focused programmes and activities, consistent with the target group need and aspirations. Evaluation of such programmes should be gender-specific, since women are a particularly disadvantaged group.

(d) International and regional cooperation and coordination

The United Nations system, through its relevant organs, organizations and bodies, in cooperation with Member States and with appropriate international and non-governmental organizations, should make poverty alleviation a major priority and should;

(a) Assist Governments, when requested, in the formulation and implementation of national action programmes on poverty alleviation and sustainable development. Action-oriented activities of relevance to the above objectives, such as poverty eradication, projects and programmes supplemented where relevant by food aid, and support and special emphasis on employment and income generation, should be given particular attention in this regard;

(b) Promote technical cooperation among developing countries for poverty eradication activities;

(c) Strengthen existing structures in the United Nations system for coordination of action relating to poverty eradication, including the establishment of a focal point of information exchange and the formulation and implementation of replicable pilot projects to combat poverty;

(d) In the follow-up of the implementation of Agenda 21, give high priority to the review of the progress made in eradicating poverty;

(e) Examine the international economic framework, including resource flows and structural adjustment programmes, to ensure that social and environmental concerns are addressed and in this connection, conduct a review of the policies of international organizations, bodies and agencies, including financial institutions, to ensure the continued provision of basic services to the poor and needy;

(f) Promote international cooperation to address the root causes of poverty. The development process will not gather momentum if developing countries are weighted down by external indebtedness, if development finance is inadequate, if barriers restrict access to markets and if commodity prices and the terms of trade in developing countries remain depressed.

Means of implementation

(a) Financial & cost evaluation

The secretariat of the Conference has estimated the average total annual cost (1993-2000) of implementing the activities of this programme to be about $30 billion, including about $15 billion from the international community on grant or concessional terms. These are indicative and order of magnitude estimates only and have not been reviewed by Governments. This estimate overlaps estimates in other parts of Agenda 21. Actual costs and financial terms, including any that are non-concessional, will depend upon, inter alia, the specific strategies and programmes Governments decide upon for implementation.

(b) Capacity-building

National capacity-building for implementation of the above activities is crucial and should be given high priority. It is particularly important to focus capacity-building at the local community level in order to support a community-driven approach to sustainability and to establish and strengthen mechanisms to allow sharing of experience and knowledge between community groups at national and international levels. Requirements for such activities are considerable and are related to the various relevant sectors of Agenda 21 calling for requisite international, financial and technological support.

Changing Consumption Patterns

This chapter contains the following programme areas:

(a) Focusing on unsustainable patterns of production and consumption;

(b) Developing national policies and strategies to encourage changes in unsustainable consumption patterns.

Since the issue of changing consumption patterns is very broad, it is addressed in several parts of Agenda 21, notably those dealing with energy, transportation and wastes, and in the chapters on economic and and the transfer of technology.

A. FOCUSING ON UNSUSTAINABLE PATTERNS OF PRODUCTION AND CONSUMPTION

Basis for action

Poverty and environmental degradation are closely interrelated. While poverty results in certain kinds of environmental stress, the major cause of the continued deterioration of the global environment is the unsustainable pattern of consumption and production, particularly in industrialized countries, which in a matter of grave concern, aggravating poverty and imbalances;

Measures to be undertaken at the international level for the protection and enhancement of the environment must take fully into account the current imbalances in the global patterns of consumption and production.

Special attention should be paid to the demand for natural resources generated by unsustainable consumption and to the efficient use of those resources consistent with the goal of minimizing depletion and reducing pollution. Although consumption patterns are very high in certain parts of the world, the basic consumer needs of a large section of humanity are not being met. This results in excessive demands and unsustainable lifestyles among the richer segments which place immense stress on the environment. The poorer segments, meanwhile, are unable to meet food, health care, shelter and educational needs. Changing consumption patterns will require a multiprolonged strategy focusing on demand, meeting the basic needs of the poor, and reducing wastage and the use of finite resources in the production process;

Growing recognition of the importance of addressing consumption has also not yet been matched by an understanding of its implications. Some economists are questioning traditional concepts of economic growth and underlining the importance of pursuing economic objectives that take account of the full value of natural resource capital. More needs to be known about the role of consumption in relation to economic growth and population dynamics in order to formulate coherent international and national policies.

Objectives

Action is needed to meet the following broad objectives:

(a) To promote patterns of consumption and production that reduce environmental stress and will meet the basic needs of humanity;

(b) To develop a better understanding of the role of consumption and how to bring about more sustainable consumption patterns.

Activities

(a) Management-related activities

Adopting an international approach to achieving sustainable consumption patterns

In principle, countries should be guided by the following basic objectives in their efforts to address consumption and lifestyles in the context of environment and development;

(a) All countries should strive to promote sustainable consumption patterns;

(b) Developed countries should take the lead in achieving sustainable consumption patterns;

(c) Developing countries should seek to achieve sustainable consumption patterns in their development process, guaranteeing the provision of basic needs for the poor, while avoiding those unsustainable patterns, particularly in industrialized countries, generally recognized as unduly hazardous to the environment, inefficient and wasteful, in their development processes. This requires enhanced technological and other assistance from industrialized countries.

In the follow-up of the implementation of Agenda 21 the review of progress made in achieving sustainable consumption patterns should be given high priority.

(b) Data and information

Undertaking research on consumption

In order to support this broad strategy, Governments, and/or private research and policy institutes. with the assistance of regional and international economic and environmental organization, should make a concerted effort to:

(a) Expand or promote databases on production and consumption and develop methodologies for analysing them;

(b) Assess the relationship between production and consumption, environment, technological adaptation and innovation, economic growth and development, and demographic factors;

(c) Examine the impact of ongoing changes in the structure of modern industrial economies away from material-intensive economic growth;

(d) Consider how economies can grow and prosper while reducing the use of energy and materials and the production of harmful materials;

(e) Identify balanced patterns of consumption worldwide which the Earth can support in the long term.

Developing new concepts of sustainable economic growth and property Consideration should also be given to the present concept of economic growth and the need for new concepts of wealth and prosperity which allow higher standards of living through changed lifestyles and are less dependent on the Earth's finite resources and more in harmony with the Earth's carrying capacity. This should be reflected in the evolution of new systems of national accounts and other indicators of sustainable development.

(c) International cooperation and coordination

While international review processes exist for examining economic, development and demographic factors, more attention needs to be paid to issues related to consumption and production patterns and sustainable lifestyles and environment.

In the follow-up of the implementation of Agenda 21, reviewing the role and impact of unsustainable production and consumption patterns and lifestyles land their relation to sustainable development should be given high priority.

Financing and cost evaluation

The conference secretariat has estimated that implementation of this programme is not likely to require significant new financial resources.

Developing national policies and strategies to enourage changes in unsustainable consumption patterns

Basis for action

Achieving the goals of environmental quality and sustainable development will require efficiency in production and changes in consumption patterns in order to emphasize optimization of resource use and minimization of waste. In many instances, this will require reorientation of existing production and consumption patterns that have developed in industrial societies and are in turn emulated in much of the world.

Progress can be made by strengthening positive trends and directions that are emerging, as part of a process aimed at achieving significant changes in the consumption patterns of industries, Governments, households and individuals.

Objectives

In the years ahead, Governments, working with appropriate organizations, should strive to meet the following objectives:

(a) To promote efficiency in production processes and reduce wasteful consumption in the process of economic growth, taking into account the development needs of developing countries;

(b) To develop a domestic policy framework that will encourage a society to more sustainable patterns of production and consumption;

(c) To reinforce both values that encourage sustainable production and consumption patterns and policies that encourage the transfer of environmentally sound technologies to developing countries.

Activities

(a) Encouraging greater efficiency in the use of energy and resources

Reducing the amount of energy and materials used per unit in the production of goods and services can contribute both to the alleviation of environmental stress and to greater economic and industrial productivity and competitiveness. Governments, in cooperation with industry, should therefore intensify efforts to use energy and resources in an economically efficient and environmentally sound mate sound manner by:

(a) Encouraging the dissemination of existing environmentally sound technologies;

(b) Promoting research and development in environmentally sound technologies;

(c) Assisting developing countries to use these technologies efficiently and to develop technologies suited to their particular circumstances;

(d) Encouraging the environmentally sound use of new and renewable sources of energy;

(e) Encouraging the environmentally sound and sustainable use of renewable natural resources:

(b) Minimizing the generation of wastes

At the same time, society needs to develop effective ways of dealing with the problem of disposing of mounting level of waste products and materials. Governments, together with industry, households and the public, should make a concerned effort to reduce the generation of wastes and waste products by:

(a) Encouraging recycling in industrial processes and at the consumed level;

(b) Reducing wasteful packaging of products;

(c) Encouraging the introduction of more environmentally sound products.

(c) *Assisting individuals and household to make environmentally sound purchasing decisions*

The recent emergence in many countries of a more environmentally conscious consumer public, combined with increased interest on the parts of some industries in providing environmentally sound consumer products, is a significant development that should be encouraged. Governments and international organizations, together with the private sector, should develop criteria and methodologies for the assessment of environment impacts and resource requirements throughout the full life cycle of products and processes. Results of those assessments should be transformed into clear indicators in order to inform consumers and decision makers.

Governments, in cooperation with industry and other relevant groups, should encourage expansion of environmental labelling and other environmentally related product information programmes designed to assist consumers to make informed choices.

They should also encourage the emergence of an informed consumer public and assist individuals and households to make environmentally informed choices by:

(a) Providing information on the consequences of consumption choices and behaviour so as to encourage demand for environmentally sound products and of products;

(b) Making consumers aware of the health and environmental impact of products, through such means as consumer legislation and environmental labelling;

(c) Encouraging specific consumer-oriented programme, such as recycling and deposit/refund systems.

(d) *Exercising leadership through governmental purchasing*

Governments themselves also play a role in consuption, particularly in countries where the public sector plays a large role in the economy and can have a considerable influence on both corporate decisions and public perceptions. They should therefore review the purchasing policies of their agencies and developments so that they may improve, where possible, the environmental content of government procurement policies, without prejudice to international trade principles.

(e) Moving towards environmentally sound pricing

Without the stimulus of prices and market signals that make clear to producers and consumers the environmental costs of the consumption of energy, materials and natural resources and the generation of wastes, significant changes in consumption and production patterns seem unlikely to occur in the near future.

Some progress has begun in the use of appropriate economic instruments to influence consumer behaviour. These instruments include environmental charges and taxes, deposit/funds system, etc. This process should be encouraged in the light of country-specific conditions.

(f) Reinforcing values that support sustainable consumption

Government and private-sector organization should promote more positive attitudes towards sustainable consumption through education, public awareness programmes and other means, such as positive advertising of products and services that utilize environmentally sound technologies or encourage sustainable production consumption patterns. In the review of the implementation of Agenda 21, an assessment of the progress achieved in developing these national policies and strategies should be given due consideration.

Means of implementation

This programme is concerned primarily with changes in unsustainable patterns of consumption and production and values that encouraged sustainable consumption pattern and lifestyles. It requires the combined efforts of Governments, consumers and producers. Particular attention should be paid to the significant role played by women and household as consumers and the potential impacts of their combined purchasing power on the economy.

Demographic Dynamics and Sustainability

This chapter contains the following programme areas:

(a) Developing and disseminating knowledge concerning the links between demographic trends and factors and sustainable development;

(b) Formulating integrated national policies for environment and development, taking into account demographic trends and factors;

(c) Implementing integrated, environment and development programmes at the local level, taking into account demographic trends and factors.

Developing and disseminating knowledge concerning the links between demographic trends and factors

Basis for action

Demographic trends and factors and sustainable development have a synergistic relationship.

The growth of world population and production combined with unsustainable consumption patterns places increasingly severe stress on the life-supporting capacities of our planet. These interactive process affect the use of land, water, air, energy and other resources. Rapidly growing cities, unless well-managed, face major environmental problems. The increase in both the number and size of cities calls for greater attention to issues of local government and municipal management. The human dimensions are key elements to consider in this intricate set of relationships and they should be adequately taken into consideration in comprehensive policies for sustainable development. Such policies should address the linkages of demographic trends and factors, resource use, appropriate technology dissemination, and development. Population policy should also recognize the role played by human beings in environmental and development concerns. There is a need to increase awareness of this issue among decision makers at all levels and to provide both better information on which to base national and international policies and a framework against which to interpret this information.

There is a need to develop strategies to mitigate both the adverse impact on the environment of human activities and the adverse impact of environmental change on human population. The world's population is expected to exceed 8 billion by the year 2020. Sixty per cent of the world's population already live in coastal areas, while 65 per cent of cities with populations above 2.5 million are located along the world coasts; several of them are already at or below the present sea level.

Objectives

The following objectives should be achieved as soon as practicable:

(a) To incorporate demographic trends and factors in the global analysis of environment and development issues;

(b) To develop a better understanding of the relationships among demographic dynamics, technology, cultural behaviour, natural resources and life support systems;

(c) To assess human vulnerability in ecologically sensitive areas and centres of population to determine the priorities for action at all levels, taking full account of community defined needs.

Activities

(a) Research on the interaction between demographic trends and factors and sustainable development

Relevant international, regional and national institutions should consider undertaking the following activities;

(a) Identifying the interactions between demographic processes, natural resources and life support systems, bearing in mind regional and subregional variations deriving from, inter alia, different levels of development;

(b) Integrating demographic trends and factors into the ongoing study of environmental change, using the expertise of international, regional and national research networks and of local communities, first, to study the human dimensions of environmental change and, second, to identify vulnerable areas;

(c) Identifying priority areas for action and developing strategies and programmes to mitigate the adverse impact of environmental change on human populations, and vice versa.

The Conference secretariat has estimated the average total annual cost (1993-2000) of implementation the activities of this programme to be about $10 million from the international community on grant or concessional terms. These are indicative and order of magnitude estimates only and have not been reviewed by Governments. Actual costs and financial terms, including any that are non-concessional will depend upon, inter alia, the specific strategies and programmes Governments decide upon for implementation.

(b) Strengthening research programmes that integrate population, environment and development

In order to integrate demographic analysis into a broader social science perspective on environment and development, interdisciplinary research should be increased. International institutions and networks of experts should enhance their scientific capacity, taking full account of community expertise and knowledge, and should disseminate the experience gained in multidisciplinary approaches and in linking theory to action.

Better modelling capabilities should be developed, identifying the range of possible outcomes of current human activities, especially the interrelated impact of demographic trends and factors, per capita resource use and wealth distribution, as well as the major migration flows that may be expected with increasing climate events and cumulative environmental change that may destroy people's local livelihoods.

(c) Developing information and public awareness

Socio-demographic information should be developed in a suitable format for interfacing with physical, biological and socio-economic data. Compatible spatial and temporal scales, cross-country and time-series information, as well as global behavioural indicators should be developed, learning from local communities perceptions and attitudes.

Awareness should be increased at all levels concerning the need to optimize the sustainable use of resources through efficient resource management, taking into account the development needs of the populations of developing countries.

Awareness should be increased of the fundamental linkages between improving the status of women and demographic dynamics, particularly through women's access to education, primary and reproductive health care programmes, economic independence and their effective, equitable participation in all levels of decision-making.

Results of research concerned with sustainable development issues should be disseminated through technical reports, scientific journals, the media, workshops, forums or other means so that the information can be used by decision makers at all levels and increase public awareness.

(d) Developing and/or enhancing institutional capacity and collaboration

Collaboration and exchange of information should be increased between research institutions and international, regional and national agencies and all other sectors (including the private sector, local communities, non-government organization and scientific institutions) from both the industrialized and developing countries, as appropriate.

Efforts should be intensified to enhance the capacities of national and local government, the private sector and non-government organizations in developing countries to meet the growing needs for improved management of rapidly growing urban area.

Formulating integrated national policies for environment and development taking into account demographic trends and factors

Basis for action

Existing plans for sustainable development have generally recognized demographic trends and factors as elements that have a critical influence on consumption patterns, production, lifestyles a long-term sustainability. But in future, more attention will have to be given to these issues in general policy formulation and the design of development plans. To do this, all countries will have to improve their own capacities to assess the environment and development implication of their demographic trends and factors. They will also need to formulate and implement policies and action programmes where appropriate. Policies should be designed to address the consequences of population growth built into population momentum, while at the same time incorporating measures to bring about demographic transition. They should combine environmental concerns and population issues within a holistic view of development whose primary goals include the alleviation of poverty; secure livelihoods; good health; quality of life; improvement of the status and income of women and their access to schooling and professional training, as well as fulfilment of their personal aspirations; and empowerment of individuals and communities. Recognizing that large increases in the size and number of cities will occur in developing countries under any likely population scenario, greater attention should be given to preparing for the needs, in particular of women and children, for improved municipal management and local government.

Objective

Full integration of population concerns into national planning, policy and decision - making processes should continue. Population policies and programmes should be considered, with full recognition of women's rights.

Activities

Government and other relevant actors could, inter alia, undertake the following activities, with appropriate assistance from aid agencies, and report on their status of implementation to the International Conference on Population and Development to be held in 1994, especially to its committee on population and environment.

(a) Assessing the implications of national demographic trends and factors

The relationships between demographic trends and factors and environmental change and between environmental degradation and the components of demographic change should be analysed.

Research should be conducted on how environmental factors interact with socio-economic factors as a cause of migration.

Vulnerable population groups (such as rural landless workers, ethnic minorities, refugees, migrants, displaced people, women heads of household) whose changes in demographic structure may have specific impacts on sustainable development should be identified.

An assessment should be made of the implications of the age structure of the population on resource demand and dependency burdens, ranging from educational expenses for the young to health care and support for the elderly, and on household income generation.

An assessment should also be made of national population carrying capacity in the context of satisfaction of human needs and sustainable development, and special attention should be given to critical resources, such as water and land, and environmental factors, such as ecosystem, health and biodiversity.

The impact of national demographic trends and factors on the traditional livelihoods of indigenous groups and local communities, including changes in traditional land use because of international population pressures, should be studied.

(b) Building and strengthening a national information base

National databases on demographic trends and factors and environment should be built and/or strengthened, disaggregating data by ecological region (ecosystem approach), and population/environment profiles should be established by region.

Methodologies and instruments should be developed to identify areas where sustainability is, or may be, threatened by the environmental effects of demographic trends and factors, incorporating both current and projected demographic data linked to natural environmental processes.

Case-studies of local level response by different groups to demographic dynamics should be developed, particularly in areas subject to environmental stress and in deteriorating urban centres.

Population data should be disaggregated by, inter alia, sex and age in order to take into account the implications of the gender division of labour for the use and management of natural resources.

(c) Incorporating demographic features into policies and plans

In formulating human settlements policies, account should be taken of resource needs, waste production and ecosystem health.

The direct and induced effects of demographic changes on environment and development programmes should, where appropriate, be integrated, and the impact on demographic features assessed.

National population policy goals and programmes that are consistent with national environment and development plans for sustainability and in keeping with the freedom, dignity and personally held values of individuals should be established and implemented.

Appropriate socio-economic policies for the young and the elderly, both in term of family and state support systems, should be developed.

Policies and programmes should be developed for handling the various types of migrations that result from or induce environmental disruptions, with special attention to women and vulnerable groups.

Demographic concerns, including concerns for

environmental migrants and displaced people, should be incorporated in the programme for sustainable development of relevant international and regional institutions.

National reviews should be conducted and the integration of population policies in national development and environment strategies should be monitored nationally.

Means of implementation

(a) Financing and cost evaluation

The Conference secretariat has estimated the average total annual cost (1993-2000) of implementing the activities of this programme to be about $90 million from the international community on grant or concessional terms. These are indicative and order of magnitude estimates only and have not been reviewed by Governments. Actual costs and financial terms, including any that are non-concessional, will depend upon, inter alia, the specific strategies and programmes Governments decide upon for implementation.

(b) Raising awareness of demographic and sustainable development interactions

Understanding of the interactions between demographic trends and factors and sustainable development should be increased in all sectors of society. Stress should be placed on local and national action. Demographic and sustainable development education should be coordinated and integrated in both the formal and non-formal education sectors. Particular attention should be given to population literacy programme, notably for women. Special emphasis should be placed on the linkage between these programmes, primary environmental care and the provision of primary health care and services.

(c) Strengthening institutions

The capacity of national, regional and local structures to deal with issue relating to demographic trends and factors and sustainable development should be enhanced. This would involve strengthening the relevant bodies responsible for population issues to enable them to elaborate policies consistent with the national prospects for sustainable development. Cooperation among government, national research institutions, non-governmental organizations and local communities in assessing problems and evaluating policies should also be enhanced.

The capacity of the relevant United Nations organs, organizations and bodies, international and regional intergovernmental bodies, non-governmental organizations and local communities should, as appropriate, be enhanced to help countries develop sustainable development policies on request and, as appropriate, provide assistance to environmental migrants and displaced people.

Inter-agency support for national sustainable development policies and programmes should be improved through better coordination of population and environment activities.

(d) Promoting human resource development

The international and regional scientific institutions should assist Governments, upon request, to include concerns regarding the population/environment interactions at the global, ecosystem and micro-levels in the training of demographics and population and environment specialists.

Implementing integrated environment and development programmes at the local level, taking into account demographic trends and factors

Population programmes are more effective when

implemented together/with appropriate cross-sectoral policies. To attain sustainability at the local level, a new framework is needed that integrates demographic trends and factors with such factors as ecosystem health, technology and human settlements, and with socio-economic structures and access to resources. Population programmes should be consistent with socio-economic and environmental planning. Integrated sustainable development programmes should closely correlate action on demographic trends and factors with resource management activities and development goals that meet the needs of the people concerned.

Objective

Population programmes should be implemented along with natural resource management and development programmes at the local level that will ensure sustainable use of natural resources, improve the quality of life of the people and enhance environmental quality.

Activities

Governments and local communities, including community-based women's organizations and national non-governmental organizations, consistent with national plans, objectives, strategies and priorities, could, inter alia, undertake the activities set out below with the assistance and cooperation of international organizations, as appropriate. Governments could share their experience in the implementation of Agenda 21 at the International Conference on Population and Development, to be held in 1994, especially its committee on population and environment.

(a) Developing a framework for action

An effective consultative process should be established and implemented with concerned groups of society where the formulation and decision-making of all components of the programmes are based on a nationwide consultative process drawing on community meetings, regional workshops and national seminars, as appropriate. This process should ensure that views of women and men on needs, perspective and constraints are equally well reflected in the design of programmes, and that solutions are rooted in specific experience. The poor and underprivileged should be priority groups in this process.

Nationally determined policies for integrated and multifaceted programmes, with special attention to women, to the poorest people living in critical areas and to other vulnerable groups should be implemented, ensurging the involvement of groups with a special potential to act as agents for change and sustainable development. Special emphasis should be placed on those programmes that achieve multiple objectives, encouraging sustainable economic development, and mitigating adverse impacts of demographic trends and factors, and avoiding long-term environmental damage. Food security, access to secure tenure, basic shelter, and essential infrastructure, education, family welfare, women's reproductive health, family credit schemes, reforestation programmes, primary environmental care, women's employment should, as appropriate, be included among other factors.

An analytical framework should be developed to identify complementary elements of sustainable development policies as well as the national mechanisms to monitor and evaluate their effects on population dynamics.

Special attention should be given to the critical role of women in population/environment programmes and in achieving sustainable development. Projects should take advantage of opportunities to link social, economic and environmental gains for women and their families. Empowerment of women is essential and should be assured through education, training and policies to accord and improve women's right and access to assets, human and civil rights, labour-saving measures, job opportunities and participation in decision-making. Population/environment programmes must enable women to mobilize themselves to alleviate their burden and improve their capacity to participate in and benefit from socio-economic development. Specific measures should be undertaken to close the gap between female and male illiteracy rates.

(b) Supporting programmes that promote changes in demographic trends and factors towards sustainability

Reproductive health programmes and services, should, as appropriate, be developed and enhanced to reduce maternal and infant mortality from all causes and enable women and men to fulfil their personal aspirations in terms of family size, in a way in keeping with their freedom and dignity and personally held values.

Governments should take active steps to implement, as a matter of urgency, in accordance with country-specific conditions and legal systems, measures to ensure that women and men have the same right to decide freely and responsibly on the number and spacing of their children, to have access to the information, education and means, as appropriate, to enable them to exercise this right in keeping with their freedom, dignity and personally held values taking into account ethical and cultural considerations.

Governments should take active steps to implement programmes to establish and strengthen preventive and curative health facilities that include women-centred, women-managed, safe and effective reproductive health care and affordable, accessible services, as appropriate, for the responsible planning of family size, in keeping with freedom, dignity and personally held values and taking into account ethical and cultural consideration. Programmes should focus on providing comprehensive health care, including pre-natal care, education and information on health and responsible parenthood and should provide the opportunity for all women to breast-feed fully, at least during the first four months post partum. Programme should fully support women's productive and reproductive roles and well being, with special attention to the need for providing equal and improved health care for all children and the need to reduce the risk of maternal and child morality and sickness.

Consistent with national priorities, culturally based information and education programme that transmit reproductive health message to men and women that are easily understood should be developed.

(c) Creating appropriate institutional conditions

Constituencies and institutional conditions to facilitate the implementation demographic activities should, as appropriate, be fostered. This requires support and commitment from political, indigenous, religious and traditional authorities, the private sector and the national scientific community. In developing these appropriate institutional conditions, countries should closely involve established national machinery for women.

Population assistance should be coordinated with bilateral and multilateral donors to ensure that population needs and requirements of all developing countries are addressed, fully respecting the overall coordinating responsibility and the choice and strategies of the recipient countries.

Coordination should be improved at local and international levels. Working practices should be enhanced in order to make optimum use of resources, draw on collective experience and improve the implementation of programmes. UNFPA and other relevant agencies should strengthen the coordination of international cooperation activities with recipeint and donor countries in order to ensure that adequate funding is available to respond to growing needs.

Proposals should be developed for local, national and international population/environment programmes in line with specific needs for achieving sustainability. Where appropriate, institutional changes must be implemented so that old-age security does not entirely depend on input from family members.

Means of implementation

(a) Financial and cost evaluation

The Conference secretariat has estimated the average total annual cost (1993-2000) of implementing the activities of this programme to be about $7 billion, including about $3.5 billion from the international community on grant or concessional terms. These are indicative and order of magnitude estimates only and have not been reviewed by Governments. Actual costs and financial terms, including any that are non-concessional, will depend upon, inter alia, the specific strategies and programme Governments decide upon for implementation.

(b) Research

Research should be undertaken with a view to developing specific action programmes; it will be necessary to establish priorities between proposed areas of research.

Socio-demographic research should be conducted on how populations respond to a changing environment. Understanding of socio-cultural and political factors that can positively influence acceptance of appropriate population policy instruments should be improved.

Survey of changes in needs for appropriate services relating to responsible planning of family size, reflecting variations among different socio-economic groups and variations in different geographical regions should be undertaken.

(c) Human resources development and capacity building

The areas of human resource development and capacity building, with particular attention to the education and training of women, are areas of critical importance and are a very high priority in the implementation of population programmes.

Workshops to help programme and projects managers to link population programmes to other development and environmental goals should be conducted.

Educational materials, including guides/workbooks for planners and decision makers and other actors of population/environment/development programme, should be developed.

Cooperation should be developed between Government, scientific institutions and non-governmental organizations within the region, and similar institutions outside the region. Cooperation with local organizations should be fostered in order to raise awareness, engage in demonstration projects and report on the experience gained.

The recommendations contained in this chapter should in no way prejudice discussions at the international Conference on Population and Development in 1994, which will be the appropriate forum for dealing with population and development issues, taking into account the recommendations of the International Conference on Populations, held in Mexico City in 1984, and the Forward-looking Strategies for the Advancement of Women, endorsed by the World Conference to Review and Appraise the Achievements of the United Decade for Women: Equality, Development and Peace, held in Nairobi in 1985.

Protecting and Promoting Human Health

Introduction

Health and development are intimately interconnected. Both insuffient development leading to poverty and inappropriate development resulting in overconsumption, coupled with an expanding world population, can result in severe environmental health problems in both developing and developed nations. Action items under Agenda 21 must address the primary health needs of the world's population, since they are integral to the achievement of the goals of sustainable development and primary environmental care. The linkage of health, environmental and socio-economic improvements requires intersectoral efforts. Such efforts, involving education, housing, public works and community groups, including businesses, schools and universities and religious, civic and cultural organization, are aimed at enabling people in their communities to ensure sustainable development. Particularly relevant is the inclusion of prevention programmes rather than relying solely on remediation and treatment. Countries ought to develop plans for priority actions, drawing on the programme areas in this chapter, which are based on cooperative planning by the various levels of government, non-governmental organizatins and local communities.

The following programme areas are contained in this chapter:

(a) Meeting primary health care needs, particularly in rural areas;

(b) Control of communicable diseases;

(c) Protecting vulnerable groups;

(d) Meeting the urban health challenge;

(e) Reducing health risks from environmental pollution and hazards.

Meeting primary health care needs, particularly in rural areas

Health ultimately depends on the ability to manage successfully the interaction between the physical, spiritual, biological and economic/social environment. Sound development is not possible without a healthy population; yet most development activities affect the environment to some degree, which in turn causes or exacerbates many health problems. Conversely, it is the very lack of development that adversely affects the health conditions of many people, which can be alleviated only through development. The health sector cannot meet basic needs and objectives on its own; it is dependent on social, economic and spiritual development, while directly contributing to such development. It is also dependent on a healthy environment, including the provision of a safe water supply and sanitation and the promotion of a safe food supply and proper nutrition. Particular attention should be directed towards food safety, with priority placed on the elimination of foot contamination; comprehensive and sustainable water policies to ensure safe drinking water and sanitation to preclude both microbila and chemical contamination; and promotion of health education, immunization and provision of essential drugs. Education and appropriate services regarding resource planning of family size, with respect for cultural, religious and social aspects, in keeping with freedom, dignity and personally held values and taking into account ethical and cultural considerations, also contribute to these intersectoral activities.

Objectives

Within the overall strategy to achieve health for all by the year 2000, the objectives are to meet the basic health needs of rural peri-urban and urban populations; to provide the necessary specialized environmental health services; and to coordinate the involvement of citizens, the health sector, the health-related sectors and relevant non-health sectors (business, social, educational and religious institution) in solutions to health problems. As a matter of priority, health service coverage should be achieved for population groups in greatest need, particularly those living in rural areas.

Activities

National government and local authorities, with the support of relevant non-governmental organizations and international organizations, in the light of countries' specific conditions and needs, should strengthen their health sector programmes, with special attention to rural needs, to :

(a) Build basic health infrastructures, monitoring and planning systems:

(i) Develop and strengthen primary health care systems that are practical, community-based, scientifically sound, socially acceptable and appropriate to their needs and that meet basic health needs for clean water, safe food and sanitation;

(ii) Support the use and strengthening of mechanisms that improve coordination between health and related sectors at all appropriate levels of government, and in communities and relevant organizations;

(iii) Develop and implement rational affordable approaches to the establishment and maintenance of health facilities;

(iv) Ensure and, where appropriate, increase provision of social services support;

(v) Develop strategies, including reliable health indicators, to monitor the progress and evaluate the effectiveness of health programmes;

(vi) Explore ways to finance the health system based on the assessment of the resources needed and identify the various financing alternatives;

(vii) Promote health education in schools, information exchange, technical support and training;

(viii) Support initiatives for self-management of services by vulnerable groups;

(ix) Integrate traditional knowledge and experience into national health system, as appropriate;

(x) Promote the provisions for necessary logistics for outreach activities, particularly in rural areas;

(xi) Promote and strengthen community-based rehabilitation activities for the rural handicapped.

(b) Support research and methodology development:

(i) Establish mechanisms for sustained community involvement in environmental health activities, including optimization of the appropriate use of community financial and human resources;

(ii) Conduct environmental health research, including behaviour research and research on ways to increase coverage and ensure greater utilization of services by peripheral, underserved and vulnerable populations, as appropriate to good prevention services and health care;

(iii) Conduct research into traditional knowledge of prevention and curative health practices.

Means of implementation

(a) Financing and cost evaluation

The Conference secretariat has estimated the average

total annual cost (1993-2000) of implementing the activities of this programme to be about $40 billion, including about $5 billion from the international community on grant or concessional terms. These are indicative and order of magnitude estimates only and have not been reviewed by Governments. Actual costs and financial terms, including any that are non-concessional, will depend upon, inter alia, the specific strategies and programmes Governments decide upon for implementation.

(b) Scientific and technological means

New approaches to planning and managing health care systems and facilities should be tested, and research on ways of integrating appropriate technologies into health infrastructures supported. The development of scientifically sound health technology resources, including the maintenance and repair of equipment used in health care. Programmes to facilitate the transfer and sharing of information and expertise should be developed, including communication methods and educational materials.

(c) Human resources development

Intersectoral approaches to the reform of health personnel development should be strengthened to ensure its relevance to the "Health for All" strategies. Efforts to enhance managerial skills at the district level should be supported, with the aim of ensuring the systematic development and efficient operation of the basic health system. Intensive, short, practical training programmes with emphasis on skills in effective communication, community organization and facilitation of behaviour change should be developed in order to prepare the local personnel of all sectors involved in social development for carrying out their respective roles. In cooperation with the education sector, special health education programmes should be developed focusing on the role of women in the health-care system.

(d) Capacity building

Governments should consider adopting enabling and facilitating strategies to promote the participation of communities in meeting their own needs, in addition to providing direct support to the provision of health care services. A major focus should be the preparation of community-based health and health-related workers to assume an active role in community health education, with emphasis on team work, social mobilization and the support of other development workers. National programmes should cover distinct health systems in urban, peri-urban and rural areas, the delivery of health programmes at the district level, and development and support of referral services.

Control of communicable diseases

Basis for action

Advances in the development of vaccines and chemotherapeutic agents have brought many communicable diseases under control. However, there remain many important communicable diseases for which environmental control measures are indispensable, especially in the field of water supply and sanitation. Such diseases include cholera, diarrhoeal diseases, leishmaniasis, malaria and schistosomiasis. In all such instances, the environmental measures, either as an integral part of primary health care or undertaken outside the health sector, form an indispensable component of overall disease control strategies, together with health and hygiene education, and in some cases, are the only component.

With HIV infection levels estimated to increase to 30-40 million by the year 2000, the socio-economic impact of the pandemic is expected to be devastating for all countries, and increasingly for women and children. While direct health costs will be substantial, they will be dwarfed by the indirect costs of the pandemic - mainly costs associated with the loss of income and decreased productivity of the workforce. The pandemic will inhibit growth of the service and industrial sectors and significantly increase the costs of human capacity building and retraining. The agricultural sector is particularly affected where production is labour-intensive.

Objectives

A number of goals have been formulated through extensive consultations in various international forums attended by virtually all Governments, relevant United Nations Organizations (including WHO, UNICEF, UNFPA, UNESCO, UNDP and the World Bank) and a number of non-governmental organizations. Goals (including but not limited to those listed below) are recommended for implementation by all countries where they are applicable, with appropriate adaptation to the specific situation of each country in terms of phasing, standards, priorities and availability of resources, with respect for cultural, religious and social aspects, in keeping with freedom, dignity and personally held values and taking into account ethical considerations. Additional goals that are particularly relevant to a country's specific situation should be added in the country's national plan of action (Plan of Action for Implementing the World Declaration on the Survival, Protection and Development of Children in the 1990s. Such national level action plans should be coordinated and monitored from within the public health sector. Some major goals are:

(a) By the year 2000, to eliminate guinea worm disease (dracunculiasis);

(b) By the year 2000, eradicate polio;

(c) By the year 2000, to effectively control onchocerciasis (river blindness) and leprosy;

(d) By 1995, to reduce measles deaths by 95 per cent and reduce measles cases by 90 per cent compared with pre-immunization levels.

(e) By continued efforts, to provide health and hygience education and to ensure universal access to safe drinking water and universal access to sanitary measures of excreta disposal, thereby markedly reducing waterborne diseases such as cholera and schistosomiasis and reducing:

  (i) By the year 2000, the number of deaths from childhood diarrhoea developing countries by 50 to 70 per cent;

  (ii) By the year 2000, the incidence of childhood diarrhoea in developing countries by at least 25 to 50 per cent;

(f) By the year 2000, to initiate comprehensive programmes to reduce mortality from acute respiratory infections in children under five years by at least one third, particularly in countries with high infant mortality;

(g) By the year 2000, to provide 95 per cent of the world's child population with access to appropriate care for acute respiratory infections within the community and at first referral level;

(h) By the year 2000, to institute anti-malaria programmes in all countries where malaria presents a significant health problem and maintain the transmission-free status of areas freed from endemic malaria;

(i) By the year 2000, to implement control programmes in countries where major human parasitic infections are endemic and achieve an overall reduction in the prevalence of schistosomiasis and of other trematode infections by 40 per cent and 25 per cent, respectively, from a 1984 baseline, as well as a marked reduction in incidence, prevalence and intensity of filarial infections;

(j) To mobilize and unify national and international efforts against AIDS to prevent infection and to reduce the personal and social impact of HIV infection;

(k) To contain the resurgence of tuberculosis, with particular emphasis on multiple antibiotic resistant forums;

(l) To accelerate research on improved vaccines and implement to the fullest extent possible the use of vaccines in the prevention of disease.

Activities

Each national Government, in accordance with national plans for public health, priorities and objectives, should consider developing a national health action plan with appropriate international assistance and support, including, at a minimum, the following components:

(a) National public health systems:

(i) Programmes to identify environmental hazards in the causation of communicable diseases;

(ii) Monitoring systems of epidemiological data to ensure adequate forecasting of the introduction, spread or aggravation of communicable diseases;

(iii) Intervention programmes, including measures consistent with the principles of the global AIDS strategy;

(iv) Vaccines for the prevention of communicable diseases;

(b) Public information and health educations:

Provide education and disseminate information on the risks of endemic communicable diseases and build awareness on environmental methods for control of communicable diseases to enable communities to play a role in the control of communicable diseases;

(c) Intersectoral cooperation and coordination

(i) Second experienced health professionals to relevant sectors, such as planning, housing and agriculture;

(ii) Develop guidelines for effective coordination in the areas of professional training, assessment of risks and development of control technology;

(d) Control of environmental factors that influence the spread of communicable diseases:

Apply methods for the prevention and control of communicable diseases, including water supply and sanitation control, water pollution control, food quality control, integrated vector control, garbage collection and disposal and environmentally sound irrigation practices;

(e) Primary health care system

(i) Strengthen prevention programmes, with particular emphasis on adequate and balanced nutrition;

(ii) Strengthen early diagnostic programmes and improve capacities programme and improve capacities for early preventative/treatment action:

(iii) Reduce the vulnerability to HIV infection of women and their offspring;

(f) Support for research and methodology development

(i) Intensify and expand multidisciplinary research, including focused efforts on the mitigation and environment control of tropical diseases;

(ii) Carry out Intervention studies to provide a solid epidemiological basis for control policies and to evaluate the efficiency of alternative approaches;

(iii) Undertake studies in the population and among health workers to determine the influence of cultural, behavioural and social factors on control policies;

(g) Development and dissemination of technology

(i) Develop new technology for the effective control of communicable diseases:

(ii) Promote studies to determine how to optimally disseminate results from research;

(iii) Ensure technical assistance, including the sharing of knowledge and know-how.

Means of implementation

(a) Financing and cost evaluation

The Conference secretariat has estimated the average total annual cost (1993-2000) of implementing the activities of this programme to be about $4 billion, including about $900 million from the international community on grant or concessional terms. These are indicative and order of magnitude estimates only and have not been reviewed by Governments. Actual costs and financial terms, including any that are non-concessional, will depend upon, inter alia, the specific strategies and programmes Governments decide upon for implementation.

(b) Scientific and technological means

Efforts to prevent control diseases should include investigations of the epidemiological, social and economic bases for the development of more effective national strategies for the integrated control of communicable diseases. Cost effective methods of environmental control should be adapted to local development conditions.

(c) Human resources development

National and regional training institutions should promote broad intersectoral approaches to prevention and control of communicable diseases, including training in epidemiology and community prevention and control, immunology, molecular biology and the application of new vaccines. Health education materials should be developed for use by community workers and for the education of mothers for the prevention and treatment of diarrhoeal diseases in the home.

(d) Capacity building

The health sector should develop adequate data on the distribution of communicable diseases, as well as the institutional capacity to respond and collaborate with other sectors for prevention, mitigation and correction of communicable disease hazards through environmental protection. The advocacy at policy and decision-making levels should be gained, professional and social support mobilized, and communities organized in developing self-reliance.

Protecting vulnerable groups

Basis for action

In addition to meeting health needs, specific emphasis has to be given to protecting and educating vulnerable groups, particularly infants, youth, women, indigenous people and the very poor as a prerequisite for sustainable development. Special attention should also be paid to the health needs of the elderly and disabled population.

Infants and children. Approximately one third of the world's population are children under 15 years old. At least 15 million of these children die annually from such preventable causes as birth trauma, birth asphyxia, acute respiratory infections, malnutrition, communicable diseases and diarrhoea. The health of children is affected more severely than other population groups by malnutrition and adverse environmental factors, and many children risk exploitation as cheap labour or in prostitution.

Youth. As has been the historical experience of all countries, youth are particularly vulnerable to the problems associated with economic development, which often weakens traditional forms of social support essential for the healthy development of young people. Urbanization and changes in social mores have increased substance abuse, unwanted pregnancy and sexually transmitted diseases, including AIDS. Currently more than half of all people alive are under the age of 25 and 4 of every 5 live in developing countries. Therefore it is important to ensure that historical experience is not replicated.

Women. In developing countries, the health status of women remains relatively low, and during the 1980s poverty, malnutrition and general ill-health in women were even rising. Most women in developing countries still do not have adequate basic educational opportunities and they lack the means of promoting their health, responsibly controlling their reproductive life and improving their socio-economic status. Particular attention should be given to the provision of pre-natal care to ensure healthy babies.

Indigenous people and their communities. Indigenous people had their communities make up a significant percentage of global population. The outcomes of their experience have tended to be very similar in that the basis of their relationship with traditional lands has been fundamentally changed. They tend to feature disproportionately in unemployment, lack of housing, poverty and poor health. In many countries the number of indigenous people is growing faster than the general population. Therefore it is important to target health initiatives for indigenous people.

Objectives

The general objectives of protecting vulnerable groups are to ensure that all such individuals should be allowed to develop to their full potential (including healthy physical, mental and spiritual development); to ensure that young people can develop, establish and maintain healthy lives; to allow women to perform their key role in society; and to support indigenous people through educational, economic and technical opportunities.

Specific major goals for child survival, development and protection were agreed upon at the World Summit for children and remain valid also for Agenda 21. Supporting and sectoral goals cover women's health and education, nutrition, child health, water and sanitation, basic education and children in difficult circumstances.

Government should take active steps to implement, as a matter of urgency, in accordance with country specific conditions and legal systems, measures to ensure that women and men have the same right to decide freely and responsibly on the number and spacing of their children, to have access to the information, education and means, as appropriate, to enable them to exercise this right in keeping with their freedom, dignity and personally held values, taking into account ethical and cultural considerations.

Governments should take active steps to implement programmes to establish and strengthen preventive and curative health facilities which include women - centred women - managed, safe and effective reproductive health care and affordable, accessible services, as appropriate, for the responsible planning of family size, in keeping with freedom, dignity and personally held values and taking into account ethical and cultural considerations. Programmes should focus on providing comprehensive health care, including pre-natal care, education and information on health and responsible parenthood and should provide the opportunity for all women to breast-feed fully, at least during the first four months post - partum. Programmes should fully support women's productive and reproductive roles and well being, with special attention to the need for providing equal and improved health care for all children and the need to reduce the risk of maternal and child mortality and sickness.

Activities

National Government, in cooperation with local and non-governmental organizations, should initiate or enhance programmes in the following areas:

(a) Infants and children

(i) Strengthen basic health - care services for children in the context of primary health - care delivery, including prenatal care, breast - feeding, immunization and nutrition programmes;

(ii) Undertake widespread adult education on the use of oral rehydration therapy for diarrhoea, treatment of respiratory infections and prevention of communicable diseases;

(iii) Promote the creation, amendment and enforcement of a legal framework protecting children from sexual and workplace exploitation;

(iv) Protect children from the effects of environmental and occupational toxic compounds;

(b) Youth

Strengthen services for youth in health, education and social sectors in order to provide better information, education, counselling and treatment for specific health problems, including drug abuse;

(c) Women

(i) Involve women's groups in decision - making at the national and community levels to identify health risks and incorporate health issues in national action programmes on women and development;

(ii) Provide concrete incentives to encourage and maintain attendance of women of all ages at school and adult education courses, including health education and training in primary, home and maternal health care;

(iii) Carry out baseline surveys and knowledge, attitude and practice studies on the health and nutrition of women throughout their life cycle, especially as related to the impact of environmental degradation and adequate resources;

(d) Indigenous people and their communities:

(i) Strengthen, through resources and self - management, preventative and curative health services;

(ii) Integrate traditional knowledge and experience into health systems.

Means of implementation

(a) Financial and cost evaluation

The Conference secretariat has estimated the average annual cost (1993-2000) of implementing the activities of this programmes to be about $3.7 billion, including about $400 million from the international community on grant or concessional terms. These are indicative and order of magnitude estimates only and have not been reviewed by Governments. Actual costs and financial terms, including any that are non-concessional, will depend upon, inter alia, specific strategies and programmes Government decide upon for implementation.

(b) Scientific and technological means

Educational, health and research institution should be strengthened to provide support to improve the health of vulnerable groups. Social research on the specific problems of these groups should be expanded and methods for implementing flexible pragmatic solutions explored, with emphasis on preventive measures. Technical support should be provided to Governments' institutions and non-governmental organizations for youth, women, indigenous people in the health sector.

(c) Human resources development

The development of human resources for the health of children, youth and women should include reinforcement of educational institutions, promotion of interactive methods of education for health and increased use of mass media in disseminating information to the target groups. This require the training of more community health workers, nurse, midwives, physicians, social scientists and educators, the education of mothers, families and communities and the strengthening of ministries of education, health, population etc.

(d) Capacity - building

Governments should promote, where necessary: (i) The organization of national, intercountry and interregional symposia and other meetings for the exchange of information among agencies and groups concerned with the health of children, youth, women and indigenous people's organizations to facilitate health and consult them on the creation, amendment and enforcement of legal frameworks to ensure a healthy environment for children, youth, women and indigenous peoples.

Meeting the urban health challenge

Basis for action

For hundreds of millions of people, the poor living conditions in urban and peri - urban areas are destroying lives, health, and social and moral values. Urban growth has outstripped society's capacity to meet human needs, leaving hundreds of millions of people with inadequate incomes, diets, housing and services. Urban growth exposes populations to serious environmental hazards and has outstripped the capacity of municipal and local governments to provide the environmental health services that the people need. All too often, urban development is associated with destructive effects on the physical environment and the resource base needed for sustainable development. Environmental pollution in urban areas is associated with excess morbidity and mortality. Overcrowding and inadequate housing contribute to respiratory diseases, tuberculosis, meningitis and other diseases. In urban environments, many factors that affect human health are outside the health sector. Improvements in urban health therefore will depend on coordinated action by all levels of government, health care providers, businesses, religious groups, social and educational institutional and citizens.

Objectives

The health and well - being of all urban dwellers must be improved so that they can contribute to economic and social development. The global objective is to achieve a 10 to 40 per cent improvement in health indicators by the year 2000. The same rate of improvement should be achieved for environmental, housing and health service indicators. These include the development of quantitative objectives for infant mortality, maternal mortality, percentage of low birth weight newborns and specific indicators (e.g. tuberculosis as an indicator of crowded housing, diarrhoeal diseases as indicators of inadequate water and sanitation, rates of industrial and transportation accidents that indicate possible opportunities for prevention of injury, and social problems such as drug abuse, violence and crime that indicate underlying social disorders).

Activities

Local authorities with the appropriate support of national Governments and international organizations should be encouraged to take effective measures to initiate or strengthen the following activities:

(a) Develop and implement municipal and local health plans:

(i) Establish or strengthen intersectoral committees at both the political and technical level, including active collaboration on linkage with scientific, cultural, religious, medical, business, social and other city institutions, using networking arrangements;

(ii) Adopt or strengthen municipal or local "enabling strategies" that emphasize "doing with" rather than "doing for" and create supportive environments for health;

(iii) Ensure that public health education in schools, workplace, mass media etc. is provided or strengthened;

(iv) Encourage communities to develop personal skills and awareness of primary health care;

(v) Promote and strengthen community-based rehabilitation activities for the urban and peri-urban disabled and the elderly;

(b) Survey, where necessary, the existing health, social and environmental conditions in cities, including documentation of intra-urban differences;

(c) Strengthen environmental health services;

(i) Adopt health impact and environmental impact assessment procedures;

(ii) Provide basic and in-service training for new and existing personnel;

(d) Establish and maintain city networks for collaboration and exchange of models of good practice.

Means of implementation

(a) Financing and cost evaluation

The Conference secretariat has estimated the average total annual cost (1993-2000) of implementing the activities of this programme to be about $222 million, including about $22 million from the international community on grant or concessional terms. These are indicative and order of magnitude estimates only and have not been reviewed by Governments. Actual costs and financial terms, including any than are non-concessional, will depend upon, inter alia, the specific strategies and programmes Governments decide upon for implementation.

(b) Scientific and technological means

Decision-making models should be further developed and more widely used to assess the costs and the health and environment impacts of alternative technologies and strategies. Improvement in urban development and management requires better national and municipal statistics based on practical, standardized indicators. Development of methods is a priority for the measurement of intra-urban and intra-district variations in health status and environmental conditions, and for the application of this information in planning and management.

(c) Human resources development

Programmes must supply the orientation and basic training of municipal staff required for the healthy city processes. Basic and in-service training of environmental health personnel will also be needed.

(d) Capacity-building

The programme is aimed towards improved planning

and management capabilities in the municipal and local government and its partners in central Government, the private sector and universities. Capacity development should be focused on obtaining sufficient information, improving coordination mechanisms linking all the key actors, and making better use of available instruments and resources for implementation.

Reducing health risks from environmental pollution and hazards

Basis for action

In many locations around the world the general environment (air, water and land), workplaces and even individual dwellings are so badly polluted that the health of hundreds of millions of people is adversely affected. This is, inter alia, due to past and present developments in consumption and production patterns and lifestyles, in energy production and use, in industry, in transportation etc., with little or no regard for environmental protection. There have been notable improvements in some countries, but deterioration of the environment continues. The ability of countries to tackle pollution and health problems is greatly restrained because of lack of resources. Pollution control and health protection measures have often not kept pace with economic development. Considerable development-related environmental health hazards exist in the newly industrializing countries. Furthermore, the recent analysis of WHO has clearly established the interdependence among the factors of health, environment and development and has revealed that most countries are lacking such integration as would lead to an effective pollution control mechanism. Without prejudice to such criteria as may be agreed upon by the international community, or to standards which will have to be determined nationally, it will be essential in all cases to consider the systems of values prevailing in each country and the extent of the applicability of standards that are valid for the most advanced countries but may be inappropriate and of unwarranted social cost for the developing countries.

Objectives

The overall objective is to minimize hazards and maintain the environment to a degree that human health and safety is not impaired or endangered and yet encourage development to proceed. Specific programme objectives are:

(a) By the year 2000, to incorporate appropriate environmental and health safeguards as part of national development programmes in all countries;

(b) By the year 2000, to establish, as appropriate, adequate national infrastructure and programmes for providing environmental injury, hazard surveillance and the basis for abatement in all countries;

(c) By the year 2000, to establish, as appropriate, integrated programme for tackling pollution at the source and at the disposal site, with a focus on abatement actions in all countries;

(d) To identify and compile, as appropriate, the necessary statistical information on health effects to support cost/benefit analysis, including environmental health impact assessment for pollution control, prevention and abatement measures.

Activities

Nationally determined action programmes, with international assistance, support and coordination, where necessary, in this area should include:

(a) Urban air pollution:

(i) Develop appropriate pollution control technology on the basis of risk assessment and epidemiological research for the introduction of environmentally sound production processes and suitable safe mass transport;

(ii) Develop air pollution control capacities in large cities, emphasizing enforcement programmes and using monitoring networks, as appropriate;

(b) Indoor air pollution

(i) Support research and develop programmes for applying prevention and control methods to reducing indoor air pollution, including the provision of economic incentive for the installation of appropriate technology:

(ii) Develop and implement health education campaigns, particularly in developing countries, to reduce the health impact of domestic use of biomass and coal;

(c) Water pollution:

(i) Develop appropriate water pollution control technologies on the basis of health risk assessment;

(ii) Develop water pollution control capacities in large cities;

(d) Pesticides:

Develop mechanisms to control the distribution and use of pesticides in order to minimize the risks to human health by transportation, application and residual effects of pesticides used in agriculture and preservation of wood:

(e) Solid waste:

(i) Develop appropriate solid waste disposal technologies on the basis of health risk assessment;

(ii) Develop appropriate solid waste disposal capacities in large cities;

(f) Human settlements:

Develop programmes for improving health conditions in human settlements, in particular within slums and non-tenured settlements, on the basis of health risk assessment;

(g) Noise:

Develop programme for maximum permitted safe noise exposure levels and promote noise assessment and control as part of environmental health programmes:

(h) Ionizing and non-ionizing radiation:

Develop and implement appropriate national legislation, standards and enforcement procedures on the basis of existing international guidelines;

(i) *Effects of ultraviolet radiation:*

Undertake, as a matter of urgency, research on the effects on human health of the increasing ultraviolet radiation reaching the earth's surface as a consequence of depletion of the stratospheric ozone layer;

(i) On the basis of the outcome of this research, consider taking appropriate remedial measures to mitigate the above-mentioned effects on human beings;

(j) *Industry and energy production:*

(i) Establish environmental health impact assessment procedures for the planning and development of new industries and energy facilities;

(ii) Incorporate appropriate health risk analysis in all major industries for the surveillance of worker's exposure to health hazards;

(iii) Establish industrial hygiene programme in all major industries for the surveillance of workers' exposure to health hazards;

(iv) Promote the introduction of environmentally sound technologies within the industries and energy sectors:

(k) *Monitoring and assessment:*

Establish, as appropriate, adequate environmental monitoring capabilities for the surveillance of environmental quality and the health status of populations;

(l) *Injury monitoring and reduction:*

(i) Support, at appropriate, the development of systems to monitor the incidence and cause of injury to allow well-targeted intervention/ prevention strategies;

(ii) Develop, in accordance with national plans, strategies in all sectors (industry, traffic and others) consistent with the WHO safe cities and safe communities programmes, to reduce the frequency and severity of injury;

(iii) Emphasize preventive strategies to reduce occupationally derived diseases and diseases caused by environmental and occupational toxins to enhance worker safety;

(m) *Research promotion and methodology development:*

(i) Support the development of new methods for the quantitative assessment of health benefits and cost associated with different pollution control strategies;

(ii) Develop and carry out interdisciplinary research on the combined health effects of exposure to multiple environmental hazards, including epidemiological investigations of long-term exposures to low levels of pollutants and the use of biological markers capable of estimating human exposures, adverse effects and susceptibility to environmental agents.

Means of implementation

(a) Financial and cost evaluation

The Conference secretariat has estimated the average total annual cost (1993-2000) of implementing the activities of this programme to be about $3 billion, including about $ 115 million from the international community on grant or concessional terms. These are indicative and order of magnitude estimates only and have not been reviewed by Government. Actual costs and financial terms, including any that are non-concessional, will depend upon, inter alia, the specific strategies and programmes Governments decide upon for implementation.

(b) Scientific and technological means

Although technology to prevent or abate pollution is readily availably for a large number of problems, for programme and policy development countries should undertake research within an intersectoral framework. Such efforts should include collaboration with the business sector. Cost/effect analysis and environmental impact assessment methods should be developed through cooperative international programmes and applied to the setting of priorities and strategies in relation to health and development.

(c) Human resource development

Comprehensive national strategies should be designed to overcome the lack of qualified human resources, which is a major impediment to progress in dealing with environmental health hazards. Training should include environmental and health officials at all levels from managers to inspectors. More emphasis needs to be placed on including the subject of environmental health in the curricula of secondary schools and universities and on educating the public.

(d) Capacity-building

Each country should develop the knowledge and practical skills to foresee and identify environmental health hazards, and the capacity to reduce the risks. Basic capacity requirements must include knowledge about environmental health problems and awareness on the part of leaders, citizens and specialists; operational mechanisms for intersectoral and intergovernmental cooperation in development planning and management and in combating pollution; arrangements for involving private and community interests in dealing with social issues; delegation of authority and distribution of resources to intermediate and local levels of governments to provide front-line capabilities to meet environmental health needs.

Promoting Human Settlement Development

Introduction

In industrialized countries, the consumption patterns of cities are severely stressing the global ecosystem, while settlements in the developing world need more raw material, energy, and economic development simply to overcome basic economic and social problems. Human settlement conditions in many parts of the world, particularly the developing countries, are deteriorating mainly as a result of the low levels of investment in the sector attributable to the overall resource constraints in these countries. In the low- income countries for which recent data are available, and average of only 5.6 per cent of central government expenditure went to housing, amenities, social security and welfare. Expenditure by international support and finance organizations is equally low. For example, only 1 per cent of the United Nations system's total grant-financed expenditures in 1988 went to human settlements, while in 1991, loans from the World Bank and the International Development Association (IDA) for urban development and water supply and sewerage amounted to 5.5 and 5.4 per cent, respectively, of their total lending

On the other hand, available information indicates that technical cooperation activities in the human settlement sector generate considerable public and private sector investment. For example, every dollar of UNDF technical cooperation expenditure on human settlement in 1988 generated a follow-up investment of $122, the highest of all UNDF sectors of assistance.

This is the foundation of the "enabling approach" advocated for the human settlement sector. External assistance will help to generate the internal resources needed to improve the living and working environments of all people by the year 2000 and beyond, including the growing number of unemployed—the -no-income group. At the same time the environmental implications of urban development should be recognized and addressed in an integrated fashion by all countries, with high priority being given to the needs of the urban and rural poor, the unemployed and the growing number of people without any source of income.

Human settlement objective

The overall human settlement objective is to improve the social, economic and environmental quality of human settlements and the living and working environments of all people, in particular the urban and rural poor. Such improvement should be based on technical cooperation activities, partnerships among the public, private and community groups and special interest groups such as women, indigenous people, the elderly and the disabled. These approaches should form the core principles of national settlement strategies. In developing these strategies, countries will need to set priorities among the eight programme areas in this chapter in accordance with their national plans and objectives, taking fully into account their social and cultural capabilities. Furthermore countries should make appropriate provision to monitor the impact of their strategies on marginalized and disenfranchised groups, with particular reference to the needs of women.

The programme areas included in this chapter are:

(a) Providing adequate shelter for all;

(b) Improving human settlement management;

(c) Promoting sustainable land-use planning and management;

(d) Promoting the integrated provision of environmental infrastructure: water, sanitation, drainage and solid-waste management;

(e) Promoting sustainable energy and transport system in human settlement;

(f) Promoting human settlement planning and management in disaster-prone areas;

(g) Promoting sustainable construction industry activities;

(h) Promoting human resource development and capacity-building for human settlement development.

Providing adequate shelter for all

Basis for action

Access to safe and healthy shelter is essential to a person's psychological, social and economic well-being and should be a fundamental part of national and international action. The right to adequate housing as a basic human right is enshrined in the Universal Declaration of Human Rights and the international Covenant on Economic, Social and Cultural Rights. Despite this, it is estimated that at the present time, at least 1 billion people do not have access to safe and healthy shelter and that if appropriate action is not taken, this number will increase dramatically by the end of the century and beyond.

A major global programme to address this problem is the Global Strategy for Shelter to the Year 2000, adopted by the General Assembly in December 1988 (resolution 43/181, annex). Despite its widespread endorsement, the Strategy needs a much greater level of political and financial support to enable it to reach its goal of facilitating adequate shelter for all by the end of the century and beyond.

Objective

The objective is to achieve adequate shelter for rapidly growing populations and for the currently deprived urban and rural poor through an enabling approach to shelter development and improvement that is environmentally sound.

Activities

The following activities should be undertaken:

(a) As a first step towards the goal of providing adequate shelter for all, all countries should take immediate measures to provide shelter to their homeless poor, while the international community and financial institutions should undertake actions to support the efforts of the developing countries to provide shelter to the poor;

(b) All countries should adopt and/or strengthen national shelter strategies, with targets based, as appropriate, on the principles and recommendations contained in the Global Strategy for Shelter to the year 2000. People should be protected by law against unfair eviction from their homes or land;

(c) All countries should, as appropriate, support the shelter efforts of the urban and rural poor, the unemployed and the no-income group by adopting and/or adapting existing codes and regulations, to facilitate their access to land, finance and low-cost building materials and by actively promoting the regularization and upgrading of informal settlements and urban slums as an expedient measure and pragmatic solution to the urban shelter deficit;

(d) All countries should, as appropriate, facilitate access of urban and rural poor to shelter by adopting and utilizing housing and finance schemes and new innovative mechanisms adapted to their circumstances;

(e) All countries should support and develop environmentally compatible shelter strategies at national, state/provincial and municipal levels through partnerships among the private, public and community sectors and with the support of community-based organizations;

(f) All countries, especially developing ones, should, as appropriate, formulate and implement programmes to reduce the impact of the phenomenon of rural to urban drift by improving rural living conditions;

(g) All countries, where appropriate, should develop and implement resettlement programmes that address the specific problems of displaced populations in their respective countries;

(h) All countries should, as appropriate, document and monitor the implementation of their national shelter strategies by using, inter alia, the monitoring guidelines adopted by the Commission on Human Settlements and the shelter performance indicators being produced jointly by the United Nations Centre for Human Settlements (Habitat) and the World Bank;

(i) Bilateral and multilateral cooperation should be strengthened in order to support the implementation of the national shelter strategies of developing countries;

(j) Global progress reports covering national action and the support activities of international organizations and bilateral donors should be produced and disseminated on a biennial basis, as requested in the Global Strategy for Shelter to the Year 2000.

Means of implementation

(a) Financing and cost evaluation

The Conference secretariat has estimated the average total annual cost (1993-2000) of implementing the activities of this programme to be about $75 billion, including about $10 billion from the international community on grant or concessional terms. These are indicative and order of magnitude estimates only and have not been reviewed by Governments. Actual costs and financial terms, including any that are non-concessional, will depend upon, inter alia, the specific strategies and programmes Governments decide upon for implementation.

(b) Scientific and technological means

The requirements under this heading are addressed in each of the other programme areas included in the present chapter.

(c) Human resource development and capacity-building

Developed countries and funding agencies should provide specific assistance to developing countries in adopting and enabling approach to the provision of shelter for all, including the no-income group, and covering research institutions and training activities for government officials, professionals, communities and non-governmental organizations and by strengthening local capacity for the development of appropriate technologies.

Improving human settlement management

Basis for action

By the turn of century, the majority of the world's population will be living in cities. While urban settlements, particularly in developing countries, are showing many of the symptom of the global environment and development crisis, they nevertheless generate 60 per cent of gross national product and, if properly managed, can develop the capacity to sustain their productivity, improve the living conditions of their residents and manage natural resources in a sustainable way.

Some metropolitan areas extent over the boundaries of several political and/or administrative entities (countries and municipalities) even though they confirm to a continuous urban system. In many cases this political heterogeneity hinders the implementation of comprehensive environmental management programmes.

Objective

The objective is to ensure sustainable management of all urban settlements, particularly in developing countries, in order to enhance their ability to improve the living living conditions of residents, especially the marginalized and disenfranchised, thereby contributing to the achievement of national economic development goals.

Activities

(a) Improving urban management

One existing framework for strengthening management is in the United Nations Development Programme/World Bank/United Nations Centre for Human Settlements (Habitat) Urban Management Programme (UMP), a concerted global effort to assist developing countries during the period 1993-2000. All countries should, as appropriate and in accordance with national plans, objectives and priorities and with the assistance of non-governmental organizations and representatives of authorities, undertake the following activities at the national, state/provincial and local levels, with the assistance of relevant programme and support agencies:

(a) Adopting and applying urban management guidelines in the areas of land management, urban environmental management, infrastructure management and municipal finance and administration;

(b) Accelerating efforts to reduce urban poverty through a number of actions, including:

(i) Generating employment for the urban poors, particularly women, through the provision, improvement and maintenance of urban infrastructure and services and the support of economic activities in the informal sector, such as repairs, recycling, services and small commerce;

(ii) Providing specific assistance to the poorest of the urban poor through, inter alia, the creation of social infrastructure in order to reduce hunger and hamelessness, and the provision of adequate community services;

(iii) Encouraging the establishment of indigenous community-based organizations, private voluntary organizations and other forms of non-governmental entities that can contribute the efforts to reduce poverty and improve the quality of life for low-income families;

(c) Adopting innovative city planning strategies to address environmental and social issues by:

(i) Reducing subsidies on, and recovering the full costs of, environmental and other services of high standard (e.g. water supply, sanitation, waste collection, roads, telecommunications) provided to higher income neighbourhoods;

(ii) Improving the level of infrastructure and service provision in poorer urban areas;

(d) Developing local strategies for improving the quality of life and the environment, integrating decisions on land use and land management, investing in the public and private sectors and mobilizing human and material resources, thereby promoting employment generation that is environmentally sound and protective of human health.

(b) Strengthening urban data systems

During the period 1993-2000 all countries should undertake, with the active participation of the business sectors as appropriate, pilot projects in selected cities for the collection, analysis and subsequent dissemination of urban data, including environmental impact analysis, at the local state/provincial, national and international levels and the establishment of city data management capabilities. United Nations organizations, such as Habitat, UNEP and UNDP, could provide technical advice and model data managements systems.

(c) Encouraging intermediate city development

In order to relieve pressure on large urban agglomerations of development countries, policies and strategies should be implemented towards the development of intermediate cities that create employment opportunities for unemployed labour in the rural areas and support rural-based economic activities, although sound urban management is essential to ensure that urban sprawl does not expandresource degradation over an ever wider land area and increase pressures to convert open space and agricultural/buffer agricultural/ buffer lands for development.

Therefore all countries should, as appropriate, conduct reviews of urbanization processes and policies in order to assess the environmental impacts of growth and apply urban planning management approaches specifically suited to the needs, resource capabilities and characteristics of their growing intermediate-sized cities. As appropriate, they should concentrate on activities aimed at facilitating the transition from rural to urban lifestyles and settlement patterns and at promoting the development of small-scale economic activities, particularly the production of food, to support local income generation and the production of intermediate goods and services for rural hinterlands.

All cities, particularly those characterized by severe sustainable development problems, should, in accordance with national laws, rules and regulations, develop and strengthen programmes aimed at addressing such problems and guiding their development along a sustainable path. Some international initiatives in support of such efforts, as in the Sustainable Cities Programme of Habitat and the Healthy Cities Programme of WHO, should be intensified. Additional initiatives involving the World Bank, the regional development banks and bilateral agencies, as well as other interested stakeholders, particularly international nad national representatives of local authorities, should be strengthened and coordinated. Individual cities should, as appropriate:

(a) Institutionalize a participatory approach to sustainable urban development, based on a continuous dialogue between the actors involved in urban development (the public sector, private sector and communities), especially women and indigenous people;

(b) Improve the urban environment by promoting social organization and environmental awareness through the participation of local communities in the identification of public services needs, the provision of urban infrastructure, the enhancement of public amenities and the protection and/or rehabilitation of older buildings, historic precincts and other cultural artifacts. In addition, "green works" programmes should be activated to create self-sustaining human development activities and both formal and informal employment opportunities of low-income urban residents;

(c) Strengthen the capacities of their local governing bodies to deal more effectively with the broad range of developmental and environmental challenges associated with rapid and sound urban growth through comprehensive approaches to planning that recognize the individual needs of cities and are based on ecologically sound urban design practices;

(d) Participate in international "sustainable city networks" to experiences and mobilize national and international technical and financial support;

(e) Promote the formulation of environmentally sound and culturally sensitive tourism programmes as a strategy for sustainable development of urban rural settlements and as a way of decentralizing urban development and reducing discrepancies among regions;

(f) Establish mechanisms, with the assistance of relevant international agencies, to mobilize resources for local initiatives to improve environmental quality;

(g) Empower community groups, non-governmental organizations and individuals to assume the authority and responsibility for managing and enhancing their immediate environment through participatory tools, techniques and approaches embodied in the concept of environmental care.

Cities of all countries should reinforce cooperation among themselves and cities of the development countries, under the aegis of non-governmental organizations active in this field, such as the International Union of Local Authorities (IULA), the International Council for Local Environmental Initiatives (ICLEI) and the World Federation of Twin Cities.

Means of implementation

(a) Financing and cost evaluation

The Conference secretariat has estimated the average total annual cost (1993-2000) of implementing the activities of this programme to be about $100 billion, including about $15 from the international community on grant or concessional terms. These are indicative and order of magnitude estimates only and have not been reviewed by Governments. Actual coasts and financial terms, including any that are non-concessional, will depend upon, inter alia, the specific strategies and programmes Governments decide upon for implementation.

(b) Human resource development anli capacity-building

Developing countries should, with appropriate international assistance, consider focusing on training and developing a cadre of urban managers, technicians, administrators and other relevant stakeholders who can successfully manage environmentally sound urban development and growth and are equipped with the skills necessary to analyse and adapt the innovative experiences of other cities. For this purpose, the full range or training methods—from formal education to the use of the mass media—should be utilized, as well as the "learning by doing" option.

Developing countries should also encourage technological training and research through joint efforts by donors, non-governmental organizations and private business in such areas as the reduction of waste, water quality, saving of energy, safe production of chemicals and less polluting transportation.

Capacity-building activities carried out by all countries, assisted as suggested above, should go beyond the training of individuals and functional groups to include institutional arrangement, administrative routines, inter-agency linkages, information flows and consultative processes.

In addition, international efforts, such as the Urban Management Programme, in cooperation with mulilateral and bilateral agencies, should continue to assist the developing countries in their efforts to develop a participatory structure by mobilizing the human resources of the private sector, non-governmental organizations and the poor, particularly women and the disadvantaged.

Promoting land-use planning and management

Basis for action

Access to land resources is an essential component of sustainable low-impact lifestyles. Land resources are the basis for (human) living systems and provide soil, energy, water and the opportunity for all human activity. In rapidly growing urban areas, access to land is rendered increasingly difficult by the conflictioning demands of industry, housing, commerce, agriculture, land tenure structures and the need for open spaces. Furthermore, the rising costs of urban land prevent the poor from gaining access to suitable land. In rural areas, unsustainable practices, such as the exploitation of marginal lands and the encroachment on forests and ecologically fragile areas by commercial interests and landless rural populations, result in environmental degradation, as well as in diminishing returns for impoverished rural settlers.

Objective

The objective is to provide for the land requirements of human settlement development through environmentally sound physical planning and land use so as to ensure access to land to all households and, where appropriate, the encouragement of communally and collectively owned and managed land. Particular attention should be paid to the needs of women and indigenous people for economic and cultural reasons.

Activities

All countries should consider, as appropriate, undertaking a comprehensive national inventory of their land resources in order to establish a land information system in which land resources will be classified according to their most appropriate uses and environmentally fragile or disaster-prone areas will be identified for special protection measures.

Subsequently, all countries should consider developing national land-resource management plans to guide land-resource development and utilization and, to that end, should:

(a) Establish, as appropriate, national legislation to guide the implementation of public policies for environmentally sound urban development, land utilization, housing and for the improved management of urban expansion;

(b) Create, where appropriate, efficient and accessible land markets that meet community development needs by inter alia, improving land registry systems and streamlining procedures in land transactions;

(c) Develop fiscal incentives and land-use control measures, including land-use planning solutions for a more rational and environmentally sound use of limited land resources;

(d) Encourage partnerships among the public, private and community sectors in managing land resources for human settlements development;

(e) Strengthen community- based land-resource protection practices in existing urban and rural settlements;

(f) Establish appropriate forms of land tenure that provide security of tenure for all land-users, especially indigenous people, women, local communities, the low-income urban dwellers and the rural poor;

(g) Accelerate efforts to promote access to land by the urban and rural poor, including credit schemes for the purchase of land and for building/acquiring or improving safe and healthy shelter and infrastructure services;

(h) Develop and support the implementation of improved land-management practices that deal comprehensively with potentially competing land requirements for agriculture, industry, transport, urban development, green spaces, preserves and other vital needs;

(i) Promote understanding among policy makers of the adverse consequences of unplanned settlements in environmentally vulnerable areas and of the appropriate national and local land-use and settlements policies required for this purpose.

At the international level, global coordination of land-resource management activities should be strengthened by the various bilateral and multilateral agencies and programmes, such as UNDP, FAO, the World Bank, the regional development banks, other interested organization and the UNDP/World Bank/ Habital Urban Management Programme, and action should be taken to promote the transfer of applicable experience on sustainable land-management practices to and among developing countries.

Means of Implementation

(a) Financing and cost evaluation

The Conference secretariat has estimated the average total annual cost (1993-2000) of implementing the activities of this programme to be about $3 billion, including about $300 million from the international community on grant or concessional terms. These are indicative and order of magnitude estimated only and have not been reviewed by Governments. Actual costs and financial terms, including any that are non-concessional, will depend upon, inter alia, the specific strategies and programmes Governments decide upon for implementation;

(b) Scientific and technological means

All countries, particularly developing countries, alone or in regional or subregional grouping, should be given access to modern techniques of land-resource management, such as geographical information systems, satellite photography/imagery and other remote -sensing technologies.

(c) Human resource development and capacity-building

Environmentally focused training activities in sustainable land-resources planning and management should be undertaken in all countries, with developing countries being given assistance through international support and funding agencies in order to:

(a) Strengthen the capacity of national, state/provincial and local educational research and training institutions to provide formal training of land-management technicians and professionals;

(b) Facilitate the organizational review of government ministries and agencies responsible for land questions, in order to devise more efficient mechanisms of land-resource management, and carry out periodic in-service refresher course for the managers and staff of such ministries and agencies in order to familiarize them with up-to-date land-resource management technologies;

(c) Where appropriate, provide such agencies with modern equipment, such as computer hardware and software and survey equipment;

(d) Strengthen existing programmes and promote an international and interregional exchange of information and experience in land management through the establishment of professional association in land-management science and related activities, such as workships and seminars.

Promoting the infrastructure like water, sanitation and drainage

Basis for action

The sustainability of urban development is defined by many parameters relating to the availability of water supplies, air quality and the provision of environmental infrastructure for sanitation and waste management. As a result of the density of users, urbanization, if properly managed, offers unique opportunities for the supply of sustainable environmental infrastructure through adequate pricing policies, educational programmes and equitable access mechanisms that are economically and environmentally sound. In most developing countries, the inadequacy and lack of environmental infrastructure is responsible for widespread ill-health and a large number of preventable deaths each year. In those countries conditions are set to worsen due to growing needs that exceed the capacity of Government to respond adequately.

An integrated approach to the provision of environmentally sound infrastructure in human settlements, in particular for the urban and rural poor, is an investment in sustainable development that can improve the quality of life, increase productivity, improve health and reduce the burden of investments in curative medicine and poverty alleviation.

Most of the activities whose management would be improved by an integrated approach, are covered in Agenda 21 as follow: chapter 6 (Protecting and promoting human health conditions), chapter 9 (Protecting the atmosphere), 18 (Protecting the quality and supply of freshwater resources) and 21 (Environmentally sound management of solid wastes and sewage related issues).

Objective
The objective is to ensure the provisions of adequate environmental infrastructure facilities in all settlements by the year 2025. The achievement of this objective would require that all developing countries incorporate in their national strategies programme to build the necessary - technical, financial and human resource capacity aimed at ensuring better integration of infrastructure and environmental planning by the year 2000.

Activities
All countries should assess the environmental suitability of infrastructure in human settlements, develop national goals for sustainable management of waste, and implement environmentally sound technology to ensure that the environmental, human health and quality of life

are protected. Settlement infrastructure and environmental programmes designed to promote an integrated human settlement approach to the planning, development, maintenance and management of environmental infrastructure (water supply, sanitation, drainage, solid-waste management) should be strengthened with the assistance of bilateral and multilateral agencies. Coordination among these agencies and with collaboration from international and national representatives of local authorities, the private sector and community groups should also be strengthened. The activities of all agencies engaged in providing environmental infrastructure should, where possible, reflect an ecosystem of metropolitan area approach to settlements and should include monitoring, applied research, capacity-building, transfer of appropriate technology and technical cooperation among the range of programme activities.

Developing countries should be assisted at the national and local levels in adopting an integrated approach to the provision of water supply, energy sanitation, drainage and solid-waste management, and external funding agencies should ensure that this approach is applied in particular to environmental infrastructure improvement in informal settlements based on regulations and standards that take into account the living conditions and resources of the communities to be served.

All countries should, as appropriate, adopt the following principles for the provision of environmental infrastructure:

(a) Adopt policies that minimize if not altogether avoid environmental damage, whenever possible;

(b) Ensure that relevant decision are preceded by environmental impact assessments and also take into account the costs of any ecological consequences;

(c) Promote development in accordance with indigenous practices and adopt technologies appropriate to local conditions.

(d) Promote policies aimed at recovering the actual cost of infrastructure services, while at the same time recognizing the need to find suitable approaches (including subsidies) to extend basic service to all household;

(e) Seek joint solutions to environmental problems that affect several localities.

The dissemination of information from existing programmes should be facilitated and encouraged among interested countries and local institutions.

Means of implementation

(a) Financing and cost evaluation

The Conference secretariat has estimated most of the costs of implementing the activities of this programme in other chapter. The secretariat estimates the average total annual cost (1993-2000) of technical assistance from the international community on grant or concessional terms to be about $50 million. These are indicative and order of magnitude estimates only and have not been reviewed by Governments. Actual costs and financial terms, including any that are non-concessional, will depend upon, inter alia, the specific strategies and programmes Governments decide upon for implementation;

(b) Scientific and technological means

Scientific and technological means within the existing programmes should be coordinated wherever possible and should;

(a) Accelerate research in the area of integrated policies of environmental infrastructure programmes and projects based on cost/benefit analysis and overall environmental impact;

(b) Promote methods of assessing "effective demand", utilizing environment and development data as criteria for selecting technology.

(c) Human resource development and capacity-building

With the assistance and support of funding agencies, all countries should, as appropriate undertake training and popular participation programmes aimed at:

(a) Raising awareness of the means, approaches and benefits of the provision of environmental infrastructure facilities, especially among indigenous people, women, low - income groups and the poor;

(b) Developing a cadre of professional with adequate skills in integrated infrastructural service planning and maintenance of resource - efficient, environmentally sound and socially acceptable systems;

(c) Strengthening the institutional capacity of local authorities and administrators in the integrated provision of adequte infrastructure services in partnership with local communities and the private sector;

(d) Adopting appropriate legal and regulatory instruments, including cross- subsidy arrangements, to extend the benefits of adequate and affordable environmental infrastructure to unserved population groups, especially the poor.

Promoting energy and transport system in human settlements

Basis for action

Most of the commercial and non-commercial energy produced today is used in and for human settlements, and a substantial percentage of it is used by the household sector. Developing countries are at present faced with the need to increase their energy production to accelerate development and raise the living standards of their populations, while at the same time reducing energy production costs and energy related pollution. Increasing the efficiency of energy use to reduce its polluting effects and to promote the use of renewable energies must be a priority in any action taken to protect the urban environment.

Developed countries, as the largest consumers of energy, are faced with the need for energy planning and management, promoting renewable and alternate sources of energy, and evaluating the life-cycle costs of current systems and practices as a result of which many metropolitan areas are suffering from pervasive air quality problem related to ozone, particulate matters and carbon monoxide. The causes have much to do with technological inadequacies and with an increasing fuel consumption generated by inefficiencies, high demographic and industrial concentrations and a rapid expansion in the number of motor vehicles.

Transport accounts for about 30 per cent of commercial energy consumption and for about 60 per cent of total global consumption of liquid petroleum. In developing countries, rapid motorization and insufficient investments in urban - transport planning, traffic management and infrastructure, are creating increasing problems in terms of accidents injury, health, noise, congestion and loss of productivity similar to those occurring in many developed countries. All of these problems have a severe impact on urban populations, particularly the low-income and no -income groups.

Objective

The objectives are to extend the provisions of more energy efficient technology and alternative/renewable energy for human settlements and to reduce negative impacts of energy production and use on human health and on the environment.

Activities

The principal activities relevant to this programme area are included in chapter 9 (Protecting the atmosphere), programme area B, subprogramme 1 (Energy development, efficiency and consumption and subprogramme 2 (Transportation).

A comprehensive approach to human settlements development should include the promotion of sustainable energy development in all countries, as follow:

(a) *Developing countries, in particular, should:*

(i) Formulate national action programme to promote and support reafforestation and national forest regeneration with a view to achieving sustained provision of the biomass energy needs of the low-income groups in urban areas and the rural poor, in particular women and children;

(ii) Formulate national action programme to promote integrated development of energy saving and renewable energy technologies, particularly for the use of solar, hydro, wind and biomass sources;

(iii) Promote wide dissemination and commercialization of renewable energy technologies through suitable measures, inter alia, fiscal and technology transfer mechanisms;

(iv) Carry out information and training programmes directed at manufacturers and users in order to promote energy -saving techniques and energy - efficient appliances;

(b) *International organizations and bilateral donors should:*

(i) Support developing countries in implementing national energy programmes in order to achieve widespread use of energy - saving and renewable energy technologies, particularly the use of solar, wind, biomass and hydro sources;

(ii) Provide access to research and development results to increase energy - use efficiency levels in human settlements.

Promoting efficient and environmentally sound urban transport systems in all countries should be a comprehensive approach to urban-transport planning and management. To this end, all countries should;

(a) Integrate land-use and transportation planning to encourage development patterns that reduce transport demand;

(b) Adopt urban-transport programmes favouring high-occupancy public transport in countries, as appropriate;

(c) Encourage non-motorized modes of transport by providing safe cycleways and footways in urban and suburban centres in countries, as appropriate;

(d) Devote particular attention to effective traffic management, efficient operation of public transport and maintenance of transport infrastructure;

(e) Promote the exchange of information among countries and representatives of local and metropolitan areas;

(f) Re-evaluate the present consumption and production patterns in order to reduce the use of energy and national resources.

Means of implementation

(a) Financing and cost evaluation

The Conference secretariat has estimated the costs of implementing the activities of this programmes in chapter 9 (Protection of the atmosphere);

(b) Human resource development and capacity - building

In order to enhance the skills of energy service and

transport professionals and institutions, all countries should, as appropriate;

(a) Provide on - the -job and other training of government officials, planners, traffic engineers and managers involved in the energy - service and transport section;

(b) Raise public awareness of the environmental impacts of transport and travel behaviour through mass media campaigns and support for non-governmental and community initiatives promoting the use of non - motorized transport, shared driving and improved traffic safety measures;

(c) Strengthen regional, national, state-provincial, and private sector institutions that provide education and training on energy service and urban transport planning and management.

Promoting human settlement planning and management in disaster-prone areas

Basis for action

Natural disasters cause loss of life, disruption of economic activities and urban productivity, particularly for highly susceptible low-income groups, and environmental damage, such as loss of fertile agricultural land and contamination of water resources, and can lead to major resettlement of populations. Over the past two decades, they are estimated to have caused some 3 million deaths and affected 800 million people. Global economic losses have been estimated by the office of the United Nations Disaster Relief Coordinator to be in the range of $30 - 50 billions per year. The General Assembly, in resolution 44/236, proclaimed the 1990s as the International Decade for Natural Disaster Reduction. The goals of the Decade bear relevance to the objectives of the present programme area.

In addition, there is an urgent need to address the prevention and reduction of man - made disasters and / or disasters caused by, inter alia, industries, unsafe nuclear power generation and toxic wastes (see chapter 6 of Agenda 21).

Objective

The objective is to enable all countries, in particular those that are disaster - prone, to mitigate the negative impact of natural and man-made disasters on human settlements, national economies and the environment.

Activities

Three distinct areas of activity are foreseen under this programme area, namely, the development of a "culture of safety", pre - disaster planning and post - disaster reconstruction.

(a) Developing a culture of safety

To promote a "culture of safety" in all countries, especially those that are disaster - prone, the following activities should be carried out:

(a) Completing national and local studies on the nature and occurrence of natural disasters, their impact on people and economic activities, the effects of inadequate construction and land use in hazard - prone areas, and the social and economic advantages of adequate pre-disaster planning;

(b) Implementing nation wide and local awareness campaigns through all available media, translating the above knowledge into information easily comprehensible to the general public and to the population directly exposed to hazards;

(c) Strengthening, and/or developing global, regional, national and local early warning systems to alert population to impending disasters;

(d) Identifying industrially based environmental disaster areas at the national and international levels and implementing strategies aimed at the rehabilitation of these areas through, inter alia:

(i) Restructuring of the economic activities and promoting new job opportunities, in environmentally sound sectors;

(ii) Promoting close collaboration between government and local authorities, local communities and non-governmental organizations and private business;

(iii) Developing and enforcing strict environmental control standards.

(b) Developing pre - disaster planning

Pre-disaster planning should form an integral part of human settlement planning in all countries. The following should be included;

(a) Undertaking complete multi-hazard research into risk and vulnerability of human settlement and settlement infrastructure, including water and sewerage, communication and transportation networks, as one type of risk reduction may increase vulnerability to another (e.g., an earthquake -resistant house made of wood will be more vulnerable to wind storms);

(b) Developing methodologies for determining risk and vulnerability within specific human settlements and incorporating risk and vulnerability reduction into the human settlement planning and management process;

(c) Redirecting inappropriate new development and human settlements to not areas prone to hazards;

(d) Preparing guidelines on location, design and operation of potentially hazardous industries and activities;

(e) Developing tools (legal, economic etc.) to encourage disaster-sensitive development, including means of ensuring that limitations on development options are punitive to owners, or incorporate alternative means of compensation;

(f) Further developing and disseminating information disaster - resistant building materials and construction technologies for buildings and public works in general;

(g) Developing training programmes for contractors and builders on disaster - resistant construction method, some programmes should be directed particularly to small enterprises, which build the great majority of housing and other small building in the developing countries, as well as to the rural populations, which build their own houses;

(h) Developing training programmes for emergency site managers, non-governmental organizations and community groups which cover all aspects of disaster mitigation, including urban search and rescue, emergency communications, early warning techniques, and pre-disaster planning;

(i) Developing procedures and practices to enable local communities to receive information about hazardous installation or situations in these areas, and facilitate their participation in early warning and disaster abatement and response procedures and plans;

(j) Preparing action plans for the reconstruction of settlements, especially the reconstruction of community life-lines.

(c) Initiating post-disaster reconstruction and rehabilitation planning

The international community, as a major partner in post - reconstruction and rehabilitation, should ensure that the countries involved derive the greatest benefits from the funds allocated by undertaking the following activities:

(a) Carrying out research on past experiences on the social and economic aspects of post-disaster reconstruction and adopting effective strategies and guidelines for post-disaster reconstruction, with particular focus on development-focused strategies in the allocation of scarce reconstruction resources, and on the opportunities that post-disaster reconstruction provides to introduce sustainable settlement patterns;

(b) Preparing and disseminating international guidelines for adaptation to national and local needs;

(c) Supporting efforts of national governments to initiate contingency planning, with participation of affected communities, for post-disaster reconstruction and rehabilitation.

Means of implementation

(a) Financing and cost evaluation

The conference secretariat has estimated the average total annual cost (1993-2000) of implementing the activities of this programme to be about $50 million from the international community on grant or concessional terms. These are indicative and order of magnitude estimates only and have not been reviewed by Governments. Actual costs and financial terms, including any that are non-concessional, will depend upon, inter alia, the specific strategies and programmes Governments decide upon for implementation.

(b) Scientific and technological means

Scientific and engineer specializing in this field in both developing and developed countries should collaborate with urban and regional planners in order to provide the basic knowledge and means to mitigate losses owing to disasters as well as environmentally inappropriate development.

(c) Human resource development and capacity-building

Developing countries should conduct training programmes on disaster - resistant construction methods for contractors and builders, who build the majority of housing in the developing countries. This should focus on the small business enterprises, which build the majority of housing in the developing countries. This should focus on the small business enterprises, which build the majority of housing in the developing countries.

Training programmes should be extended to government officials and planners and community and non-governmental organizations to cover all aspects of disaster mitigation, such as early warning techniques, pre-disaster planning and construction, post-disaster construction and rehabilitation.

Promoting construction activities

Basis for action

The activities of the construction sector are vital to the achievement of the national socio-economic development goals of providing shelter, infrastructure and employment. However, they can be a major source of environmental damage through depletion of the natural resource base, degradation of fragile eco-zones, chemical pollution and the use of building materials harmful to human health.

Objective

The objectives are, first, to adopt policies and technologies and to exchange information on them in order to enable the construction sector to meet human settlement development goals, while avoiding harmful side-effects on human health and on the biosphere, and, second, to enhance the employment-generation capacity of the construction sector in achieving these objectives.

Activities

All countries should, as appropriate and in the accordance with national plans, objectives and priorities;

(a) Establish and strengthen indigenous building materials industry, based, as much as possible, on inputs of locally available natural resources;

(b) Formulate programmes to enhance the utilization of local materials by the construction sector by expanding technical support and incentive schemes for increasing the capabilities and economic viability of small-scale and informal operatives which make use of these materials and traditional construction techniques;

(c) Adopt standards and other regulatory measures which promote the increased use of energy Activities efficient designs and technologies and sustainable utilization of natural resources in an economically and environmentally appropriate way;

(d) Formulate appropriate land-use policies and introduce planning regulations specially aimed at the protection of eco-sensitive zones against physical disruption by construction and construction-related activities;

(e) Promote the use of labour-intensive construction and maintenance technologies which generate employment in the construction sector for the underemployed labour force found in most large cities, while at the same time promoting the development of skills in the construction sector;

(f) Develop policies and practices to reach the informal sector and self-help housing builders by adopting measures to increase the effordability of building materials on the part of the urban and rural poor, through, inter alia, credit schemes and bulk procurement of building materials for sale to small-scale builders and communities.

All countries should:

(a) Promote the free exchange of information on the entire range of environmental and health aspects of construction, including the development and dissemination of databases on the adverse environmental effects of building materials through the collaborative efforts of the private and public sectors;

(b) Promote the development and dissemination of databases on the adverse environmental and health effects of building materials and introduce legislation and financial incentives to promote recycling to energy-intensive materials in the construction industry and conservation of waste energy in building-materials productions methods;

(c) Promote the use of economic instruments, such as product charges, to discourage the use of construction materials and products that create pollution during their life cycle;

(d) Promote information exchange and appropriate technology transfer among all countries, with particular attention to developing countries, for resource management in construction, particularly for non-renewable resources;

(e) Promote research in construction industries and related activities, and establish and strengthen institutions in this sector.

Means of implementation

(a) Financing and cost evaluation

The conference secretariat has estimated the average total annual cost (1993-2000) of implementing the activities of this programme to be about $40 billion, including about $4 billion from the international community on grant or concessional terms. These are indicative and order of magnitude estimates only and have not been reviewed by Governments. Actual costs and financial terms, including any that are non-concessional, will depend upon, inter alia, the specific strategies and programmes Governments decide upon for implementation.

(b) Human resource development and capacity-building

Developing countries should be assisted by international support and funding agencies in upgrading the technical and managerial capacities of the small entrepreneur and the vocational skills of operatives and supervisors in the building materials industry, using a variety of training methods. These countries should also be assisted in developing programmes to encourage the use on non-waste and clean technologies through appropriate transfer to technology.

General education programmes should be developed in all countries, as to increase builder awareness of available sustainable ecologies.

Local authorities are called upon to play a pioneering role in promoting the increased use of environmentally sound building materials and construction technologies, e.g., by pursuing an innovative procurement policy.

Promoting human resource development and capacity-building for human settlement developments

Basis for action

Most countries, in addition to shortcomings in the availability of specialized expertise in the areas of housing, settlement management, land management, infrastructure, construction, energy, transport, and pre-disaster planning and reconstruction, face three cross-sectoral human resource development and capacity-building shortfalls. First is the absence of an enabling policy environmental capable of integrating the resources and activities of the public sector, the private sector and the community, or social sector, second is the weakness of specialized training and research institutional; and third is the insufficient capacity for technical training and assistance for low-income communities, both urban and rural.

Objectives

The objective is to improve resource development and capacity-building in all countries by enhancing the personal and institutional capacity of all actors, particularly indigenous people and women, involved in human settlement development. In this regard, account should be taken to traditional cultural practices of indigenous people and their relationship to the environment.

Activities

Specific human resource development and capacity-building activities have been built into each of the programme areas of this chapter. More generally, however, additional steps should be taken to reinforce those activities. In order to do so, all countries, as appropriate, should take the following action:

(a) Strengthening the development of human resources and of capacities of public sector institutions through technical assistance and international cooperation so as to achieve by the year 2000 substantial improvement in the efficiency of government activities.

(b) Creating an enabling policy environmental supportive of the partnership between the public, private and community sectors;

(c) Providing enhanced training and technical assistance

to institutions providing training for technicians, professionals and administrators, and appointed, elected and professional members of local governments and strengthening their capacity to address priority training needs, particularly in regard to social, economic and environmental aspects of human settlement development;

(d) Providing direct assistance for human settlement development at the community level, inter alia, by:

(i) Strengthening and promoting programmes for social mobilization and raising awareness of the potential of women and youth in human settlements activities;

(ii) Facilitating coordination of the activities of women, youth, community groups and non-governmental organizations in human settlements development;

(iii) Promoting research on women's programmes and other groups, and evaluating progress made with a view to identifying bottlenecks and needed assistance;

(e) Promoting the inclusion of integrated environmental management into general local government activities.

Both international organizations and non-governmental organizations should support the above activities by, inter alia, strengthening subregional training institutions, providing updated training materials and disseminating the results of successful human resource and capacity-building activities,

Means of implementation

(a) Financial and cost evaluation

The Conference secretariat has estimated the average total annual cost (1993-2000) of implementing the activities of this programme to be about $65 million from the international community on grant or concessional terms. These are indicative and order of magnitude estimates only and have not been reviewed by Governments. Actual costs and financial terms, including any that are non-concessional, will depend upon, inter alia, the specific strategies and programmes Governments decide upon for implementation.

(b) Scientific and technological means

Both formal training and non-formal types of human resource development and capacity-building programmes should be combined, and use should be made of use-oriented training methods, up-to-date training materials and modern audio-visual communication systems.

20 Resolutions of the General Assembly

An Agenda for Development

The General Assembly,

Recalling the Charter of the United Nations, in particular the commitment to employ international machinery for the promotion of the economic and social advancement of all peoples,

Taking note of the report of the Secretary-General on the work of the Organization, in particular the reference to an agenda for development,

Reaffirming the unique position of the United Nations as a forum for the promotion of international cooperation for development,

Emphasizing the need to give due consideration to the broad scope of themes related to international cooperation and international economic relations in order to address effectively the issue of development, particularly of developing countries,

Stressing the importance of continuing to strengthen the capacity of the United Nations to foster international cooperation in order to address fully the wide range of issues pertaining to development, particularly that of developing countries,

Stressing also that the objectives and commitments with regard to development adopted by the General Assembly, especially the Declaration on International Economic Cooperation, in particular the Revitalization of development, adopted by the Group of 77 on 24 June 1994 (A/49/204-E/1994/90);

(c) Letter dated 27 June 1994 from the Permanent Representative of Algeria to the United Nations addressed to the Secretary-General transmitting the Ministerial Statement adopted on the occasion of the thirtieth anniversary of the Group of 77 (A/49/205-E/1994/91);

(d) Letter dated 29 June 1994 from the Charge d'affaires a.i. of the Permanent Mission of Yugoslavia to the United Nations addressed to the Secretary-General (E/1994/101).

4. At the 9th meeting of the Council, on 27 June, the President of the Council made a statement.

5. At the same meeting, the Council began its policy dialogue and discussion on important developments in the world economy and international economic cooperation with the heads of multilateral financial and trade institutions of the United Nations system.

6. Statements were made by the President of the World Bank, the Managing Director of the International Monetary Fund, the Officer-in-charge of the United Nations Conference on Trade and Development and the Deputy Director-General of the General Agreement on Tariffs and Trade.

7. During the exchange of views, statements were made by the representatives of the United States of America, Belgium, Germany, Norway and Greece.

8. The President of the World Bank, the Managing Director of the International Monetary Fund, the Officer-in-charge of the United Nations Conference on Trade and Development, the Deputy Director-General of the General Agreement on Tariffs and Trade and the Under-Secretary-General for Policy

Coordination and Sustainable Development responded to questions raised during the exchange of views.

9. At the 10th meeting, on 27 June, the Council continued its policy dialogue. During the exchange of views, statements were made by the representatives of Denmark, India, Egypt, the Russian Federation, Nigeria, Chile, China, the United Kingdom of Great Britain and Northern Ireland, Bangladesh, Japan, Indonesia and Belarus and the observers for Algeria and Morocco.

10. The observer for the European Community also made a statement.

11. The Managing Director of the International Monetary Fund, the Officer-in-charge of the United Nations Conference on Trade and Development, the Deputy Director-General of the General Agreement on Tariffs and Trade, the Under-Secretary-General for Policy Coordination and Sustainable Development and the representative of the World Bank responded to questions raised during the exchange of views.

12. The President of the Council made some concluding remarks on the policy dialogue and discussion.

13. At the 11th meeting, on 28 June, the Council began its consideration of an agenda for development (agenda item 2).

14. The Secretary-General made a statement.

15. The President of the General Assembly also made a statement.

16. Statements were then made by the Permanent Representative of Algeria to the United Nations (on behalf of the States Members of the United Nations that are members of the Group of 77 and China); the

Alternate Minister for Foreign Affairs of Greece (on behalf of the States Members of the United Nations that are members of the European Union); the Secretary of State (Asia-Pacific) of Canada; the Secretary-General of the Ministry of Foreign Affairs of France, the Administrator of the United-States Agency for International Development; the Minister for Development of Denmark; the Permanent Representative of Senegal to the United Nations; the Permanent Representative of Mexico to the United Nations; the Minister for Foreign Affairs of Paraguay.

17. The Director-General of the Food and Agriculture Organization of the United Nations also made a statement.

18. At the 12th meeting, on 28 June, statements were made by the Deputy to the Minister for Foreign Economic Relations of Indonesia; the Deputy Secretary, Overseas Development Administration of the United Kingdom of Great Britain and Northern Ireland; the Minister of State for External Affairs of India; the Minister of State of Germany; the Under-Secretary of State, Ministry of Foreign Affairs of Poland; the Minister of Planning and Economic Development of Ethiopia; the Deputy Minister for Foreign Affairs of Romania; the Special Representative of Brazil to the high-level segment; the Deputy Foreign Minister for International Affairs of the Islamic Republic of Iran; the Permanent Representative of Sri Lanka to the United Nations; the Minister, Department of the Prime Minister of Malaysia; the Under-Secretary of State for Development Cooperation of Finland; the Secretary of State for Development Cooperation of Belgium; the Minister for Foreign Affairs of Costa Rica; the Planning Commissioner of the National Economic

Planning Commission, Office of the President of Zimbabwe; the Under-Secretary of State of Sweden; the Secretary of the Economic Relations Division, Ministry of Finance of Bangladesh; the Deputy Prime Minister of the Republic of Croatia.

19. Statements were also made by the Director-General of the World Health Organization, the Director-General of the United Nations Educational, Scientific and Cultural Organization and the Director-General of the United Nations Industrial Development Organization.

20. At the 13th meeting, on 29 June, statements were made by the Charge d'affaires of the Permanent Mission of Colombia to the United Nations; the Secretary of the General People's Committee for Economic and Commercial Affairs of the Libyan Arab Jamahiriya; the Minister of State of Ireland; the State Secretary of Norway; the State Secretary (Deputy Foreign Minister) of Slovenia; the Permanent Representative of China to the United Nations; the Special Assistant to the Prime Minister of Pakistan on Social Affairs; the Parliamentary Secretary, Office of the Prime Minister of the Bahamas; the First Deputy Minister for Foreign Affairs of Ukraine; the Deputy Minister for Minister for Foreign Affairs of Bulgaria; the Under-Secretary of State of Italy.

21. The observer for the European Community made a statement.

22. Statements were also made by the Administrator of the United Nations Development Programme, the Executive Director of the United Nations Children's Fund, the Executive Director of the United Nations Population Fund and the Executive Director of the World Food Programme.

23. The President of the Council made a statement to launch the dialogue, in which the Minister for Development of Denmark participated.

24. At the 14th meeting, on 29 June, statements were made by the Deputy Permanent Representative of Japan to the United Nations; the Deputy Minister for Foreign Affairs of the Russian Federation; the Permanent Representative of Austria to the United Nations; the Secretary of State for Cooperation, Ministry of Foreign Affairs of Portugal; the First Deputy Minister of the Ministry of Foreign Affairs and Permanent Representative of Cuba to the United Nations; the Permanent Representative of Venezuela to the United Nations; the Deputy Permanent Representative of Australia to the United Nations; the Ambassador Extraordinary and Plenipotentiary of Israel, the Permanent Representative of Jamaica to the United Nations, the Permanent Representative of Nepal to the United Nations; the Permanent Representative of Belarus to the United Nations; the Ambassador from the Ministry of Foreign Relations of the Former Yugoslav Republic of Macedonia; the Minister for Economic Affairs of Morocco; the Permanent Representative of the Republic of Korea to the United Nations; the Minister of Information and Minister of State of Jordan; the Minister for Economic Planning and Development of Swaziland; the Permanent Representative of Egypt to the United Nations; the Director of the Department for International Organizations of Switzerland.

25. Statements were made by the observers for the Latin American Economic System and the Organization of African Unity.

26. Statements were made by the Secretary-General of the International Civil Aviation Organization, the

Deputy Director-General of the International Labour Organization and the Deputy High Commissioner for Refugees.

27. The representative of Greece made a statement.

28. At the 15th meeting, on 29 June, statements were made by the Deputy Permanent Representative of Madagascar to the United Nations; the Director General for International Organizations, Royal Foreign Office of Spain; the Permanent Representative of Turkey to the United Nations; the Under-Secretary of Social Labour of Kuwait.

29. At the same meeting, the Council entered into a dialogue during which statements were made by the representatives of Angola, the United Kingdom of Great Britain and Northern Ireland, Germany, Benin, the Netherlands, Japan, Egypt, Senegal, China, Canada, France, Pakistan, Brazil, the United States of America, India, Australia and Nigeria and the observers for Algeria and the Netherlands.

30. Statements were also made also made by the representatives of the United Nations Development Programme and the World Bank.

31. The President of the Council made some concluding remarks.

B. Conclusions of the high-level segment

32. At the 35th meeting, on 18 July, the President of the Council presented the summary and conclusions of the high-level segment (E/1994/109).

33. At the same meeting, statements were made by the representatives of the United States of America, the Russian Federation, Germany (on behalf of the States Members of the United Nations that are members of the European Union), Ukraine, China, Paraguay, the Libyan Arab Jamahiriya and Belarus and the observers for Algeria (on behalf of the States

Members of the United Nations that are members of the Group of 77) and Kyrgyzstan.

34. The representative of the Food and Agriculture Organization of the United Nations also made a statement.
35. The President of the Council made some concluding remarks.
36. The principal elements emerging from the discussions are summarized below [see following page].

Summary and conclusions by Ambassador Richard Butler, AM, President of the Economic and Social Council

The state of affairs

"The following main relevant features of current global economic and social conditions were identified:

"While growth has resumed in the world economy overall, it is spread very unevenly and is by no means secure;

"A number of developing countries now play a key role in the world economy, yet the magnitude and spread of extreme poverty has increased greatly. Today, more than 1 billion people live in extreme poverty;

"Overall, the gap between developed and developing countries continues to widen. It reflects the marginalization of developing countries in respect of the main determinants of international trade, money, finance, technology, and information and communication flows;

"Notwithstanding stronger growth in some developed countries, unemployment rates remain alarmingly high;

"Integration/globalization in the global economy is now one of its fundamental pervasive features;

"Sustainable development needs to be pursued;

"Levels of official development assistance continue to decline. There is a crisis of official development assistance characterized by a stagnation, in some cases a reduction, in aid budgets, contrary to the target of 0.7 per cent of gross national product, as agreed;

"Globally, levels of direct private investment in developing countries are increasing, although such investment is spread unevenly and cannot, in many cases, be a substitute for official development assistance;

"Emergency assistance is now absorbing a significant proportion of the resources being made available to developing countries by the United Nations;

"An increasing portion of growth in world trade is being generated by some developing countries. This is positive for the global economy and points further towards the need to support growth in developing countries;

"The completion of the Uruguay Round of multilateral trade negotiations of the GATT and the creation of the World Trade Organization hold out the prospect of significant benefits to the world economy. While the benefits of the Uruguay Round should be equal to all, they could be uneven initially. They will depend, in part, on sound export-oriented policies. Their wider or complete realization requires the implementation of the transition arrangements for developing countries and the forging, as appropriate, of greater coherency between trade, monetary and finance policies, as well as the prevention and redress of unilateral actions of a protectionist nature;

"In the present decade, a considerable number of developing countries have implemented trade liberalization measures, such as reducing their tariff rates. This is a positive trend, which should be accompanied by similar measures on the part of developed countries where that has not already occurred;

"The debt burden remains a constraint on the development efforts of many developing countries, particularly in Africa and the least developed countries, which continue to experience severe debt-service difficulties. This situation continues to impede development efforts;

"Special attention needs to be given to the least developed countries and the most vulnerable groups. The continuing critical economic situation of Africa constitutes a failure of serious proportions in itself and in the global economy;

"The obstacles to economic and social development being experienced in the economies in transition are serious intrinsically and in global terms;

"The situation of women in the global economy, especially in poorer countries, is a cause for deep concern in human and social terms and constitutes a serious failure of utilization of a highly productive resource in economic terms.

Priorities

"In the debate on the theme 'An agenda for development', the following issues were identified as being basic to contemporary circumstances and/or needing to be addressed if a new agenda is to be implemented:

"The need for political agreement among all States to assign priority in policy, actions, and allocation of resources for global economic and social development—that is, for improving significantly the standard of life of the very considerable number of the world's people who live in developing countries. A new agenda must be action-oriented, based on a spirit of partnership, and give due attention to national specificities;

"This commitment would be based on recognition of both qualitative and quantitative goals, the need to distinguish between urgent and deep-seated tasks, and the fundamental importance of economic growth and of sustainable development;

"Recognition of the fundamental right to development, as stated in the Vienna Declaration adopted by the World Conference on Human Rights, and of the linkage between peace and development, and recognition that democracy, development and respect for human rights and fundamental freedoms are interdependent and mutually reinforcing;

"The importance of economic growth and social justice which includes the promotion of equality of opportunity for all members of society;

"The United Nations has a unique opportunity to act now on a new agenda for development. Present circumstances will not necessarily prevail for long. Failure to seize this opportunity could have widespread and deeply damaging effects because of the existence of conditions in the world economic and social situation which are global and interlocked;

"Development is a global issue. There is a need to recognize the diversity of the developing world and to strengthen differentiated and comprehensive approaches, as well as both North-South and South-South cooperation;

"It is essential that all relevant actors be involved in a new agenda institutions of civil society, non-governmental organizations and the private sector, as well as Governments and international organizations. An agenda which is simply auto-suggestive will fail;

"A new agenda for development must be centred primarily on people. While recognizing the importance of overall economic development needs, action programmes must give appropriate priority to the education, health and welfare of people. Within this framework, institutions-both governmental and those of civil society need to be strengthened;

"A concerted attack must be made on the grinding poverty that afflicts over 1 billion people. Action must be directed particularly towards the elimination of its underlying causes. Special attention must be given to the least developed countries and, in particular, to Africa;

"The status of women must be given particular attention. Women must be integrated into decision-making and mainstream economic activities. The economic and social return on investment in their education, health and welfare is greater than that on almost any other comparable investment;

"Among the constraints to development is rapid population growth. A new agenda should incorporate clear and effective population policies within the context of overall sustainable development;

"The issue of declining national official development assistance and the growing proportion of multilateral development funds being devoted to emergency rather than development purposes must be addressed;

"An agenda for development must consider the fundamental role of science and technology, particularly for developing countries. It should identify ways and means of improving and facilitating the access and transfer of technology to developing countries;

"External factors such as trade, debt, commodity prices, transfer of technology and financial flows are critical to the success of failure of the domestic efforts of developing countries;

"Regional economic integration is complementary to multi-lateralism. The Process of regional integration should contribute towards an open trode system;

"Governments have a prime responsibility to ensure the framework conditions for development based on self-help efforts;

"It has become clear that United Nations machinery operates today in ways that are inadequate to the present challenge. There is no support for the establishment of new machinery but an insistence that the present machinery be made to function vastly more effectively than at present, particularly at Headquarters. At the field level, the resident coordinator system must continue to be strengthened;

"Action to make United Nations machinery operate more effectively should begin by identifying the areas of works in which the United Nations has a comparative advantage and shedding those areas in which it does not;

"A stronger role for the United Nations in development, including in the operational field, is needed. The role of the United Nations in relation to that of other actors also needs to be clarified. This would facilitate action-oriented recommendations by the Secretary-General for the United Nations system in the implementation of an agenda for development;

"There is considerable room for improvement in the relationship between the United Nations and the Bretton Woods institutions. The social dimensions of structural adjustment programmes also require further attention.

Conclusions

"The statements made during the high-level segment of the Economic and Social Council, the World Hearings on Development and further consultations with members of the Council, pointed towards issues of central priority for action on an agenda for development. Decisions on such action will be considered by the General Assembly.

"To facilitate that consideration, the Secretary-General will submit a further report on an agenda for development to the General Assembly at its forty-ninth session. I hope that, in formulating his report, he will take into account the priorities recorded in the present document.

"In addition, with respect to the activities of the United Nations development system, much was said in the Council about the need for greater clarity with respect to the comparative advantages of that system.

"In this context, I believe two basic considerations are relevant:

"The United Nations disposes directly of only a fraction of global resources relevant to development:

"At the same time, the United Nations has uniquely at its disposal the ability to build consensus for globally relevant political decisions. This is its central comparative advantage.

"If that advantage is exercised on the basis of an accurate analysis of relevant data, it should assist those who dispose of very significant resources to commit them in ways compatible with the priorities identified by the United Nations and thus join with the United Nations in the crucial enterprise of development.

Index